LIVERPOOL STUDIES IN SPANISH

LITERATURE

FOURTH SERIES

AMS PRESS
NEW YORK

PUBLISHED BY THE INSTITUTE OF
HISPANIC STUDIES

Liverpool Studies in Spanish Literature :
  I.—*From Cadalso to Rubén Darío.*
  II.—*Spanish Golden Age Poetry and Drama.*
  III.—*Tirso de Molina : Studies in Dramatic Realism.*

I. L. McClelland : *The Origins of the Romantic Movement in Spain.*

E. Piñeyro : *The Romantics of Spain* (tr. E. Allison Peers).

E. Allison Peers : *Spanish—Now.*

Bulletin of Hispanic Studies.

Spanish Plain Texts.

Booklet Series.

Monograph Series.

LIVERPOOL STUDIES IN SPANISH LITERATURE—IV

A SHORT HISTORY
of the
ROMANTIC MOVEMENT
IN SPAIN

BY
E. ALLISON PEERS

LIVERPOOL
INSTITUTE OF HISPANIC STUDIES
1949

Library of Congress Cataloging in Publication Data

Peers, Edgar Allison.
    A short history of the romantic movement in Spain.

    (Liverpool studies in Spanish literature; 4)
    Reprint of the 1949 ed. published by Institute of
Hispanic Studies, Liverpool, Eng.
    Includes index.
    1. Spanish literature—19th century—History and
criticism. 2. Romanticism—Spain—History. I. Title.
II. Series.
PQ6070.P4   1976   860'.9'14   76-28478
ISBN 0-404-15034-9

Reprinted from an original copy in the collections
of the University of Chicago Library

From the edition of 1949, Liverpool
First AMS edition published in 1976
Manufactured in the United States of America

International Standard Book Number:
Complete Set: 0-404-15030-6
Volume IV: 0-404-15034-9

AMS PRESS INC.
NEW YORK, N.Y.

PREFACE

This book is an abridgment of my two-volume *History of the Romantic Movement in Spain*, published in 1940. Because it was the first organic history of that movement, and brought together the results of much research not previously co-ordinated, a considerable amount of documentation had to be included in it. It has often been suggested to me that a shorter History would be useful, alike to the general reader, to the non-specialist student of Spanish literature and to the student who wishes to make a preliminary survey of the field before specializing in it. As many who use it will wish to refer to the longer History, it follows the plan of that book exactly, chapter by chapter and section by section : at the head of each chapter and each section reference is given to the corresponding pages in it.

The omission of much detail, numerous footnotes and many minor names will, I hope, allow the essentials of the narrative to stand out more clearly. For, although until comparatively recently literary historians, in treating the history of the Movement, were compelled to be vague and obscure, research has now made its course perfectly plain. It resembles a five-act drama : Origins, Growth, Success, Apparent Failure, Eventual Penetration. The first chapter of the book goes back to the initial stirrings of romanticism, perceptible early in the eighteenth century, and shows how small a part, at this stage in its development, was played by foreign influences. Two chapters then reveal the Romantic movement emerging as a phenomenon of genuinely Spanish growth, and, considering it in turn as a revival and as a revolt, trace its history, past the climax which political happenings had delayed for more than a decade, down to the crucial year of 1837. The fourth chapter describes and accounts for the failure of romanticism to establish itself in Spain as a constructive movement, a militant force or a self-conscious entity. The fifth traces the rise and growth of the Eclectic ideal which supplanted romanticism in the late eighteen-thirties and appeared to have swept it away. The last three chapters describe the nature—the idea-content—of romanticism in Spain, and show how, from 1837 onward, though failing to establish itself as a cohesive and constructive movement, it succeeded in penetrating literature as a force which has never wholly lost its power.

The abridgment, first drafted four years ago, has been thoroughly tested during the intervening period by use in lectures and seminars at the University of Liverpool. My warm thanks are due to my colleague and former pupil, Mr. H. B. Hall, who has read the book for me in proof.

E.A.P.

UNIVERSITY OF LIVERPOOL,
July 10, 1949.

PRINCIPAL ABBREVIATIONS

B.A.E.—Biblioteca de Autores Españoles.

B.B.M.P.—*Boletín de la Biblioteca Menéndez y Pelayo.* Santander, 1919 ff.

H.R.—*Hispanic Review.* Philadelphia, 1933 ff.

H.R.M.S.—E. Allison Peers : *A History of the Romantic Movement in Spain.* Cambridge, 1940. 2 vols.

M.A.E.—*Memorias de la Academia Española.* Año I. Madrid, 1870. 2 vols.

M.L.R.—*Modern Language Review.* Cambridge, 1905 ff.

Piñeyro-Peers.—Enrique Piñeyro : *The Romantics of Spain.* Translated by E. Allison Peers. Liverpool, 1934.

R.F.E.—*Revista de Filología Española.* Madrid, 1914 ff.

R.H.—*Revue Hispanique.* New York-Paris, 1894-1933.

CONTENTS

CHAPTER I

THE ANTECEDENTS OF THE ROMANTIC
MOVEMENT[1]

I. ROMANTIC SPAIN :
THE ROMANTICISM OF THE GOLDEN AGE[2]

Well over a century has passed since the term *romanticism*
was invented to describe that peculiarly elusive literary and
artistic mode which preceding generations had attempted to
define by such adjectives as *romanesque, romancesco, romántico,
romantique, romantic.*[3] During the whole of that time the word
has been freely used to describe a fundamental characteristic
of literature and art in Spain. It was Spain, again and again,
that inspired the leaders of the Romantic movement in France
and Germany. To the brothers Schlegel, Spanish drama,
down to the time of Calderón, was " almost entirely
Romantic,"[4] while Spanish poetry " remained purely
Romantic throughout."[5] Sismondi described Spanish literature as " wholly Romantic and chivalric."[6] They were right.
In every phase and epoch of Spanish literature the Romantic
tendencies of the Spanish character find expression—most
markedly so in the Middle Ages, when literature in Western
Europe had hardly taken definite form and Classical ideals

---

[1] *H.R.M.S.*, I, 1-81. [2] *H.R.M.S.*, I, 1-12.

[3] Cf. E. Allison Peers, in *R.H.*, 1933, LXXXI (2e partie), 411-418 ;
H. Becher, in *B.B.M.P.*, 1931, XIII, 31-3.

[4] A. W. von Schlegel : *Über Dramatische Kunst und Litteratur*, Heidelberg,
1809, 1811 (Zwölfte Vorlesung, II, ii, 12-13).

[5] F. von Schlegel : *Sämmtliche Werke*, Vienna, 1822-5, II, 125.

[6] Sismondi : *De la Littérature du Midi de l'Europe*, Paris, 1829, III, 497-8,
IV, 254-5.

were still imperfectly assimilated, and in the period of Spain's most triumphant art, the so-called " Age of Gold."

Even during the Renaissance, when literature was characterized by an increasing attention to form, the formlessness of those innumerable and influential " books of chivalry " may be contrasted with the precision of Nebrija and Valdés, and alongside tales that are mere objective adaptations of Latin models were published others, sentimental, emotional and violently passionate. By the middle of the sixteenth century Spain's native romanticism had overwhelmed the rival ideal and inspiration had become mistress of the literary art and the criterion of greatness. Around that greatest of improvisers, Lope de Vega, grew up a school distinguished by spontaneity, freshness and imagination, and almost any of Lope's major contemporaries illustrate the impatience of the Golden Age with restraint. Though many of them are open to Classical influences, their primary inspiration is Romantic. The greatest of them—Luis de León, San Juan de la Cruz, Cervantes—unite the two ideals as only the greatest of artists can. The latest of them, Calderón, was acclaimed by German and Italian, as well as by Spanish, critics of the early nineteenth century as " in all circumstances, and compared with all other dramatic poets, the most Romantic." [1]

There are, of course, aspects of Golden Age literature which are the reverse of Romantic : the unnatural rigidity and conventionality, for example, of much of its drama ; its comparative weakness in subjectivity ; its indifference to cosmopolitanism in art. But these are traits which one would expect to find in an age of success, achievement and prosperity : social history frequently modifies literary development. The nineteenth-century Romantics certainly accepted the masters of the Golden Age as their fellows, and that view was shared by their adversaries as well as by those whose attitude to the conflict was one of neutrality. As Durán, a leading pre-Romantic, put it just when the Movement was about to burst into its short life :

[1] F. von Schlegel : *Op. cit.*, II, 123-4. Cf. A. W. von Schlegel : *Op. cit.*, II, ii, 374 (Vierzehnte Vorlesung).

Yo considero a Lope, Góngora y sus contemporáneos como los primeros que comprendieron el destino de la poesía castellana, y que, abandonando la imitación de modelos latinos e italianos, establecieron el verdadero romanticismo español, tanto en la lírica como en la dramática.[1]

II. THE EIGHTEENTH CENTURY : EARLY SIGNS OF A NEW ROMANTICISM[2]

" El verdadero romanticismo español " : for its historical significance the phrase is worth remembering. But, when the Golden Age ended, this "true romanticism" was succeeded by nearly a century of desolation, during which, as Larra put it, " el gusto se asentó sobre las ruinas del genio."[3] From about 1680 to 1760, neo-classicism presided over all forms of literature ; and both poets and dramatists glorified the letter of art at the expense of its spirit. After 1760, neo-classicism began to lose its power and to pass slowly into obscurity—a process hastened by its having produced no literature worthy of that name. Even before its decline, however, we can discover signs of the new romanticism. As early as 1750 it became clear that men were seeking a more inspiring ideal than that of the preceptist Luzán—the revivifying of literature by the codifying of rules for it. Fortunately they had not to look far. A young cleric from Granada, Porcel, one of the leading members of the " Academy of Good Taste " which met from 1749 to 1751, declared that poetry knew no law save that of genius.[4] A much older man, the Benedictine, Feijóo, described the " rules " as " unas luces estériles . . . que alumbran, y no influyen"[5] and invoked an all-important "something"—a "no sé qué que agrada, que enamora, que

[1] A. Durán : *Romancero de romances caballerescos e históricos, etc.*, Madrid, 1832, p. xxx.

[2] *H.R.M.S.*, I, 13-39.

[3] Review of Maury's *Espagne poétique* (*Obras*, Madrid, 1855, II, 215).

[4] Porcel : *Juicio lunático*, 1750, fol. 9. On this general subject, cf. I. L. McClelland : *The Origins of the Romantic Movement in Spain*, Liverpool, 1937.

[5] Feijóo : *Cartas eruditas*, Madrid, 1748-51, Vol. II, Carta 6.

hechiza ", a " primor que no se explica ", a " regla superior, que existe en su mente, distinta de aquellas comunes que la escuela enseña."[1]

Soon after the middle of the century appeared more definite and more general signs of Romantic revivification. The two main currents of the new movement emerged slowly from their underground channels and began to flow toward the point where they would unite. These two aspects of the Romantic movement in Spain are in no sense mutually exclusive and the distinction made between them in these pages is chiefly one of convenience. They did, in fact, often appear to those who witnessed them to be distinct and separate, but informing them both was the same spirit, seeking diverse ways of self-expression. The one—too often misinterpreted, both then and now, as being merely negative —claimed liberty for authors to write as they pleased, expressed discontent with certain fashions and conventions already tending to become outmoded and eventually grew into a determined and even vehement revolt against the limitations which the neo-Classicists were seeking to impose upon literature. The other also desired liberty, but desired it in order to bring about a revival, both in theme and in treatment, of the literature of the Middle Ages and of the Age of Gold.

These parallel movements will be designated respectively as the Romantic revolt and the Romantic revival. Not only was each inspired by the same ideal, but to some extent each implied the other. The attempt to revive two closely related but long neglected types of literature was itself a revolt, both against the neglect and against those who persistently defended it. Revolt, on the other hand, against past, or current, traditions would have been meaningless had the rebels not had something to put in their place, which, in fact, belonged to a past still more remote.

The two movements developed surely, if somewhat slowly, during the second half of the eighteenth century, and were well advanced by 1800—the year generally, though incorrectly, considered as marking the approximate beginnings

[1] Feijóo : *Discursos*, B.A.E., LVI, 349-53, *passim*.

of Spanish pre-romanticism. Each of them, in its own way, expressed the primary and essential characteristic of the Romantic ideal—the desire for freedom—and at the same time there began to reappear the secondary or derived characteristics of that ideal, which were not for many decades to be considered as normal traits of the national literature. Continually, amid the otherwise unrelieved conventionality of the early eighteenth century, the reader may light upon poems marked by spontaneity, even by passion ; upon manifestations of subjectivity and melancholy which fringe the Romantic ; and upon occasional, though rarer, suggestions of romanticism in form.

Early signs of romanticism in lyric poetry are few—the lachrymosity of Verdugo y Castilla, the subjectivity and sentimental melancholy of García de la Huerta, the semi-Romantic devices of Nicolás Fernández de Moratín—but, as the eighteenth century advances, both the primary and the secondary characteristics of the Movement appear in the works of the Arcadian group of poets known as the " Salamancan School."

José Cadalso, for example, though no conscious revolutionary, was a true poet whose temperament prevented him from completely surrendering his inspiration to the neo-classicism which moulded the form of his chief works. We find in him the impatience with restraint, the subjectivity, the sensibility and the melancholy of the Romantic. He would like to re-name his *Ocios de mi juventud* " Alivio de mis penas," " porque los hice todos en ocasión de acometerme alguna pesadumbre."[1] Of his prose works, the *Noches lúgubres*, though not uniformly spontaneous, conforms very closely to the Romantic type of personal and passionate lament. In the often uncouth vigour of its style and the unrestraint of its vocabulary it is markedly pre-Romantic.

Like Cadalso, José Iglesias de la Casa abounds in a passionate, restless energy—" la actividad de un fuego penetrante," " la inquietud que en mi interior yo siento "[2]

[1] Cadalso : *Obras,* Madrid, 1818, III, 4.

[2] Idilio VI.

—which, when it reaches its maximum force, approaches delirium. His predominant note, however, is gloom. His frankly individualistic disillusion—" mi mal," " mi dolor callado "[1]—is intimately connected with a love of solitude. Notable, too, is his appreciation of certain specific aspects of Nature, especially the " natural desorden " of the open country :

> Aquel confuso amontonar de cosas
> arrojadas acaso y diferentes ;
> acá hiedra, allá espinas, allá fuentes,
> riscos, peñascos, ríos, flores, rosas.[2]

Gaspar Melchor de Jovellanos, though closest to the Romantic movement in his lachrymose play *El Delincuente honrado*, foreshadows it also in a few of his poems, in which emotionalism breaks through lines stiff with artificiality. Several of his epistles and sonnets are markedly personal, particularly the " Epístola de Fabio a Anfriso," which contains a description of El Paular instinct with sensibility and the truly Romantic quality of intimacy with Nature.

Comparable with this epistle are " La Primavera," " El Otoño," " Mi Paseo solitario de primavera " and " La Rosa del desierto " of Nicasio Álvarez de Cienfuegos. Despite his emotion-ridden nature and his occasionally unrestrained and passionate diction, Cienfuegos delights in calm and solitude :

> O salve, salve, soledad querida . . . .[3]
> Busco la soledad y en su silencio
> sin esperanza mi dolor exhalo.[4]

In " La Escuela del sepulcro " he joins the graveyard school, combining with the melancholy which we find in almost the whole of the group a somewhat morbid asceticism highly suggestive of nineteenth-century Romantic *desengaño*.

Even the neo-Classical Manuel José Quintana has his Romantic affinities. His ruling passion is love of freedom and independence. His ideas belong to the eighteenth

---

[1] Idilio V.

[2] Canción II.

[3] " El Otoño."

[4] " Mi Paseo solitario de primavera."

century, and in many respects he is an ultra-conservative in literary criticism, but he is by no means unsympathetic with some of the new tendencies. His language constantly betrays a Romantic's impatience with accepted terminology : though he would not banish all rhyme from verse, he was not, as he wrote to young Manuel de Cabanyes, one of those " desesperados *filorímicos* " against whom the latter made so determined a stand.[1] He is strongly drawn towards the Middle Ages ; and, if their principal attraction for him seems to have been patriotic rather than literary, their literary appeal becomes more pronounced as the years go on. It is not surprising to find that, though he never became an addict to romanticism, he was looked up to with respect by the Romantics and by the neo-Classics alike. He is one of the noblest literary figures of his age.

But the most important of the Romantics' eighteenth-century precursors was Juan Meléndez Valdés, in whom we find a love of Nature more intense than that of his contemporaries, more obviously sincere, and, above all, more particularized. It is not merely a spring or a summer day that moves him, but the " dark green " meadows, the banks of mist hanging over the river, the " delightful freshness " of the trees that fringe its margin and the flowers as they tremble in the gentlest breeze. And they do more than give him a pleasant thrill :

> Me enajenan y me olvidan
> de las odiosas ciudades,
> y de sus tristes jardines,
> hijos míseros del arte.[2]

Some of Meléndez Valdés' poems, including that just quoted, have an almost Wordsworthian sensibility. When had a Spanish poet last declared that he " abandoned him-self to the impulse " which came to him from Nature, walk-ing unquietly from one scene to another and seeking spiritual solace from each, while open to the influences of them all ?[3]

[1] Cf. *Poems of Manuel de Cabanyes*, Manchester, 1923, p. 12, and p. 92, below.
[2] Romance XXXIV : " La Tarde."
[3] *Ibid.*

2

He plucks a flower—and

> Me confundo, me abismo : el alma mía
> se pierde, una flor sola contemplando. [1]

He knows

> . . . . que don tan funesto
> es . . . . un corazón sensible
> cual débil muro puesto
> de un mar airado al ímpetu terrible. [2]

He affects a sentimentality which at times borders on the lachrymose : he can sentimentalize over a fallen tree,[3] over the autumn leaves,[4] or over the coming of spring,[5] and equally so over such pathetic types, to be exploited to the full by the Romantics, as the beggar,[6] the criminal[7] or the poverty-stricken peasant[8], or over such abstract qualities as beneficence,[9] humanitarianism[10] or rustic virtue.[11] He passes readily from sentimentality to melancholy and disillusion. The elegy to Jovino (Jovellanos) entitled " El Melancólico " is in sentiment, though not in form, a pure product of the Romantic spirit, not least so because it links its author's feelings with Nature. In all his moods of disillusion, however, he tends to fade into conventional insincerity and his emotions are too easily quenched by a formalism from which he seems unable for long to escape.

As an artist, Meléndez Valdés tends to observe more closely than his fellow-poets and to describe more faithfully, not least when faced with the "grato desorden"[12] which they detested but which he was inclined to admire. In form he is no revolutionary, yet his metrical innovations drew upon him

---

[1] Discurso III.

[2] Oda XXXI.

[3] Romance III.

[4] Oda XXVI.

[5] Oda XXII.

[6] *Discursos forenses*, Madrid, 1821, pp. 273-310.

[7] *Ibid.*, Cf. pp. 194, below.

[8] Epístolas VI, III.

[9] Epístola IV.

[10] Epístolas, *passim*.

[11] Epístola VI.

[12] Oda XXXII.

neo-Classical censure and he played an important part in the restoration of the *romance* to Spain.

It is important not to allow the judgment to be biassed in favour of Meléndez Valdés by admiration for his purple patches—a caution even more applicable as regards his contemporaries. Whatever suggestions of revolt or revival they may convey are heavily overweighted with pseudo-classicism. This is particularly true of the " Sevilian " group of poets, whose activities were centred in the Academia de Letras Humanas, founded at Seville in 1793. Though this group stands chronologically between the Salamancan School and the Romantics of the eighteen-thirties, it is in the main retrogressive. Alberto Lista, for example, was an outspoken critic of romanticism, whose academically restrained fervour is characteristic of his temperament. Félix José Reinoso displays a cold conventionality. José Marchena, on the other hand, a priest who renounced his orders and found a home in revolutionary France, is a prophet of liberalism, though hardly of liberalism in literature, who invokes liberty in his verses, and also indulges in Romantic doubts and questionings.[1] His fellow-renegade, Blanco White (José María Blanco y Crespo), who became a Unitarian minister in England, not only insinuated the theme of freedom into many unpromising contexts, but often wrote in a way which betrayed his genuine feelings. Though always restrained in manner, he conveys unmistakable suggestions of hidden power, and the vigour of his imagination seems continually to be promising greater achievements than he accomplished.

The strongest literary link between the Sevilians and the Romantics is Manuel María de Arjona, whose poetry, though more pretentious than that of the best of the Salamancans, is as strongly impregnated as theirs with subjectivity, melancholy and sensibility to Nature. Perhaps his chief merit as a pre-Romantic lies in the discontent which he felt with eighteenth-century verse-forms and the original contributions which he made to Spanish versification. These

---

[1] Marchena : *Obras literarias*, Seville, 1892-6, I, 51, 54, 131-2. Félix María Hidalgo (*e.g.*, in B.A.E., LXVII, 738-9) also apostrophizes liberty.

did not escape the censure of later critics, but they were signs, if faint ones, of the impending revolution.

No novel of the period carries us far from neo-classicism, save P. Isla's satire, *Fray Gerundio* (1758, 1768). This, though written in an age predominantly Classical, has less of classicism than the prose works of Cervantes and Quevedo, while its length, its formlessness and the fantastic nature of its satire stamp it indelibly. The novels of the last third of the century are, in direction as in intrinsic merit, a retrogression.[1] Even Pedro Montengón, the translator of Ossian and a writer of great fertility, has nothing to offer but didacticism and conventionality. Antonio Valladares de Sotomayor's highly moral and amorously sentimental *La Leandra* (1797) foreshadows Romantic drama with its coincidences and surprises. Francisco de Tójar's *Filósofa por amor* (1799) has all the lachrymosity and sentimentalism of the most advanced Romantics, combined, however, with an unimpeachable rectitude which they might have been less ready to embrace.

On the stage, there were numerous signs of changing tendencies long before 1800.[2] In none of the *genres* was precept so sacrosanct as in drama : the " rules " had to be followed unswervingly. In practice, most of the second-rate or third-rate neo-Classical plays current in Spain during the eighteenth century came from, or by way of, France. But by the end of the sixties this type of play was beginning to lose favour. A widespread dissatisfaction with the state of the theatre made itself felt, and various kinds of drama, which may be described as " non-literary," became popular. Some of the authors of these plays respected the main tenets of neo-classicism, though in spirit they may seem to us nearer to the Romantic than to the Classical. Others approached romanticism still more closely, neither aiming nor expecting to please the critics, but simply ignoring them.

Of the three types of non-literary play, the one that best

---

[1] Cf. *H.R.M.S.*, I, 29-32.

[2] For a fuller discussion of this subject, see McClelland, *op. cit.*, Chaps. v-viii.

answered to that description was the *comedia de magia*. It was a fantastic production in which ridiculously marvellous stage effects were attained by the use of apparatus : its characters were entirely divorced from reality and its plot was often a mere string of impossible happenings. The *tragedia urbana* was closely allied to the lachrymose play familiar in eighteenth-century England and France. The Spanish variant of the type, of which the best-known example is Jovellanos' *El Delincuente honrado* (1774), was largely an importation. Founded on emotion, and prolific in Romantic devices, it clearly foreshadows Romantic drama despite its outward adherence to neo-Classical standards. Finally, the *comedia heroica* looks back to the Golden Age, is distinctively Spanish in character, maintains a lofty tone, uses virile language, incorporates characteristics of all the other types, is usually non-Classical in structure and lays particular stress upon sensation and mystery.

With each of these types was mingled a spice of what to-day is called melodrama. This word was first used in Spain in its etymological sense of " a play with music " —almost as a synonym of opera. It then developed a connection with the lachrymose play, and at the same time, while still implying the use of music, came to denote also an attention to theatrical effect. Finally, in the early nineteenth century, the word began to assume something of the sense it bears to-day. It is not treated here as a separate *genre* because, though many plays were announced and described as melodramas, the type quickly disintegrated and its various characteristics began to be found in productions coming within almost every category.[1]

Of the numerous authors who produced work of so little intrinsic merit, three are more prominent than the rest : Luciano Francisco Comella, 'the least estimable, the most sentimental and the nearest to the neo-Classics ; Gaspar Zavala y Zamora, at his most vehement a positive rebel, whose freshness of imagination, overlaying his indebtedness to the Golden Age, often gives the reader the illusion of

[1] Cf. McClelland, *op. cit.*, pp. 182-4.

reading one of the Romantics ; and Antonio Valladares de Sotomayor, who, despite his great regard for the Middle Ages, is perhaps the most modern of the three, though he recalls the exaggerations of the later Romantics rather than their virtues.

These non-literary types, which were highly popular, and were decried by many serious people, [1] represent the element of revolt in pre-romanticism. For, in the first place, they owed their popularity to the reaction of the public against neo-classicism in drama, and, in the second, certain of their characteristic traits were to be extolled and emulated by the literary revolutionaries of the nineteenth century. Another type of play belongs to the Romantic revival. This was the *refundición*, or drama adapted from the *comedia* of the Golden Age—in its origins a compromise invented to reconcile neo-Classical principles with the taste of the public. To modern readers, these *refundiciones* are worse than failures, for they suppress or mutilate precisely what seems to-day to have constituted the beauty of their originals. But, as the period advanced, they came to reflect less the ideals of neo-classicism and more the spirit of their originals. And even before that they served two important purposes in the evolution of Romantic drama. First, they sent the public back to an epoch of dramatic greatness, at a time when some at least of its foremost names were in danger of being forgotten. Secondly, they acted to some extent as an antidote to the non-literary plays and provided the playgoer with drama acceptable to him, yet not without merit.

III. THE ROMANTIC REVIVAL BEFORE 1800 [2]

(i) *The Revival of Mediaeval Literature*

Of the eighteenth-century pioneers of the mediaeval Revival in Spain the chief is Tomás Antonio Sánchez,

---

[1] *E.g.*, by Leandro Fernández de Moratín, in " Lección poética, etc." and in *Comedia nueva*, I, iv, II, v.   *Cit. H.R.M.S.*, I, 36.

[2] *H.R.M.S.*, I, 40-73.

librarian to the King and author of a four-volume *Colección de poesías castellanas anteriores al siglo xv* (1779-90) which comprised the works of the Marqués de Santillana, the *Poema del Cid*, the poems of Berceo and Juan Ruiz and the *Libro de Alexandre*. Anxious to demonstrate that Spanish " rhymed poetry did not begin with Juan de Mena, Boscán and Garcilaso, as some have affirmed,"[1] he thought he could best do this by publishing

> una colección de nuestras primeras poesías para que el tiempo, los incendios, la polilla y otros enemigos que tienen los códices no acabaran con ellos y se perdiera del todo su memoria. Siempre he creído que un gran caudal de nuestra lengua, de nuestra historia, de nuestras costumbres y literatura antigua, yacía como mudo entre las tinieblas del más profundo olvido y abandono.[2]

Sánchez, though the most notable of the eighteenth-century mediaevalists, was not the first of them. In 1743, Fray Martín Sarmiento made a list of twelve collections— one an anthology of mediaeval Spanish verse—which he would like to see published, " ya para la pureza de la lengua, ya por que en (los Cancioneros) hay pensamientos delicados, que después se nos vendieron por nuevos."[3] A later book of Sarmiento's, *Memorias para la historia de la poesía y poetas españoles* (1775), discusses the origins of Spanish poetry and the history of its various metres ; reproduces a large part of Santillana's letter to the Constable of Portugal as the foundation of a discourse on poetics ; and treats of the very authors whom Sánchez shortly afterwards reprinted.

Towards the end of the century, Spanish mediaevalists became more numerous. Rafael Floranes, an outstanding critic, advocated the study of palaeography and laboured with unusual care over problems of mediaeval literature. Francisco Cerdá y Rico published mediaeval chronicles, an annotated edition of Jorge Manrique's *Coplas*, Gil Polo's continuation of Montemayor's *Diana*, and works by Ginés de Sepúlveda, Luis de León and many others, including the

---

[1] *Colección*, etc., I, fol. 6r. [2] *Op. cit.*, I, fol. 4v, 5r.
[3] *Reflexiones literarias para una biblioteca real*, etc., Madrid, 1743, p. 228.

twenty-one-volume *Obras sueltas* of Lope de Vega, still widely used. Though primarily a conservative and a bibliophile, he was deeply interested in recalling the attention of his contemporaries to Spain's past ; at one time he had intended to collaborate with Juan José López de Sedano in his *Parnaso español* (1768).

This was one of the first, most ambitious and best known of the eighteenth-century collections of Spanish poetry. True, the extracts which fill its nine volumes by no means always commend the anthologist's taste and he begins only at the sixteenth century. But his preface, which glances with interest at the Middle Ages, is eloquent of the spirit of revival. " La renovación o el desentierro de la antigua poesía castellana," wrote the distinguished critic Böhl von Faber, over sixty years later, " se debe en gran parte a las diligencias del buen Sedano, editor del *Parnaso español*." [1]

In drama, the mediaeval history of Spain was by no means being neglected. Some of the worst neo-Classical plays of the eighteenth century, indeed, were Spanish in theme. Favourite subjects were the beginnings of the Spanish nation, the exploits of the Cid, of Fernán González and of James I of Aragon, the union of the various Spanish kingdoms and the reconquest of Granada. Montiano portrayed Visigothic Spain in *Ataulfo* (1753) ; Jovellanos celebrated the birth of the Spanish nation in *Munuza* (1769 : also known as *Pelayo*) ; Nicolás Moratín found two home-themes in *Hormesinda* (1770) and *Guzmán el Bueno* (1777) ; Cadalso clothed the most artificial plot in Spanish dress in *Sancho García* (1771) ; and García de la Huerta took the " Jewess of Toledo " theme for his *Raquel* (1778). In face of such evidence, the common fallacy that the return to mediaeval themes was an exclusively Romantic achievement is clearly indefensible.

As the eighteenth century drew to a close, the number of mediaevally inspired plays greatly increased ; fewer of them were neo-Classical in treatment ; and the characteristics of later Romantic drama began to appear. To take a single

[1] Cf. *B.B.M.P.*, 1921, III, 95. Two other collections of this period are described in *H.R.M.S.*, I, 45-6.

illustration, Valladares de Sotomayor's *El Católico Recaredo* (1785), set in royal Toledo, is patriotic and religious in tone ; it breaks one of the Unities ; it has a great many characters ; allegorical figures mingle with others from real life ; lengthy stage directions pay great attention to *décor ;* and very considerable use is made of local colour. Here we have in germ both Revival and Revolt.

In strong contrast with drama, prose fiction cares for none of these things : an occasional exception, such as Montengón's treatment of the Roderick-legend (*El Rodrigo*, 1793), only emphasizes the rule. Lyric poetry, on the other hand, took its full share in the mediaeval Revival, patriotism, in particular, directing poets to the heroes of Spanish history, which means, in large measure, to the Middle Ages. " Sean tu objeto," wrote Jovellanos to a fellow-poet of the Salamancan School,

> Sean tu objeto los héroes españoles,
> las guerras, las victorias y el sangriento
> furor de Marte . . . .
> los triunfos de Pelayo y su renombre,
> las hazañas, las lides, las victorias
> que el imperio de Carlos, casi inmenso,
> y al Evangelio santo un nuevo mundo
> más pingüe y opulento sujetaron.[1]

(ii) *The Revival of Golden Age Literature*

The revival of every branch of Golden Age literature, too, had its roots deep in the eighteenth century. No complete break with the traditions of that age was ever made. Zamora, who died as early as 1728, was an ineffective enough dramatist, but, like his contemporary Cañizares, he drew freely upon Lope, Tirso and Calderón and as a matter of course paid them tributes of admiration. A little later, Añorbe y Corregel, attacked by Luzán, Montiano and others, defended himself by decrying authority and precept.[2] Feijóo realized clearly how deeply indebted was European comedy to Lope

---

[1] " Jovino a sus amigos de Salamanca."

[2] Cf. McClelland, *op. cit.*, pp. 12-15.

de Vega. Even Luzán expressed admiration for Lope de Vega and Calderón, while the *Diario de los literatos de España*, neo-Classical though its general outlook might be, was lenient in its interpretation of the Rules and defended tragicomedy by using the argument, so popular later with the Romantics, that drama of that type abounds in real life.

Towards 1750, neo-classicism became more aggressive, but defenders of the Golden Age became more active too. Erauso y Zavaleta, a critic drawn upon by Böhl von Faber, made a spirited defence, in his *Discurso crítico sobre . . . las comedias de España* (Madrid, 1750), of the plays of Lope de Vega and Calderón :

> Son las comedias de España, y en especial las de los venerados Lope de Vega, Calderón y sus imitadores, el más dulce agregado de la sabiduría, de la discreción, de la enseñanza, del ejemplo, del chiste y de la gracia : en ellas se retrata, con propios apacibles coloridos, el genio grave, pundonoroso, ardiente, agudo, sutil, constante, fuerte y caballero, de toda la nación.[1]
>
> Sólo Calderón y Lope tocaron felizmente la delicada línea del acierto, y del primor, con los hallazgos de su altivo ingenio.[2]

Both Erauso y Zavaleta and others vigorously defended the *autos sacramentales*, which were being attacked with great vehemence,[3] mainly, however, in the field, not of literature, but of moral and religious propriety. Juan Cristóbal Romea y Tapia, in *El Escritor sin título* (1763), passionately upheld the *autos* as " legitimate sacred poetry," with precedents in Scripture, and placed Calderón, with all his " so-called defects ", above Metastasio, and even above Molière.[4] In the same year, Francisco Mariano Nipho, who, in his *Cajón de sastre* (1760), had published extracts from Golden Age writers, eulogized Calderón as " never more glorious than when most severely impugned, yet unconquered " ;[5] and

---

[1] *Discurso crítico*, etc., Dedication.

[2] *Op. cit.*, " Papel circular." Cf. *H.R.M.S.*, I, 51-3, and McClelland, *op. cit.*, pp. 28-40.

[3] On this controversy, see *H.R.M.S.*, I, 53-5.

[4] *El Escritor sin título*, pp. 16-17, 24, 25.

[5] *Diario extranjero*, April 12, 1763. Cf. McClelland, *op. cit.*, pp. 75-8.

when, in 1765, the conflict over the *autos* ended with their prohibition, Calderón suffered no loss of prestige. Indeed, soon after 1765, the neo-Classical tide began to turn more markedly in favour of Golden Age drama, which both in critical theory and in stage practice now slowly recovered its reputation. Francisco Nieto de Molina, who had already placed Lope de Vega, Góngora and Quevedo among the immortals, dilated upon " lo grande, superior, excelso y eminente que fué Lope " : " vive Lope y vivirá inmortal-mente" (1768).[1] He had many like-minded contemporaries. López de Sedano (1768) believed that Golden Age literature would have an important influence on a revival of letters which he thought he saw close at hand.[2] Tomás Sebastián y Latre (1772), while lamenting the defects of Golden Age dramatists, recognized their genius : had they but exercised more restraint, " qué perfectos modelos no tendríamos hoy para su imitación ! "[3]

Cerdá y Rico, Lope's editor, made much less difficulty about Lope's greatness (1776) :

> La increíble copia de sus escritos y la grandeza de su ingenio y numen poético ha extendido su nombre por todo el orbe literario . . . . Cuando quiso pulir sus composiciones, no es inferior a los más perfectos dechados de nuestra poesía ; . . . . en el ingenio, invención y pureza de estilo excede a muchos ; y en la abundancia dejó a todos muy atrás.[4]

Even García de la Huerta, no admirer of the Golden Age, had moments (1785) in which he appeared to realize its greatness : particularly significant is his praise of the *comedia heroica*, as containing some of the finest passages in all dramatic literature, ancient and modern.[5]

In 1789 appeared the second and posthumous edition of Luzán's *Poética*, which, as regards its attitude to the Golden Age, has generally been considered a retrogression from the

---

[1] *Obras en prosa*, etc., Madrid, 1768, pp. 43-4.

[2] *Parnaso español*, I, iv, vii.

[3] *Ensayo sobre el teatro español*, Zaragoza, 1772, *cit. H.R.M.S.*, I, 58, n.2.

[4] Lope de Vega : *Obras sueltas*, etc., Madrid, 1776-9, I, iv, v, vi.

[5] *Theatro Hespañol*, Pt. III, Vol. I, Madrid, 1785, p. ii.

first edition. It is true that it omitted certain significant eulogies of Lope, Calderón and others, but for these omissions it made some atonement. If unflattering to Lope de Vega, Luzán is enthusiastic about Calderón and Moreto : Calderón, he says, raised Spanish drama " to its greatest height and almost to the greatest degree of perfection to which the type of comedy that he wrote was capable of attaining."[1]

In 1792 appeared the *Comedia nueva* of Leandro Moratín, in which the well-known words of Don Pedro, preferring Golden Age drama to modern " tonterías," seem to represent the standpoint of the author :

> No, señor, menos me enfada cualquiera de nuestras comedias antiguas, por malas que sean. Están desarregladas, tienen disparates ; pero aquellos disparates y aquel desarreglo son hijos del ingenio y no de la estupidez. Tienen defectos enormes, es verdad ; pero entre estos defectos se hallan cosas que, por vida mía, tal vez suspenden y conmueven al espectador en términos de hacerle olvidar o disculpar cuantos desaciertos han precedido. Ahora compare usted nuestros autores adocenados del día con los antiguos, y dígame si no valen más Calderón, Solís, Rojas, Moreto, cuando deliran, que estotros cuando quieren hablar en razón.[2]

From this point to the end of the century the chorus of approval and eulogy of Golden Age drama grows ever stronger and the testimonies of leading writers are reinforced by others from the periodical press.[3] The question now arises how far the attitude of the critics was reflected in the interest of the public. During the period under review the plays of Calderón, Moreto and Rojas Zorrilla had been continuously performed and published. Calderón was the most popular Golden Age dramatist : a six-volume edition of his *autos* (1759-60) was followed by an eleven-volume edition of his *comedias* (1760-3). " Conserva Calderón," says the second edition of Luzán's *Poética* (1789), " casi todo su primitivo aplauso : sirvió y sirve de modelo ; y son sus

---

[1] *Poética*, ed. cit., II, 37.   [2] *Comedia nueva*, II, v.
[3] For illustrations, see *H.R.M.S.*, I, 63-8.

comedias el caudal más redituable de nuestros teatros."[1] Lope and Tirso followed Calderón back to popularity only gradually, Lope returning the more slowly of the two.[2] In a single month (April) of 1763 there were twenty-five performances in Madrid of plays by Calderón, six of Rojas' and six of Moreto's, but not one of Lope's. Between 1783 and 1800 only twenty-one references to Lope can be found in the press against 173 to Calderón. Not until Lope's plays won increasing notice through the increasing popularity of the *refundiciones* did his position improve, and even in their altered form they had still to meet much obscurantist criticism.

Of non-dramatic works of the Golden Age, the first in popularity was *Don Quijote*. Some thirty editions of that work appeared in Spain during the eighteenth century ; and, if Montiano preferred Avellaneda's *Don Quijote* to Cervantes' and Maruján abused Cervantes for destroying Spain's honour and making her the butt of all, such judgments were fiercely combated as soon as they were emitted.[3] With the publication of the Academy edition of *Don Quijote* (1780) the fame of Cervantes in Spain began to mount steeply. Forner (1786) placed him in merit above Descartes and satirized critics who despised him.[4] Sánchez wrote a vigorous defence of him against a fantastic attack by Estala (1788).[5] Quintana's biographical study (1797) was prefaced to an edition of the *Quijote* which rivalled that of the Academy.

Next to Cervantes, the most popular of the non-dramatic writers of the Golden Age during the eighteenth century was the inspirer of the " Salamancan School," Fray Luis de León, a writer whom it would be difficult to assign to the Classical or the Romantic category. Other leading poets who regained some degree of popularity were Boscán, Garcilaso de la Vega, Herrera, Acuña and the Argensolas.

---

[1] *Poética, ed. cit.*, II, 30.

[2] On Tirso's return, see *H.R.M.S.*, I, 70-1.

[3] Cf. *H.R.M.S.*, I, 71-2.

[4] *Oración apologética*, etc., Madrid, 1786, p. 13.

[5] *Carta publicada en el Correo de Madrid*, etc., Madrid, 1788. Cf. *R.H.*, 1908, XVIII, 295-431.

But, so far as the early history of the Romantic movement is concerned, Golden Age means Golden Age drama, and in so brief a survey as this it is unnecessary to follow the vogue of the other *genres* any farther.

IV   THE ROMANTIC REVOLT BEFORE 1800[1]

During the whole of the eighteenth century, and for some time afterwards, the Romantic revolt was much less active than the Romantic revival. From about 1750 onwards, however, it began to gather force. Practically all the progressive critics already mentioned make their contributions to the Revolt, though these are often so vague that they cannot easily be summarized, still less quoted. We shall content ourselves, therefore, with referring to some representative opinions and indicating their general nature.

The majority of the complainants desired greater freedom, chiefly in drama. Anxious to uproot the custom of drawing for plays upon France, they not only asserted the superiority of home products, but made frequent and violent attacks upon foreign importations. " Es plaga de España, o castigo de Dios," exclaimed Erauso y Zavaleta, " el irremediable y excesivo amor que tenemos a todo lo extranjero."[2] These sentiments were echoed by many of his contemporaries.

Other critics desired freedom for the artist, whether in prose, verse or drama, to express himself without hindrance. They also claimed the right to do a number of things that were prohibited : to take themes from Christian poetry, to mingle tragedy with comedy, to use a variety of metres, and so on. But incomparably their most frequent and effective protests were those made against the rules of the Unities, which are not only, again and again, the true objects of the continual vague complaints against " rules " and " laws," but are referred to, specifically, by nearly all the critics quoted in this chapter. In the non-literary plays, of course,

---

[1] *H.R.M.S.*, I, 73-8.
[2] *Discurso crítico*, etc., p. 44.

the Unities were broken more often than they were kept, and broken quite unashamedly. And many serious critics were hardly more conservative than the popular playwrights. Few of them rejected the Unities entirely and desired to see Cervantes' " niño en mantillas " of the first act of a play " salir ya hecho hombre barbado " in the second.[1] Some recommended that they should be strictly observed within variously defined limits. Some preferred them to be kept wherever possible but inveighed against grammarians who misinterpreted Aristotle and " burdened dramatic art with arbitrary little rules which serve only to impede the progress of genius."[2] Some condoned the non-observance of the Unities of time and place provided the Unity of action was followed. There is clearly much variation of opinion here.

Such were the murmurings of revolt during the latter half of the eighteenth century : three decades of the nineteenth were to pass before they became appreciably louder. While we have not reached the Romantic revolt, however, in the proper sense of that term, we have discovered that the inspiration of Romantic ideals was beginning to stir, and that, even at this early stage in its history, romanticism in Spain was not all revival.

V THE LATENESS OF THE NEW ROMANTICISM

The foregoing pages have shown that the immediate origins of the Romantic movement in Spain are far earlier in date than is generally imagined. Popular chronology puts those origins at approximately 1800 ; dates their termination, and the beginning of the Romantic movement proper, in 1835 ; and to the end of that movement assigns no date at all. We shall endeavour, in the following chapters, to correct the last two of these ideas : this chapter should have disposed of the first.

[1] Cf. p. 51, below.
[2] Estala : *Edipo Tirano*, Madrid, 1793, p. 3.
[3] *H.R.M.S.*, I, 78-81.

The resurgence of the primary Romantic principle—that of freedom—occurs, as we have seen, in the first half of the eighteenth century. The beginnings of both the Romantic revolt and the Romantic revival can be traced to a date not much later. The characteristics of Romantic literature which underlie the Revolt appear with frequency between 1750 and 1800. The Revival proceeds actively during the whole of this same period. By its close, the historian who examines his phenomena with impartiality and care may be forgiven for thinking that the emergence of a coherent and self-conscious Romantic movement is imminent.

But, in actual fact, for over one-third of the new century, nothing even approaching such a movement appeared. Why was this, if so many of the elements of Spanish romanticism were present in Spain before 1800 ? The chief reason is to be found in the political history of the years 1808 to 1833. Not only did the Napoleonic invasion check original literary productiveness, but for some time after its close it dried up the springs of subjectivity, so that patriotic and impersonal odes were preferred to lyrics charged with melancholy, sensibility and emotion. Mediaevalism, as such, lost its attraction, though the patriotic aspect of mediaevalism was still observable, principally in drama, and the waves of anti-Gallic feeling favoured the vogue of the dramatists of the Golden Age.

Then came the defeat of the invaders, the accession of Ferdinand VII and the two epochs of tyranny (1814-20 and 1823-33), which saw the exile of the most progressive of Ferdinand's subjects, including most of those who were on the way to becoming liberals in literature. During the War of Independence, there was little opportunity or inclination for literary pursuits, and, when it was over, exiled men of letters had to accept routine, or even menial, employment lest they starved. During the second period of absolutism (1823-33), when the Romantic movement was making such headway in France, the development of Spanish literature was almost completely arrested. " Literature," wrote one close observer and shrewd judge, was " enveloped in a dense cloud." Genius was " completely silent," and " the public completely indifferent." [1] The press was muzzled, books and reviews were constantly banned from circulation, foreign works (frequently non-political ones) were stopped at the frontiers and schools and universities were closed lest (to quote the notorious phrase applied to the short-lived University of Cervera) they should disseminate " the disastrous mania for thinking." When, after the death (1833) of the " tirano de las letras," as Ferdinand was commonly termed, the exiles returned to Spain, they found their country highly receptive and were able to make up for lost time. But, while Ferdinand reigned, it was impossible for new ideas to flourish ; a literary revolution in his time could only have come, as it had come in France, on the heels of a political one.

That is the main answer to the question : Why was the precipitation of the Romantic movement so long delayed ? But this " political " answer, as we may call it, is not com-pletely satisfactory. We shall see in due course that there was a fundamental weakness in nineteenth-century Spanish romanticism which is discernible in its history from the period during which the Revival and the Revolt began to unite until the time when the movement which resulted from their union was seen to be, to a large extent, a failure. As we look back upon those first thirty years of the nineteenth century, we cannot but interpret the dilatoriness of the Romantic movement in declaring itself as a sign of its inherent debility. True, many Spanish writers were in exile, but even in exile they wrote freely. With the fertility which has always characterized the national genius, they main-tained a number of more or less literary reviews, besides publishing books in considerable quantity. But anyone who turns up the files of *El Emigrado observador* or of *Ocios de españoles emigrados* will realize with what lifeless, conven-tional work the great majority of them were content. Nor were all Spain's foremost literary men among the emigrants. Some of them returned home long before the 1833 amnesty ; some of them never left the country at all ; in any case, as we shall presently see, there were quite enough writers there

[1] Ramón de Mesonero Romanos : *Memorias de un Setentón*, Madrid, 1891, II, 22.

during Ferdinand's reign to form literary coteries which were galaxies of potential talent. And yet, even with the glowing example of the French Romantics before them, these coteries achieved nothing in common and very little even as individuals, the chief part of that little being the antithesis of Romantic.

Viewed in the light of later events, these happenings must be taken as indications of weakness, of lack of enthusiasm for Romantic ideals, of the absence of any sense of solidarity. Had Ferdinand's death preluded the inauguration of a Romantic movement notable for strength, cohesion and vigour, the literary phenomena of the years preceding it might be interpreted very differently. At this stage of our narrative it is premature to go into further detail ; but, when we look back upon the position hereafter, it will become clearer.

CHAPTER II

THE ROMANTIC REVIVAL, 1800-1837[1]

I. FOREIGN INFLUENCES UPON THE ROMANTIC REVIVAL[2]

When the whole of the Romantic movement is viewed in its true perspective, by far the broader of the two currents described in the last chapter is seen to be the Romantic revival. This was in the main a native development, and foreign influences upon it have often been given more than their due importance, not least commonly by Spanish critics. The misconception—no doubt partly attributable to the habit, so general in Spain, of underrating the achievements of one's own countrymen—has become altogether too widely current. France has been given sole credit for the Romantic revolt in Spain, while France, Germany, Italy and England have jointly been credited with the Romantic revival.

This, like many unsound generalizations, sounds plausible enough, and—to foreigners at least—attractive enough, but it will not stand a moment's examination. Foreign influences there were, in plenty, upon the Revival, as also upon the Revolt ; they played, as it were, the part of foreign legionaries in the Classical-Romantic conflict. But once we realize how much of the Revival had been accomplished in Spain before the Napoleonic period the true position of these legionaries becomes clear. They came in from without, upon a battleground long since marked out for them, to help carry an engagement which, if not already won, was at any rate veering definitely in the direction which they favoured.

For convenience we shall first consider, in turn, the various foreign influences upon the Romantic revival, before returning to the native origins which we studied in the last chapter.

---

[1] *H.R.M.S.*, I, 82-204.   [2] *H.R.M.S.*, I, 82-115.

(i) *The Influence of Germany*

First in chronological order comes the influence of Germany, where the Romantic movement began about the end of the eighteenth century. In 1808 the Vienna lectures of August Wilhelm von Schlegel, and in 1812 a course by his brother Friedrich, gave a very high place to Spanish poetry and drama. To August Wilhelm, Romantic drama was indigenous only to England and to Spain ; Shakespeare and Calderón were the only two poets who could properly be called great. Calderón was his principal hero : " in audacity, fullness and profundity " he outsoared all his Spanish contemporaries ; " in him the Romantic drama of the Spaniards reached the summit of perfection." [1]

Friedrich, in his admiration for Calderón, went farther even than this ; but August Wilhelm had by far the wider and deeper influence ; he was reviewed, and excerpted in translation, even in Ferdinand VII's Spain. The influence of one of his translators, however, Böhl von Faber, father of the novelist Fernán Caballero, was greater still. A Hamburg merchant, educated abroad, who had settled in Cádiz, married a Spanish girl and become known as a book-collector and man of letters, he gradually won himself a firm place in the esteem of Spanish critics. His translations of Schlegel brought him into conflict with a conservative journalist, José Joaquín de Mora, and in September and October 1814 and throughout 1818-19 a controversy raged in the press, chiefly around the merits of Golden Age drama. On paper the conflict was indecisive but Böhl von Faber was generally held to have won a moral victory. [2]

This enthusiast from Hamburg also stimulated interest in the Revival with his *Floresta de rimas antiguas castellanas* (Hamburg, 1821), which, with its two supplements (1823, 1825), brought together no less than one thousand poems

---

[1] A. W. von Schlegel : *Über dramatische Kunst und Litteratur*, Heidelberg, 1809, 1811 (Vierzehnte Vorlesung, II, ii, 357-8).

[2] Cf. Camille Pitollet : *La Querelle calderónienne de Johan Nikolas Böhl von Faber et José Joaquín de Mora*, Paris, 1909. The course of the conflict is summarized in *H.R.M.S.*, I, 89-90, 115-9.

with annotations. This was only one of many publications illustrating the interest of Germans in Spanish balladry and having a direct repercussion in Spain—as well as in England. Herder's posthumously published verse translation of the Cid romances (*Der Cid : nach Spanischen Romanzen besungen :* Tübingen, 1805) was actually translated into English, while Grimm's *Silva de romances viejos* (Vienna, 1815), which had a Spanish introduction, was described by Lockhart as a "small but very elegant collection."[1] Better known in Spain than either of these was Depping's *Sammlung der besten alten Spanischen . . . Romanzen* (Altenburg and Leipzig, 1817), which was republished in London, in Spanish, by some Spanish refugees, in 1825, and finally re-issued, with a critical preface by Antonio Alcalá Galiano, in 1844.

(ii) *The Influence of France*

The other three countries which chiefly influenced the Revival—France, England and Italy—have this in common, that their influence came directly, through the diffusion in Spain of the works of a small number of their greatest creative writers, rather than indirectly, by means of the publication at home either of Spanish anthologies or of critical works on Spanish literature.

Of French authors the most important was Chateaubriand,[2] whose cult of melancholy, religiosity, picturesqueness, exoticism and local colour, together with the interest in Spain displayed in his *Itinéraire* and *Dernier Abencerrage*, combined to win him popularity in that country. The years 1800 to 1830 were marked by the steadily increasing vogue of his novels, after which his political and historical works became popular also. Though all his imaginative writings were translated early into Spanish, by far the most widely read was *Atala*, of which a Spanish version was published in Paris in the very year (1801) of its appearance, and in Spain

---

[1] *Ancient Spanish Ballads*, London, 1853, 4th ed., p. viii.

[2] Cf. E. Allison Peers : " La influencia de Chateaubriand en España," in *R:F.E.*, 1924, XI, 351-82 ; J. Sarrailh : " La fortune d'*Atala* en Espagne," in *Homenaje ofrecido a Menéndez Pidal*, Madrid, 1925, I, 255-68.

two years later. Nineteen translations of this novel in all appeared during these thirty years. " Cuando a principios de este siglo leyeron los españoles la *Atala*," wrote the Valencian publisher, Cabrerizo,

> sorprendióles el nuevo género de novela con que el joven Chateaubriand acababa de enriquecer la literatura ; .... aquella narración tan fácil y animada, ... las variadas y magníficas descripciones, el florido lenguaje, y aquella poesía, en fin, tan brillante a la vez y tan sencilla como el país y las costumbres que describe. El nombre de Chateaubriand corrió ya desde entonces de boca en boca.[1]

Though Chateaubriand seems to have exercised no fundamental influence on any prominent Spanish writer, with the exception of Enrique Gil, he counted for much in the development of the Romantic revival and many would think of him as nearer in spirit to Spain than any other foreign author associated with it.

(iii)   *The Influence of England*

In England, the political refugees from Ferdinand VII's Spain absorbed a good deal of English literature, though there is little evidence as to how much of it they carried back to Spain. Any such influence, however, as they may have exerted upon the Spanish Revival cannot be compared with the stupendous influence of Sir Walter Scott.[2] References to Scott can be traced in Spanish periodical literature from as early as 1818. Before 1824 he was " recognized (*sc.*, in Spain) as the first Romantic of this century."[3] By the thirties he was being discussed in every fashionable Madrid drawing-room. " Donde hay una novela de Walter-Scott," remarks a society weekly in 1834, " calle todo el mundo."[4]

---

[1] *Obras completas del Vizconde de Chateaubriand*, Valencia, Cabrerizo, 1843. Vol. I : Prólogo del editor español.

[2] Cf. Philip H. Churchman and E. Allison Peers : *A Survey of the influence of Sir Walter Scott in Spain*, New York, Paris, 1922 ; E. Allison Peers : *Studies in the influence of Sir Walter Scott in Spain*, New York, Paris, 1926.

[3] *El Europeo*, February 14, 1824.

[4] *Correo de las Damas*, Cf. *H.R.M.S.*, I, 107.

The " Cervantes of Scotland," as Scott was frequently termed, found numerous translators : he figured in the lists of no less than nineteen Madrid publishers, while in Barcelona twenty-five separate translations from his works appeared in as many years. But the remarkable feature of his vogue is the way in which Spaniards paid him the flattering honour of imitation. His imitators, writes a contemporary, were " as numerous as toads after a shower of rain in summer.[1] And they included well-known writers, who did not scruple to borrow freely. López Soler's *Los Bandos de Castilla* (1830) was described by Mesonero Romanos as " *Ivanhoe* in disguise".[2] Espronceda's *Sancho Saldaña* (1834) was based on the same novel and probably influenced by others.[3] Enrique Gil's *El Señor de Bembibre* (1844) has marked similarities with *The Bride of Lammermoor*.[4] López Soler and Espronceda not only imitate *Ivanhoe*, but translate whole passages from it, altering nothing but proper names, allusions or other phrases which Spaniards would not understand. A more intelligent and significant use of Scott is to be found in the *Moro expósito* (1834) of the Duque de Rivas,[5] who in that same year attributed publicly to that author's " admirable romances," and also to the originality of Byron and Hugo, the beginnings of a new interest in Spanish national history.[6] " The peerless Walter Scott," wrote Milá y Fontanals ten years later, " can up to a certain point be called the inventor of the (historical) novel."[7] He was certainly the father of that *genre* in nineteenth-century Spain.

Of minor English influences on the Revival, the chief is probably that of Ossian,[8] translated in 1788 and again in 1800.   Ossianic references and terminology persist right through the first half of the nineteenth century.   In the

[1] Cf. Churchman and Allison Peers, *op. cit.*, p. 24.

[2] Cf. E. Allison Peers : *Studies*, etc., pp. 12-39.

[3] *Op. cit.*, pp. 40-69.   [4] *Op. cit.*, pp. 70-91.

[5] Cf. E. Allison Peers : *Rivas and Romanticism in Spain*, Liverpool, 1923, pp. 94-101, and *Ángel de Saavedra, Duque de Rivas, a Critical Study*, New York, Paris, 1923, pp. 275-303.

[6] Cf. Churchman and Allison Peers, *op. cit.*, p. 33.   [7] *Op. cit.*, p. 39.

[8] Cf. E. Allison Peers : " The influence of Ossian in Spain," in *Philological Quarterly*, Iowa City, 1925, IV, 121-38.

" bardo caledón," as he was termed, Spanish poets found, not only that remote civilization which so greatly attracted them, but also, and in the crudest form, most of the qualities called " Romantic " : vagueness and mystery, subjectivity, melancholy, sensitiveness to Nature—and, of course, a vast assortment of novel phrases with which one could mystify the uninitiated reader. The wonder is that Ossian's vogue was not far greater.

Milton was greatly admired by Meléndez Valdés, and among his translators were Cadalso and Jovellanos, but he exercised no fundamental influence on Spanish literature.[1] The same may be said of Shakespeare, translated again and again, but generally through the French.[2] Young, on the other hand, had a considerable vogue, and influenced Cadalso, Cienfuegos and Meléndez Valdés.[3]   Southey's Hispanic activities were often eulogized in the Spanish press, but his original work seems to have attracted little attention.[4]

(iv) *The Influence of Italy*

In Italy we find no author who helped to mould the Romantic revival in Spain as the Schlegels did in Germany, Chateaubriand in France and Scott in England. Alessandro Manzoni, however, had a certain vogue in Spain ;[5] and, considering the sympathy which he had with the ideals of the Revival, it is surprising that it was not earlier or more general. His famous novel, *I Promessi Sposi*, was translated into Spanish in 1833 and again in 1836-7 ; in 1837, Martínez de la Rosa placed him on a level of merit with Sir Walter

[1] Cf. E. Allison Peers : " Milton in Spain," in *Studies in Philology*, Chapel Hill, N.C., 1926, XXIII, 169-83.

[2] Cf. A. Par : *Shakespeare en la literatura española*, Madrid, 1935, 2 vols. ; E. Juliá Martínez : *Shakespeare en España*, Madrid, 1918 ; Ramon Esquerra : *Shakespeare a Catalunya*, Barcelona, 1937.

[3] Cf. E. Allison Peers : " The influence of Young and Gray in Spain," in *Modern Language Review*, Cambridge, 1926, XXI, 404-18.

[4] Cf. L. Pfandl : " Robert Southey und Spanien," in *R.H.*, 1913, XXVIII, 1-315.

[5] Cf. E. Allison Peers : " The influence of Manzoni in Spain," in *A Miscellany of Studies*, Cambridge, 1932, pp. 370-84.

Scott. His dramas and poems (particularly the " Cinque Maggio ")[1] also had some vogue in Spain at this time. A new wave of interest in him invaded the country about 1841 and yet another some nine years later. But his formative influence upon the Romantic revival must be limited to that of his great novel.

Besides Manzoni, and Alfieri (who belongs principally to the Revolt), Metastasio, Goldoni, Ugo Foscolo, Silvio Pellico and Tommaso Grossi were commonly read in Spain during the early years of the Romantic revival. A version of the *Ultime Lettere di Jacopo Ortis* appeared in 1833. *Le Mie Prigioni* was translated twice (1836, 1837) within five years of its first appearance. The influence of Grossi belongs chiefly to Catalan literary history : though it was in Castilian that Aribau published (1824) some selections from his novel *Ildegonda*, the only translation of any one of his complete works was in Catalan. [2] The popularity of Manzoni, Pellico and Foscolo, as well as of Grossi, in Barcelona emphasizes their connection with the Revival rather than with the Revolt, for, as we shall see, the Revival-aspect of the Romantic movement was predominant in that city.

(v) *A Cosmopolitan Influence : Sismondi*

One isolated instance of foreign influence upon the Romantic revival may be added here. Simonde de Sismondi, a Genevan whose work for a time enjoyed a European reputation, published (Paris, 1813) a four-volume history of Romance literature, *De la Littérature du Midi de l'Europe*, which went into eight editions, was translated into three languages and was quoted frequently in Spain (notably during the Böhl-Mora controversy) between 1813 and 1835. Though differing from the Schlegels in his low èstimate of Calderón, he agrees with them in commending the literature of Spain to the rest of Europe as wholly Romantic, unsurpassed in fertility and imaginative power, and particularly

---

[1] M. Gasparini : " Traducciones españolas del ' Cinco de Mayo ' de Alejandro Manzoni," Rome, 1948.

[2] Cortada's version of the dialectal *Fuggitiva* (*La Noya fugitiva*, Barcelona, 1834).

in holding up its neglected Golden Age drama as thoroughly worthy of study.

II. AN EARLY MILESTONE : THE *EUROPEO* (1823-4)[1]

Nowhere did foreign influence upon the Revival show itself more strikingly than in the *Europeo*, a little weekly " review of science, arts and literature " which appeared in Barcelona from October 1823 to April 1824 and may most properly be thought of as cosmopolitan. Though contemporary periodicals hardly noticed either its advent or its demise, it is of great importance historically, not only as an attempt to incorporate Spain in the intellectual movement of Europe, but also, and chiefly, for its literary position *vis-à-vis* romanticism.

Of its five editors, one, Ernest Cook, was an English scientist ; two, Fiorenzi Galli and Luigi Monteggia, were Italian literary men exiled from their country ; and two, Buenaventura Carlos Aribau and Ramón López Soler, were Spaniards. The foreign literary influence comes through Monteggia, who finds three elements in the " essence of romanticism " : a style " simple, melancholy and full of feeling " ; arguments drawn from the modern world as well as from the ancient ; and an execution in which form is subordinated to theme and " overmuch regularity rejected."[2] This very moderate standpoint is also taken by López Soler. He thinks of romanticism as a kind of " Ossianism," with its origin in chivalry and the Crusades : its heroes and its atmosphere are more attractive, more picturesque and more poetic than those of antiquity :

> No podemos negar que al tomar la pluma para describir algún objeto de la edad media se apodere de nosotros un venerable entusiasmo. Sobre todo cuanto tiene referencia con la caballería sorprende de antemano la fantasía y excita algún sentimiento de ternura en el corazón.[3]

[1] *H.R.M.S.*, I, 119-23.

[2] *Europeo*, I, 48-56, October 25, 1823. Reproduced in *Bulletin of Spanish Studies*, Liverpool, 1931, VIII, 144-9.

[3] From an article " Las costumbres de los antiguos caballeros " in *Europeo*, Vol. II, No. 2 (1824).

When he analyses " the burning issue between Romantics and Classicists," he comes out as more moderate even than Monteggia, advocating reconciliation between the two opposing forces before they are so much as drawn up in battle array—that is to say, in his own country—almost, indeed, before the term " Romantic " has become naturalized there.[1]

We shall be able later to appreciate the significance of this reconciliatory attitude : for the moment we may be content with summarizing the principal services which the *Europeo* rendered to Spanish letters. It was an early purveyor of cosmopolitanism, not only publicizing such prominent writers as Scott and Byron, but introducing to Spaniards, by means of translations or reviews, many less known authors—*e.g.*, Collins, Moore, Millevoye, Grossi. It popularized Oriental and mediaeval subjects. It encouraged investigation and criticism. It printed creative work, some of it Romantic or semi-Romantic in character. But its principal importance lies in its early date, hardly later than that of the beginnings of self-conscious romanticism in France ; in its diffusion of a conception of Romantic art which belonged essentially to the Revival ; and in its sane and conciliatory attitude to classicism—an attitude which, once romanticism as a movement had fallen into discredit, was to dominate Spain.

III. THE REVIVAL OF MEDIAEVAL LITERATURE[2]

Having now discussed the direct and indirect influences of other countries upon the Romantic revival in Spain, we return to the beginning of the new century to trace the history of the Revival as a whole—first, as regards mediaevalism, and then in relation to the Golden Age.

It was about 1800, or rather later, that interest in the Middle Ages became so concentrated that it assumed the character of a concerted revival. Although the popularizers

---

[1] *H.R.M.S.*, I, 121.
[2] *H.R.M.S.*, I, 123-67.

of mediaevalism had neither an agreed programme nor a common plan of campaign, the number of works which they produced during the first third of the nineteenth century is so large, and their scope is so varied, that they convey the impression of a co-operation which reaches its climax in a series of works to be referred to later in this section—the *Romanceros* (1828-32) of Agustín Durán.

(i) *The Revival in Drama*

In drama, no great progress in mediaevalization was made until the Romantic revival was reinforced by the full weight of the Revolt, but mediaeval Spanish subjects continued to attract dramatists as they had been doing during the late eighteenth century, though they were treated either in a frigidly pseudo-Classical or in an unashamedly melo-dramatic way. From time to time political events lent these subjects additional popularity, and, though cosmopolitanism was often a characteristic of them, patriotism was a more powerful attraction during the War of Independence and the years which immediately followed it. Martínez de la Rosa's *La Viuda de Padilla* was written during the siege of Cádiz and first played in an improvised theatre of that city, while the very soldiers, marching to battle, would declaim stirring snatches from Quintana's *Pelayo*.[1]

The outbursts of liberalism which occurred in 1820 and 1833 drew much of their literary inspiration from a history in which ideals of freedom and independence are very prominent. A typical play of 1820, *La Libertad restaurada*,[2] drags Pelayo and the Cid into the company of Daoiz and Velarde during a single act in which the " Genio Español " breaks the fetters that bind him, while patriotic songs are sung by a " chorus of shades," against a background distinctly Romantic :

[1] Louis Viardot : *Etudes sur l'histoire des institutions . . . en Espagne*, Paris, 1835, p. 361.

[2] *La Libertad restaurada*. Representación dramática patriótica escrita . . . . por los ciudadanos Ubariso (=Aribau), Martilo (=? F. de P. Martí), Lopecio (=López Soler) y Selta Rúnega (=Altés y Casals), Barcelona, 1820.

Representa el teatro un templo magnífico rodeado de sepulcros : en los bastidores, si es posible, sarcófagos y esqueletos ; varias lámparas moribundas esparcidas por la escena.

Equally typical, and of greater merit, is the *Lanuza* (1823) of Ángel de Saavedra, later Duque de Rivas,[1] in which the famous Justice of Aragon symbolizes liberalism defying monarchical oppression and declamatory speeches make almost overt reference to the tyranny which the Liberals of 1823 believed to be vanquished.

Soon after the amnesty of 1833, the history of the Romantic movement became virtually that of the Classical-Romantic battle to be described in the next two chapters. Throughout the four years, 1834-7, during which that battle was at its height, the Revolt lent a powerful stimulus to the drama of the mediaeval Revival : many of the plays with mediaeval themes published or acted between 1800 and 1837 belong to those years, during which the Revolt was making itself felt and every dramatist was considering how far he should associate himself with it. The most important of these plays, and the new type of drama which they represented, will be described later. They represent the climax of the mediaeval Revival on the stage ; their treatment is in complete harmony with their theme ; and they show no remnants whatever of pseudo-classicism. In any summary view of the drama of this period, it must not be forgotten how important a part is played by the few years at its close.

(ii) *The Revival in Prose Fiction*

The advance made in the mediaeval Revival during the first third of the nineteenth century is much more marked in prose fiction than in drama. This was perhaps natural, since in the seventeenth century the novel had been mainly Romantic and in the eighteenth had almost disappeared. There was nothing to protest or to fight against, as there was

---

[1] Though not strictly mediaeval in theme, *Lanuza* is an example of the type of play most commonly associated with mediaeval subjects during this period. Its authorship gives it additional interest.

in poetry and drama. No conventions had to be uprooted. The new novelists could work almost upon a *tabula rasa*. They needed, not incentives to revolution, but the breath of inspiration, which came to them mainly from Spain's early history.

This provided them with an ample number of themes full of power : the exploits of semi-legendary heroes, such as Pelayo, Fernán González and Bernardo del Carpio, the prowess of the Cid, the expansion of Catalonia-Aragon, the reconquest of Granada, the discovery of America, and so forth. What they lacked was original genius to interpret those themes and to give them some permanence of expression. Because of this, the early historical novel in Spain was an almost complete failure. On the other hand, it was an almost pure product of the Romantic revival, and, for all its mediocrity, it was highly popular. The success of innumerable poor novels by third-rate authors testifies eloquently to the movement's strength. For years before authors of the merit of Larra, Escosura and Espronceda tried their hands at prose fiction, the public had a craving for novels which should re-create past history—especially that of Spain—and this craving had at first to be satisfied by means of translations.

"¡ Y qué traducciones ! " as the younger Moratín had exclaimed towards the end of the preceding century. "Hechas casi todas sin conocimiento de la materia que en ellas se trata, sin poseer bastantemente ninguno de los dos idiomas."[1] Yet, bad as they were, they found an eager public, and formed the staple part of many collections of fiction. Apart from Scott, who came easily first in popularity, the chief British authors translated were Richardson, Fielding, Monk Lewis and Ann Radcliffe.[2] As an antidote to the English " novel of terror," the young person of the time could assimilate such genteel French novelists as Mme. Cottin and Mme. Genlis, together with the effusive Florian. Rousseau,

---

[1] *La Derrota de los pedantes*, Madrid, 1789, p. 68.

[2] Cf. Ada M. Coe : " Richardson in Spain," in *H.R.*, 1935, III, 56-63 ; E. Allison Peers : " Minor English influences on Spanish romanticism," in *R.H.*, 1924, LXII, 443-5.

too, was popular : of his *Nouvelle Héloise* six Spanish editions
(two of them reprints) appeared between 1814 and 1823 ;
of *Emile*, either five or six between 1817 and 1822.[1] These
authors, of course, had little or nothing in common with the
mediaeval tradition ; they are enumerated here partly as
examples of the type of rivalry against which that tradition
had to contend and partly in order to give a balanced account
of the state of prose fiction during the period under survey.

Let us preface our examination of the original novels of
the Romantic revival with a brief account of the types of
prose fiction chiefly in vogue in Spain during the first third of
the nineteenth century.   Some of the novels were of an
inspiring character, written to serve the ends of morality or
religion. The majority, however, kept their moral aim well
in the background and concentrated upon entertainment.
Often they were ridiculously sentimental and couched in an
exaggerated poetic diction. Less commonly, they catered for
the reader who liked melodrama at home as well as at the
theatre, as in the twelve volumes of the notorious *Galería
fúnebre de historias trágicas* (Madrid, 1831), pilloried by Larra
and Mesonero Romanos.[2]

To all these types the historical novel offered a refreshing
contrast. It may be said to have begun with two works
written in English, and published in London, by a young
exile from Santander, Telesforo Trueba y Cosío[3] : *Gómez
Arias* (1828) and *The Castilian* (1829). Though not translated
into Spanish until 1831 and 1845 respectively, these books
would have been familiar to the Spanish exiles : Menéndez y
Pelayo went so far as to call Trueba " the father of the
(Spanish) historical novel."[4] *Gómez Arias*, while owing much
of its technique to Scott, is founded upon Calderón's play
La Niña de Gómez Arias, derives some of its characters from
Cervantes or from Golden Age drama and draws freely on
Spanish history. *The Castilian* goes back to the time of Peter

---

[1] Cf. J. R. Spell, in *H.R.*, 1934, II, 134-52.

[2] Its author was a certain Agustín Pérez Zaragoza Godínez. Cf. *H.R.M.S.*,
I, 135-6.

[3] Cf. M. Menéndez y Pelayo : *Trueba y Cosío*, Santander, 1876.

[4] *Op. cit.*, p. 248.

the Cruel, and, like *Gómez Arias*, contains elucidatory notes and a historical introduction. In it he writes with ease, sometimes even with fire and spirit, on a subject " affording, perhaps, one of the most striking romantic series of incidents in the annals of any people."[1] We need not enquire too carefully into his interpretation of the word " romantic."

These two London romances were closely followed, in Spain, by López Soler's plagiarism of Scott, *Los Bandos de Castilla, o El Caballero del Cisne* (1830),[2] in which mediaeval history is reinforced by the Romantic traits of sensitiveness, melancholy and love of Nature. The Caballero del Cisne, whose heart is " sobradamente tierno," sighs and groans for a true friend, yet flees from man and indulges his " inclinación desabrida y melancólica " by taking solitary walks and losing himself in forests. The two heroines, Blanca and Matilde, are of a similar type : Blanca, referred to as "ángel de la melancolía," is apt to be plunged into sad reveries by the beauties of Nature. The author's ideal spot is the " plácido recinto, verdaderamente romántico y solitario," and his Nature scenes greatly surpass those of his immediate predecessors. The novel received the warmest and widest of eulogies and many at this time looked upon López Soler as a future literary leader.

Between 1830 and 1834 historical novels became more and more plentiful. Estanislao de Cosca Vayo, in *La Conquista de Valencia por el Cid* (1831), which he intended to be the first of a series of novels illustrating " the principal events and customs of the (Spanish) nation in different ages," treated his hero with the most exaggerated idealism and introduced into his background an abundance of local colour. López Soler's *Jaime el Barbudo* (1832), though not strictly historical, portrays a well-known Romantic type, the noble bandit ; his *Henrique de Lorena* is a tragic love-story written around the France of the Guises, full of Romantic devices and preceded by an introduction which stresses the importance to the historical novel of appropriate atmosphere. Patricio de la Escosura's first novel, *El Conde de Candespina* (1832),

---

[1] *The Castilian*, London, 1829, I, v.   [2] Cf. p. 29, above.

indebted to Scott, is equally full of faults and of promise. López Soler's *El Primogénito de Alburquerque* (1833-4) adapts episodes from the reign of Peter the Cruel, without great success. Juan Cortada's first novel, *Tancredo en el Asia* (1833), a " historical romance of the time of the Crusades," has a preface, written with the " impetuosity of youth," which attacks the "sinnúmero de novelas insulsas y despreciables " that fill the bookshops and calls upon " true Spaniards " to "show the fertility of their talent and the liveliness of imagination with which Nature has dowered them " by reconstructing the Middle Ages and the epoch of chivalry. These are the chief of the mediocre productions of this quinquennium.

The year 1834 marks the zenith of the early historical novel in Spain, which was enriched by the work of two writers of experience and repute, both of whom essayed it for the first time.

José de Espronceda, in *Sancho Saldaña*, made as free use of *Ivanhoe* as López Soler had done, and his dependence upon Sir Walter Scott increases as he proceeds. His novel is not a good one : the plot is too full of incident and loosely knit ; the characters are, at best, only types—at worst, caricatures ; and the style is prolix, repetitive and heavy. Even the chief contribution made by the book to the Romantic movement —its use of the mysterious and the supernatural—is a much less effective one than we should expect of the author of *El Estudiante de Salamanca*.[1] On the other hand, the novel has some striking descriptive passages, introduces the mysterious and the supernatural, manifests a concern for exactness in local colour and shows an evident interest in Nature.

Mariano José de Larra's *El Doncel de Don Enrique el Doliente*, on a theme which he also treated in his play *Macías*, reminds one less of Scott than of the French Romantics. " Procede en línea recta," wrote Julio Nombela, " del ultra-romanticismo francés, superficial y declamatorio, tendencioso y efectista. Es una serie de peregrinos lances que se desarrollan en un ambiente malsano, donde dominan la

---

[1] Cf. E. Allison Peers : *Studies*, etc., pp. 40-69 ; N. B. Adams : " Notes on Espronceda's *Sancho Saldaña*," in *H.R.*, V, 304-8.

fatalidad del amor y las traiciones de melodrama."[1] But the *Doncel* is much more readable than this description would suggest. Though it lacks some of the beauties of *Macías*, its greater length and permissible discursiveness soften much of the violence of its sentiment and action, without in the least impairing its evident sincerity. It is, on the whole, well constructed, and its characters, if not consistently life-like, could at least have existed. The prominence which it gives to the theme of unbridled love makes it one of the few early novels which contributed anything to the Revolt. The Revival it served by its author's zeal for mediaeval local colour, though the zeal was not always according to knowledge.

From 1834 onwards, the historical novel becomes more definitely Romantic : the technique of the new mode is now not merely tolerated in the author, but expected of him. Vayo's " original historical novel, belonging to the year 1254," entitled *Los Expatriados, o Zulema y Gazul* (1834) preaches a political idealism which extends to literature and colours narrative and characterization throughout. Escosura's second novel, *Ni Rey ni Roque* (1835), contains a public profession of his Romantic faith as well as nearly all the characteristics of romanticism. José García de Villalta's *El Golpe en vago* (1835) contributes to the Revival only occasional archaeological descriptions but lays a stress on the purely horrible quite out of keeping with native Spanish romanticism, though, as we shall see, it is found elsewhere about this time. Cortada's *La Heredera de Sangumí* (1835) has a typically exaggerated Romantic ending, while his *El Rapto de Doña Almodis* (1836) is bathed in mystery, melancholy and tears.

By 1837, the *genre* was frankly on the decline, and this became accentuated in the years immediately following. Martínez de la Rosa's *Doña Isabel de Solís* (1837)[2] stands out as a contribution to the Revival by its substantial length and the reputation of its author. In Eugenio de Ochoa's *El Auto*

---

[1] *Larra*, Madrid, 1906, p. 120.

[2] The first volume was published in 1837 ; the second in 1839 and the third in 1846.

de fe (1837), as in most other historical novels of this date, Revival and Revolt meet.

(iii) *The Revival in Lyric and Narrative Poetry*

In lyric and narrative poetry the mediaeval Revival takes two forms : the introduction into original poetry of mediaeval ideas, sentiments, technique and local colour, and the continuing re-publication and popularization of the mediaeval ballads. These two forms will be considered in that order.

Despite a considerable persistence of the pseudo-Classical manner in Spanish poetry, Romantic art returned tardily and slowly to Spanish verse, and one of the first signs of its return was a free use of mediaeval themes. Examples will be found in the early poems of Ángel de Saavedra (*El Paso honroso*, 1812 ; *Florinda*, 1824-6 ; and a few of the shorter pieces) [1] and in the *Pelayo* (c. 1824-6) of the youthful and still unemancipated Espronceda. [2] Even in such un-Romantic authors as Quintana, Gallardo and Noroña one can find lyrical and narrative reminiscences of the Middle Ages, while the early volumes of *Cartas españolas*, a review greatly addicted to mediaevalism, printed a number of semi-Romantic poems and tales of mediaeval inspiration by Serafín Estébanez Calderón.

The revival of interest in the mediaeval *romances*, or ballads, is generally associated with Agustín Durán, but in reality goes back far beyond him. The opinion which he emitted, in 1828, that the ballad stood for the " verdadera y original poesía lírica castellana," [3] had already been voiced by the still Classically-minded Martínez de la Rosa : " El romance es en realidad la poesía nacional de España . . . El romance es propiamente la poesía lírica de los españoles." [4]

---

[1] Cf. E. Allison Peers : *Ángel de Saavedra, etc.*, pp. 115, 132-45, 153-5, 186-98.

[2] *H.R.M.S.*, I, 154-5.

[3] *Romancero de romances moriscos*, Madrid, 1828. Prólogo.

[4] *Poética* (*Obras literarias*, Paris, 1827, I, 276).

When a preceptist of the more pedantic type, Gómez Hermosilla, made bold, in 1826, to depreciate mediaeval Spanish poetry, he was answered by two critics, Gómez de la Cortina and Hugalde y Mollinedo :

> Al público nunca se le engaña : . . . Sostendremos eternamente que nuestros buenos Romances son modelos que nunca debe perder de vista el que aspire a la perfección poética, sea cual fuere el género de poesía que haya adoptado.[1]

Imitations of mediaeval ballads were frequently published during the eighteen-twenties. Even unromantics like Mendibil and Silvela, in their four-volume anthology of Spanish literature (1819), mingled mediaeval ballads with conventional poems of the preceding century. The Cid was now once again a national hero, and the *Poema del Cid*, though it had been known to Spaniards for little more than fifty years, was already a national classic. In 1818 was re-published, " en lenguaje antiguo," Juan de Escobar's *Romancero del Cid* (Alcalá, 1612), " adorned " with an " epitome of the genuine history of the Cid " and with " various notes and compositions of the same time and on the same subject."

Another work which in some quarters was hailed as a contribution to the mediaeval Revival was the *Espagne poétique* (Paris, 1826-7) of an elderly ex-politician living in Paris, Juan María Maury.[2] The attribution was unduly flattering. The book was, in its own words, a two-volume " selection of Castilian poetry from the time of Charles V to our own day, done into French verse," accompanied by an introduction and notes. The first volume, it is true, contains some mediaeval selections, beginning with *Mío Cid* and Berceo, and going down to Boscán. But it is fairly clear that these were included for the sake of completeness : no critic who dated the " restoration of taste " from 1700, and described Luzán as in any respect a poet of the first order,[3]

---

[1] In F. Bouterwek : *Historia de la literatura española, etc.*, Madrid, 1829, p. 172.

[2] Cf. the review by Larra in *Revista española*, April 24, 1834, reprinted in his works.

[3] *Espagne poétique*, Paris, 1826-7, II, 219, 237.

could have much sympathy with the Middle Ages. None the less, Maury's versions were widely read, especially in France and England, and must have exercised some indirect influence upon Spain.

All this prepared the way for the work of Agustín Durán, a man who contributed to every stage in the progress of the Romantic movement. A Madrilenian, for some time Director of the Biblioteca Nacional, he produced a substantial amount in his mature years : a collection of Golden Age plays under the title of *Talía española* (1834),[1] an edition of Tirso de Molina (1839-42), a collection of Ramón de la Cruz's *sainetes* (1843), and, last in date but first in importance, a *Romancero general* (1849-50). The piece of work by which he is chiefly remembered, however, was completed before he was forty and it is to the formative years of the Romantic movement that he essentially belongs. The publication, in 1828, of his great Academy discourse on modern criticism and old Spanish drama[2] is a milestone of progress comparable with the Böhl-Mora polemic and the foundation of the *Europeo*. He was for many years in constant touch with Böhl von Faber, who admired his work greatly, and the association enhanced the excellent effect which his contentions produced upon the younger and more progressive critics. " His name," wrote one of these, " will be graven upon the hearts of all good Spaniards."[3]

The value of the *Discurso* lies in its author's keen appreciation of earlier literature, in the sincerity of his convictions and in the attractiveness and suggestiveness both of his arguments and of his defence of them. Though sympathetic to the Revolt, its chief contribution is to the Revival. It prepared the way for a genuinely Spanish renaissance. It makes no mention of Victor Hugo or of any other contemporary foreign Romantics. It is inspired, as it; peroration

---

[1] Cf. p. 53, below.

[2] *Discurso sobre el influjo que ha tenido la crítica moderna en la decadencia del teatro antiguo español, y sobre el modo con que debe ser considerado para juzgar convenientemente de su mérito peculiar.* Madrid, 1828. It can be conveniently read in *M.A.E.*, II, 280-336.

[3] Juan Donoso Cortés : *Obras*, Madrid, 1903-4, III, 28.

tells us, by a " patriotic impulse " [1] for the Spain which in the Middle Ages was " mistress and model " of all other nations, [2] and by a deep conviction that the Spanish dramatists whom it is defending are " perhaps the greatest poets in the world." [3] Since the pamphlet as a whole is concerned chiefly with these, the dramatists of the Golden Age, it will be considered at greater length in the next section : we can form from it, however, a fairly clear idea of Durán as a mediaevalist.

Its opening paragraphs indulge in a glorification of the days when all nations flocked to the Spanish universities, to sit under Moslem teachers, the rest of Europe being " submerged in the darkness of ignorance." [4] The first love-poets of southern France learned their melodies in Toledo, Córdoba and Seville. Catalonian and Aragonese troubadours came to the court of John II of Castile and the peculiar characteristics of their poetry blended with those of the Moors of Andalusia. Spanish poetry, declares Durán, unites more dissimilar elements and is thus richer than the poetry of any other country in the south of Europe. [5] The national character is in sympathy with the " noble and generous gallantry" of the Middle Ages, [6] for which reason even heroes of antiquity can be made acceptable on the Spanish stage if they are represented as acting like mediaeval Spanish gentlemen. [7] And it is in the " heroic mediaeval centuries " that we find " the germ of the sublime and beautiful creations of the Romantics," [8] so very much finer than anything belonging to antiquity.

The patriotic note in Durán's mediaevalism is unmistakable. As he conceived it, the Romantic revival was before all things Spanish. From the very first line of the *Discurso*, he appeals for the restoration of " la gloria patria." His pride in all that " Spain can boast," he declares, should be shared by all Spaniards.

A practical patriot, he reinforced his exhortations by his own example, carrying farther the rehabilitation of Spain's ballad-literature begun by Sarmiento, Sánchez, Floranes

[1] *M.A.E.*, II, 321.
[2] *M.A.E.*, II, 283.
[3] *M.A.E.*, II, 319.
[4] *M.A.E.*, II, 283-4.
[5] *M.A.E.*, II, 284.
[6] *M.A.E.*, II, 315.
[7] *M.A.E.*, II, 302-3.
[8] *M.A.E.*, II, 305-6.

and others in his own country and by Herder, Grimm, Depping and Böhl von Faber in Germany. His five-volume ballad-collection, published between 1828 and 1832, comprised : (i) *romances moriscos;* (ii) *coplas y canciones de arte menor, letras, letrillas, romances cortos,* etc. ; (iii) *romances doctrinales, amatorios, festivos, jocosos, satíricos y burlescos ;* and (iv), (v) two volumes of *romances caballerescos e históricos.* These last two volumes have a long preface, dealing chiefly with theories on the origin of the Spanish ballad, which describes the editor's frankly popular principle of selection, his aim being to provide " roses rather than thorns " and thus to " cajole the imaginations " of readers who had been brought up on eighteenth-century literature and criticism. He admits that he has included bad work with good ; but, despite this, and despite his debts to Böhl von Faber and Depping, his achievement is great enough to give him without question first place among the early leaders of the mediaeval Revival.

One other work, and perhaps only one, may be considered of comparable importance with Durán's *Romanceros :* the *Moro expósito* (1834) of Ángel de Saavedra, later Duque de Rivas.[1] This long narrative poem was begun at Malta in September 1829, finished there in May 1833, and published at Paris early in the year following. It is important for its length, for its combination of erudition and artistry, and above all for the manifold uses which it makes of the Middle Ages. Antonio Alcalá Galiano, in his unsigned preface to the poem, remarks that mediaeval Spanish history, a " most fertile field," has been " greatly neglected by our poets, except by a few dramatists ; and, if our modern writers of tragedy have occasionally treated this theme, they have treated it in the so-called ' Classical ' spirit—that is to say, in a way unbefitting to it."[2]

Rivas, he claims, has " pointed out a path untrodden until now by his compatriots," and has " ventured to tread it boldly."[3] Many later critics have since echoed that judgment. His poem " has no precedent in our literature,"

---

[1] E. Allison Peers : *Ángel de Saavedra, etc.,* pp. 58-62, 211-378, 575-91.
[2] *Obras completas,* Madrid, 1894-1904, III, xxxi.
[3] *Op. cit.,* III, vii.

wrote Juan Valera, " nor does it resemble anything of an earlier date." [1] Whatever degree of merit we may ascribe to it, we must perforce agree. Rivas achieved something more than a vast *leyenda* or a loosely strung collection of *romances ;* he has given us a semi-epic treatment of a mediaeval and national theme [2] and raised a monument to mediaevalism which is of great historical significance as well as of intrinsic merit.

There is much in the *Moro expósito* which will repay study. Rivas had examined his sources with care and his treatment of them was skilful. [3] He introduced mediaeval local colour with a freedom previously unknown in the history of the mediaeval Revival. [4] He embodied suggestions (and occasionally whole passages) from Sir Walter Scott, thus blending elements from the Spanish and the Scottish revival. [5] He modernized the character of his hero, Mudarra, and to a lesser extent some of the minor characters, in accordance with the artistic conceptions current in his day. [6] Similarly, he incorporated in his technique various principles which were being exploited in different countries as befitting modern art and held up in contrast to others which the Romantics were ridiculing and despising.

One important final remark must be made upon the *Moro expósito*. It is a common fallacy to credit only the drama of the Spanish Romantic movement with the exaggerations of romanticism commonly associated with the parallel movement in France. A careful study of this poem should remove that impression entirely. All the exaggerations of French Romantic drama are here: coincidence, antithesis, surprise, the grotesque, the horrible, and, not least, the unintentionally comic can be found as easily as in Dumas or Hugo. Yet " the poem aroused none of the opposition caused later by *Don Álvaro* . . . It dealt with a familiar legend ; it presented its subject in the familiar form of the *romance ;* and it did not

---

[1] *Ángel de Saavedra, etc.*, p. 213, n. 2.

[2] *Op. cit.*, pp. 212-13.   [3] *Op. cit.*, pp. 240-74, 575-91.

[4] Rivas : *Obras completas*, III, xxxi-xxxii.

[5] *Ángel de Saavedra, etc.*, pp. 275-303.

[6] *Op. cit.*, pp. 356-78.

appear on the traditional literary battlefield—the stage." [1]
To represent the Romantic revival as purely indigenous and
the Romantic revolt as purely exotic is a facile generalization
which cannot possibly be squared with the facts.

IV. THE REVIVAL OF GOLDEN AGE LITERATURE [2]

The revival of Golden Age literature during these years,
which is largely, though not entirely, a revival of drama,
received a temporary, but very effective, stimulus from
politics. The reaction against it in the eighteenth century
had been largely bound up with the vogue of France—of
French pseudo-classicism, of original French drama and of
French adaptations of Spanish plays. Not until the taste for
these should have ceased could original Spanish drama come
back again ; yet, as soon as it did cease, it was natural that
the type of play to come back should be anti-Classic. Such a
state of affairs would of itself suggest a return to the Golden
Age, for, since the close of that age, scarcely half-a-dozen
dramatists above the third rank had arisen.

It is convenient to begin by considering the history of the
Golden Age revival between 1800 and 1835, which can be
roughly divided into three stages. In the first (c. 1800-1808),
the late eighteenth-century tradition continues, though there
are many signs that the attraction of French pseudo-Classical
drama for Spaniards is growing less. In the second (1808-14),
the French invasion and the War of Independence kill the
taste for French drama and give an impetus to the growing
reaction in favour of the Golden Age. In the third (1814-35),
the activity on both sides is greater. On the one hand, the
pseudo-Classical play comes back, up to a certain point, on
the crest of a counter-reaction. On the other, there is much
greater interest in the Golden Age and the Revival makes
rapid progress. And all the time the exiles abroad, and their
compatriots at home, are developing the " new " Romantic
drama which will be described in the next chapter.

[1] *Op. cit.*, p. 214.   [2] *H.R.M.S.*, I, 167-92.

(i) 1800—1808

During this period there was still life in the old ideals, but at the same time many authors and critics were growing weary of French drama in Spanish dress and were therefore recommending and furthering Golden Age revivals. *Refundiciones* became increasingly common. Among the well-known plays produced during those eight years, some of them under fresh titles, were *La Estrella de Sevilla*, which between 1802 and 1818 went into five editions, Lope de Vega's *La Melindrosa*, *La Moza de cántaro*, and *Lo cierto por lo dudoso*, and a considerable number of plays by Tirso de Molina, including *La Prudencia en la mujer, El Vergonzoso en palacio* and *Don Gil de las calzas verdes*. In 1805, we learn that the plays performed at the Teatro de la Cruz, in Madrid, were either Golden Age *comedias*, " farsas maravillosas " or *comedias de figurón*.[1] The same might have been said of a number of theatres in the provinces.

Outside the field of drama, and apart from a few Cervantes reprints, the chief tribute paid to the Golden Age in these years was Quintana's *Poesías selectas castellanas, desde el tiempo de Juan de Mena hasta nuestros días* (Madrid, 1807). The merit and importance of these three bulky volumes lie less in the poems selected than in the introduction, which sketches the history of Spanish poetry from its beginnings. We may not approve Quintana's eulogies of the " restorers of good taste," especially of the restorer-in-chief, Luzán. But we cannot be insensitive to his reserved but patently sincere tribute to the earliest of the poems which he was reprinting :

> Aunque contemplo nuestras poesías antiguas a bastante distancia de la perfección, todavía sin embargo producen en mi espíritu y en mi oído el placer suficiente para disimular en gracia suya los descuidos y lunares que encuentro.[2]

(ii) 1808—1814

During the French invasion, fewer books than usual were published and there was naturally an almost total cessation in the performance of dramas translated from the French.

---

[1] *Variedades de Ciencias, Literatura y Artes*, Madrid, 1805, No. 8, II, ii, 115.
[2] *Poesías selectas castellanas, etc.*, I, lxxxiii.

This was partly compensated by the increased number of topical patriotic plays, but it also meant an increased vogue for the great national dramatists, and a further growth in the number of *refundiciones*. Cándido María Trigueros, the chief of the earlier *refundidores*, had died about 1800, but Dionisio Solís, who outlived him by thirty years, devoted himself during the years under review to adapting Calderón, as well as Lope de Vega, Rojas Zorrilla, Tirso de Molina, Moreto and a number of their contemporaries. Not all these, however, were published, partly through their re-shaper's indifference to their ultimate fate and partly on account of the censorship. When Calderón's *Peor está que estaba* was prohibited for its supposed allusion to Calomarde's government, when Lope's *Los Milagros del desprecio* was banned because only God could work miracles, and when Cervantes' *La Numancia*, given in a mutilated form, was officially withdrawn because it aroused applause,[1] it could hardly be wondered at if playwrights were unwilling to submit themselves to the caprice of authority more often than was essential.

(iii) 1814—1835

Between 1814 and 1835 there was increasing activity in the field of drama, and also an increasing confusion, caused by the struggle for pre-eminence of various types of drama and the gradual emergence of a new type distinct from them all. This state of confusion was aggravated by the instability of political and social conditions and the artificial situation created by the emigrations. During the decade following the Liberal triennium, Golden Age drama received a great impetus for the curious reason that so many contemporary dramatists were victims of the proscription. " La generalidad del público," reports Durán in 1828,

> llenaba los coliseos cuando veía en la escena a Lope, Tirso, Calderón y Moreto ; y tal vez sus detractores salían del teatro tan conmovidos como avergonzados de haber participado del entusiasmo general, contra las ordenanzas de Aristóteles y del espíritu de partido.[2]

[1] J. E. Hartzenbusch : *Ensayos poéticos y artículos en prosa, etc.*, Madrid, 1843, p. 213. " Son hechos," the critic assures us.
[2] " Discurso, etc.", in *M.A.E.*, II, 291.

Tributes to individual authors now become frequent. Even neo-Classics like Quintana and Javier de Burgos join the chorus ; one of them, Manuel Silvela, describes Lope de Vega as

> el ingenio más fecundo y más universal que presenta la historia de la poesía antigua y moderna, el verdadero Hércules del Parnaso, por lo gigantesco de sus proporciones y la fecundidad de su numen.[1]

Editions of Golden Age writers appear in great number—a severely censored but valuable and significant *Colección general* of thirty-three volumes, edited by Durán and others (1826-34) ; twenty-six volumes of Calderón (1826-33) ; and twelve editions of *Don Quijote* between 1815 and 1837, exclusive of the numerous editions published abroad during the emigrations. The first nineteenth-century edition of Cervantes' *entremeses* appeared at Cádiz in 1816 and a new selection of his plays came from Madrid in 1829.

These are representative indications of the progress made by the Golden Age during this period. There is, however, another side to the picture. Despite the eulogies showered on Calderón from abroad, there was still much indifference and opposition to him in his own country : his *autos sacramentales*, in particular, were written of with great disfavour. " Calderón and Lope, Moreto and Montalbán, Solís and Candamo, seldom occupy the Spanish stage," wrote an English observer, Sir John Bowring, in 1819.[2] Literary critics and historians could still write disparagingly of the Golden Age, or ignore it entirely, and yet achieve reputations. An indifferent anthology, compiled by an exile in London, Antonio Garrido,[3] whose preface mentions neither Lope, nor Tirso, nor Calderón, and gives only six lines to Cervantes, went into four editions within a year.

The attack upon Golden Age literature was led by a number of mainly elderly and highly respectable critics,

---

[1] *Obras póstumas*, Madrid, 1845, I, 164.

[2] *Observations on the state of religion and literature in Spain*, etc. N.p., n.d. (? 1820), p. 14.

[3] *Floresta española*, etc., London, 1826.

whose influence, though waning, was still considerable.
José Gómez Hermosilla, the pedantic author of an *Arte de
hablar en prosa y verso* which had a wide circulation, described
Lope de Vega as

> la prueba más irrefragable de que el hombre de mayor
> talento, aunque sea también muy sabio y erudito, no hará
> jamás una composición literaria perfecta, si ignora o
> quebranta voluntariamente las reglas.[1]

Another Classicist, Manuel Norberto Pérez de Camino,
poured scorn and ridicule by turns upon Golden Age drama.
Neglect of the Unities, he declared, led it into absurdities :

> Héroe en el primer acto tierno infante,
> te sorprende barbado en el segundo.[2]

And these Lope de Vega not only defended but boasted
about :

> Lope impudente se jactaba,
> lecciones dando a literatos graves,
> de encerrar los preceptos con tres (*sic*) llaves.[3]

With such critics it is usual to class Espronceda's master,
Lista, but he, despite his frequent tirades against the more
modern Romantics, managed to preserve a more judicial
attitude to Golden Age drama. To a certain point he even
defends it. His greatest obstacle is Lope's facility—a defect
of his age, to which he was a victim. But in spite of Lope's
prosiness, Tirso's immorality, Rojas Zorrilla's habitual
gongorisms and the like, the drama of the Golden Age, to
Lista, remains great. " It annoys us," he wrote, " to hear
Montiano y Luyando, author of two detestable tragedies,
utter . . . any amount of nonsense against our old drama. It
wearies us to find the elder Moratín, in the prologue to his
wretched comedy *La Petimetra*, declaiming against the
comedies of Lope de Vega. And who can tolerate . . .
Velázquez's dogmatic tone and extravagant judgments on
what he neither understood nor was capable of understanding ? These criticisms were unjust, because they were
stupid."[4]

---

[1] *Arte de hablar, etc.*, I, iii, 20.   The work went into at least thirteen editions.
[2] *Poética y sátiras*, Bordeaux, 1829, p. 296. Cf. p. 21, above.
[3] *Ibid.*
[4] *Ensayos literarios y críticos*, Seville, 1844, I, 36-7.

But a head and shoulders above all these, both detractors and defenders, stands the stalwart Durán. The greater part of his 1828 *Discurso* is devoted to a defence of " old Spanish drama," which, " to avoid periphrases and circumlocutions," he described as " Romantic."[1] All mediaeval literary history is for him but a prelude to that of the Golden Age, when, " from Lope de Vega to Calderón the glory of our drama grew and became more nearly perfect daily."[2] Now, he continues, all that glory has departed. Great drama is neither produced nor recognized as such by the critics. Why is this so ? Why do they not dwell upon the many beauties in the dramas of their own countrymen instead of upon their defects, or upon the merits of dramatists from abroad ? What nation, in any period of its history, can produce rivals to the playwrights of Spain's Golden Age ?

> ¿ Quién . . . . podrá competir con Lope en fecundidad e invención ? ¿ Quién a Calderón podrá negarle la primacía en el arte de combinar los planes, de dirigir y sacar el mayor partido de las situaciones, en la perfección de las narraciones, en el modo de presentar sus ideas eminentemente poéticas, y en el noble artificio con que supo hacer el verso octosílabo, o romance, digno y capaz de expresar los más sublimes pensamientos ? ¿ Quién no admirará en Tirso la armoniosa riqueza de rimas, la elegancia del lenguaje, las gracias de elocución, y las sales cómicas que abundan en sus obras dramáticas ? ¿ Y qué diremos del ingenioso Moreto, el primer poeta que supo poner en la escena la verdadera comedia de carácter, y desempeñarla con tanta perfección como pudo hacerlo el famoso Molière ?[3]

All these dramatists, he adds, and many others, have been freely used by the French to aid their own powers of invention, while we ourselves have forgotten them.

Durán, therefore, proposes the republication of some of the dramas of the Golden Age—" not only those which have some analogy with Classical drama "[4] but also those " belonging exclusively to our national Romantic drama."[5] As

[1] *M.A.E.*, II, 282 n.
[2] *M.A.E.*, II. 285.
[3] *M.A.E.*, II, 319.

[4] *M.A.E.* II, 293.
[5] *M.A.E.*, II, 318.

with mediaeval literature, so with the Golden Age, he himself reinforced precept with practice. The first volume of his *Talía española* (1834), a collection of three of Tirso's plays, containing a fervid defence of their author by way of introduction, was to have been followed by volumes of plays by his contemporaries, but financial support failed and no more were issued. The first volume was well received, however, not only by the Romantically inclined, but by the Press in general,[1] and its reception confirms other evidence that, before ever the Classical-Romantic battle began, that of the Golden Age had been won. Larra, in a review of Durán's *Discurso*, was writing of " the grandiose and colossal productions of our Lopes and Calderóns."[2] " Imitate Cervantes, Lope, Calderón, Tirso, Moreto," was the slogan of Salas y Quiroga. " If any French author is worth studying," he added, " the credit is due to Spain—*nosotros le hemos formado.*"[3] " Today in Spain," wrote Rivas' friend Alcalá Galiano, who had once sided with Mora in the Calderonian quarrel, " Lope, Calderón and Moreto are justly venerated."[4] In the same year Rivas made an almost identical assertion before the Spanish Academy.[5] The time had also come for popularizing less famous dramatists than Lope and Calderón. Böhl von Faber's *Teatro español anterior a Lope de Vega* (Hamburg, 1832), for example, prints, in a slightly modernized form, four plays by Encina, eight (in Spanish) by Gil Vicente, four by Torres Naharro and four by Lope de Rueda. To this collection Gallardo devoted forty-four out of the forty-eight pages of one issue of his *Criticón* (1836)[6] and filled most of the following issue with the reprint of another play by Encina and one by the almost wholly forgotten Lucas Fernández.[7] " El teatro español," he declares in justification, and the context shows that he is referring to the Golden

---

[1] *H.R.M.S.*, I, 188-9.

[2] *Revista española*, April 2, 1833.

[3] Salas y Quiroga : *Poesías*, Madrid, 1834, p. xiii.

[4] In his preface to *El Moro expósito* (1834).   Rivas : *Obras, ed. cit.*, p. xxix.

[5] *Cit. Ángel de Saavedra, etc.*, p. 529 n.

[6] *El Criticón*, 1836, No. 4, pp. 1-44.

[7] *Ibid.*, 1836, No. 5.

Age, " aparece desde luego como un astro brillante en los tiempos obscuros, en que tuvo su oriente. Nuevo, original y característico, posee cual ninguno de los conocidos en el mundo el don de suspender y regalar la fantasía." [1]

(iv) 1835—1837

By the date of the publication of the *Talía,* the battle between Classicists and Romantics, to be described in the next chapter, was already joined, and the story of the Golden Age revival, like that of the Mediaeval revival, during those years, will be more appropriately told in that context. We can, however, briefly summarize the progress of the Golden Age revival from 1835 to 1837 and so complete this part of our survey.

Strange to say, the republication of outstanding works of the Golden Age ceased almost entirely during this triennium and for some few years longer. One play by Calderón, nothing by Tirso and one edition of *Don Quijote* typify the output. As original creative activity, which for years had been at a standstill, was now becoming more intense, there was less need for reproductions.

In the historical novel, as we have seen, the tendency, both now and earlier, was to go right back to the Middle Ages rather than to stop short at the sixteenth century. The same is true of narrative poetry, which depended for its inspiration chiefly on mediaeval ballads. The periodicals gave considerable space to Golden Age biography. On the stage there were two years almost devoid of Golden Age themes, and then, in 1837, they leapt into popularity. Looking back over the whole period 1800-37, we can assert that the influence of Golden Age drama extends and deepens continuously. From eulogizing the great plays of that time and reprinting them, men passed to reading and assimilating them ; and, when the principal Romantic dramas began to appear, it became evident that the influence had gone deep and would not quickly be lost.

[1] *Ibid.,* 1836, No. 4.

V. The Romantic Revival in the Provinces [1]

Having traced the main course of the Romantic Revival down to the year 1837, we have now to examine its progress in the provinces.

It is impossible fully to understand nineteenth-century literature in Spain without studying its history in provincial centres, the literary life of these being strongly developed, and also, for various reasons, much more remote from that of the capital than was the case in most other countries. Of some of these centres this is true even to-day ; it is not surprising, then, if more than a century ago the inefficiency of Peninsular communications, now vastly bettered, should have accentuated a natural tendency to decentralization.

Five centres stand out during the first half of the nineteenth century as having a literary life independent of that of Madrid : namely (in descending order of importance) Barcelona, Valencia, Cádiz, Seville and Granada. These cities had their own literary heroes, their own periodicals, their own tastes in plays and their own literary coteries. Research has shown that the Revival had much more influence in them than the Revolt. Provincial men of letters had little of the rebel in their make-up ; on the other hand, many of them had an insatiable curiosity for new themes, fresh modes of expression and new treatment. Only as the right to develop along those lines was denied them—which happened seldom—did they become rebels. Their interest in the Revival more than warrants a brief separate treatment of them here.

(i) *The Revival in Catalonia*

It was in Catalonia, where, even during the reign of Ferdinand VII, there was great literary activity, that the revival-aspect of the Spanish Romantic movement had the greatest importance. In Barcelona, as in Valencia, it transcended the revolt-aspect completely.

This, no doubt, was partly due to the influence of the

---

[1] *H.R.M.S.*, I, 192-204.

Europeo—published, it will be remembered, in Barcelona—but much more, it may safely be asserted, to the connection between the ideals of the revivalists and those of the renaissance of the Catalan language and of literature written in that language. This movement, though the product of a long period of slow evolution, actually declared itself very suddenly in 1833, with the publication, in Catalan, of Aribau's *Oda a la pàtria*, and gathered strength till it was permanently established by the restoration of the Jocs Florals (Floral Games) in 1859. Thus its development was approximately contemporary with the Romantic movement in Spain as a whole.[1] Almost exclusively it was a revival, for it was in the Middle Ages that the Catalan language had had its long period of splendour. " Which of us," asked a Catalan writer in 1832, " does not experience a profound impression, an inexplicable delight, as he reads the Moorish and chivalric *romances*? For it was this type of composition that gave the greatest scope to the luxuriant talent of óur old poets." [2]

A striking illustration of the popularity of the revival-movement in Catalonia may be found in a comparison of the number of translations published in Barcelona from Byron and from Scott. Byron, as will shortly be seen, represents the violent, rebellious type of romanticism which came into Spain chiefly from France ; Scott represents the native historical ideal. In spite of Byron's vogue in Spain, only one translation from him seems to have been published in book form in Barcelona before 1850, while there appeared at least twenty-two translations from Scott, coming from seven publishers.

It is difficult to-day to recapture any idea of the immense popularity enjoyed by Scott in those early years of the Romantic movement in Barcelona. Not only was he translated, adapted and imitated ; not only did he inspire Carbó, Piferrer, Semís, Milá y Fontanals and many others ; not only was Aribau's *Oda a la pàtria* presented to its first readers

---

[1] For a brief account of the Catalan Renaissance, see E. Allison Peers : *Catalonia Infelix*, London, 1937, pp. 99-111, 307-14.

[2] *Diario de Barcelona*, May 2, 1832.

" con el patriótico orgullo con que presentaría un escocés los versos de sir Walter Scott a los habitantes de su patria ;"[1] but persons who never aspired to the height of reading Scott, even in Spanish, were engulfed in the prevailing fashion, and the *rasgo escocés* became a feature of popular art, sartorial modes and the adornment of shop-fronts. Milá is said to have remarked that if anyone had been anxious to get together a body of young men to form a society animated by one common ideal, a method more effective even than the creation of a political group would have been to enlist them as " admirers of Walter Scott."[2]

Chateaubriand may be taken as having represented to Spaniards similar ideals to those of Scott, with the additional elements of cosmopolitanism and Catholicism. Although it was in Valencia that Chateaubriand achieved his greatest popularity, as many as twelve translations from him were published in Barcelona during the first forty years of his vogue in Spain as against fourteen in Valencia.[3] Like Scott, wrote a Barcelona periodical, Chateaubriand " will never pass away " ; and it added this significant contrast :

El genio de Chateaubriand *es lo bello y lo sublime* . . . .
El genio de V. Hugo *es lo feo y lo horrible.*[4]

It was Catalonia, too, that first learned to appreciate Lamartine, a poet whose works represent the gentler aspect of the Romantic movement and make no appeal at all to the rebels.

These and similar tendencies were stimulated by the establishment in Barcelona, in 1833, by López Soler, of a new periodical, ·less important than *El Europeo* only because later in date, to which he gave the symbolic title of *El Vapor*. This he himself edited until 1835, and, for some five years from its foundation, it represented Catalonian romanticism

[1] *El Vapor*, August 24, 1833.

[2] A. Rubió y Lluch y C. Parpal Marqués : *Milá y Fontanals y Rubió y Ors. Discursos*, etc. Barcelona, 1919, pp. 26-7.   Cf. *El Vapor*, June 17, 1834.

[3] Cf. E. Allison Peers : " La influencia de Chateaubriand en España," in *R.F.E.*, 1924, XI, 351-82.

[4] *La Civilización*, Barcelona, 1841, III, 145-86.

in so far as this expressed itself in the Castilian language, which is equivalent to saying that, although it was influenced by the Revolt, it steadily and continuously represented the Revival. Aribau joined its staff and among its early contributors was Manuel Milá y Fontanals, then only a boy, who was to become one of the greatest literary traditionalists of the century.

The Romantic revival, then, took very deep root in Barcelona. An occasional writer, like Cabanyes or Ribot y Fontseré, might be something of an emancipator or even a mild iconoclast. But for every one of these we can find a dozen whose sole thought was revival. Such are Cabanyes' friend Joaquín Roca y Cornet ; Pablo Piferrer and Juan Francisco Carbó, popularizers of the *romance ;* Juan Cortada, already mentioned as a historical novelist of the Middle Ages ; Tomás Aguiló and José María Quadrado, two Majorcans who collaborated in the foundation of a weekly review called *La Palma* (1840) ; Joaquín Rubió y Ors, a mediaevalist and a leader of the Catalan Renaissance who also wrote voluminously in Castilian ; and Víctor Balaguer, born a few years later than all these, but early enough to be associated with the Revival while its chief exponents still lived.

(ii) *The Revival in Valencia*

We should expect the Romantic movement in Valencia and Barcelona to follow similar lines, since the revival of the Valencian language as a medium of literary expression followed the general direction of the Catalan Renaissance, though at a considerable distance. The foreign author chiefly favoured in Valencia was Chateaubriand : both *Atala* and *René* were published there ten years before the *Europeo* appeared in Barcelona and eight translations of Chateaubriand between 1813 and 1832. One of the few Spanish translations, too, of Bernardin de St. Pierre's *Paul et Virginie* was published (1816) in Valencia.[1]

---

[1] Valencia had at this time a small group of progressive publishers who were partly responsible for these editions. Cf. *H.R.M.S.*, I, 200.

More striking than this early interest in French pre-romanticism is the prevalence between 1835 and 1850 of a type of romanticism which follows quite naturally upon it— a romanticism marked by a lofty, at times even a puritanical standard of morality, suspicious of any kind of literary excess, unconnected with revolt, impervious to the attractions of melodrama, and dominated, occasionally by patriotism, but more often by a melancholy, now merely lachrymose, now approaching an attitude of reasoned pessimism.

Three Valencian Romantics are principally associated with the prevalence of this literary fashion. The best-known of them is Juan Arolas, a priest who mingles home-made orientalism with religion, mediaevalism and love. One is apt to be dazzled by the brilliance of his imagination or lulled into an uncritical frame of mind by the easy flow of his attractive verse-style and thus to fail to perceive how strongly he is influenced by Chateaubriand. The other two were friends : Vicente Boix y Ricart, later known as a historian, and José María Bonilla. Both these vehemently attack the exaggerations of " el romanticismo galo-pésimo,"[1] invent Romantic character-types, use many and varied metres and exhale melancholy and a resigned *desengaño*. " El autor de estas poesías," writes Boix in a preface to Bonilla's verses, " ha llorado grandes sentimientos, y ha probado que la felicidad es una ilusión, o solamente es el producto de las dulces sensaciones del alma."[2] The remark would be equally applicable to his own.

(iii) *The Revival in Cádiz, Granada and Seville*

The three remaining centres can be described more briefly. The articles of Böhl von Faber and the early interest

---

[1] *El Cisne*, 1840, I, 38-40, 55 ff. and Bonilla : *Poesías*, Valencia, 1840, pp. 134-7. Cf. *H.R.M.S.*, II, 408-9.

[2] *Poesías*, Valencia, 1840, *loc. cit.* The reviews to which Arolas, Boix and Bonilla chiefly contributed (*El Liceo Valenciano*, 1838-9, 1841-2 ; *El Cisne*, 1840 ; *El Fénix*, 1844-6) are rather later in date than the period under review, but the same characteristics as are here described are found earlier.

taken by the Cádiz theatres in Golden Age drama suffice to attach that city to the Revival. Its literary importance, of course, belongs mainly to the pre-Romantic period, and is reflected in the *Diario mercantil de Cádiz* (1803-30). Besides featuring the Böhl-Mora controversy (1817-19), it shows (1825-8) great interest in English literature, especially in Scott. Even as late as 1828 Böhl and his defence of the Golden Age are not forgotten.

Granada, with only one literary periodical of note (*La Alhambra*, 1839-41), and Seville, with a little group of short-lived reviews (1837-45), merely reflect opinion in Madrid, whither most of their promising writers migrated while still young. In a brief survey, therefore, both writers and periodicals may be disregarded.

CHAPTER III

THE ROMANTIC REVOLT, 1800-1837[1]

I. THE ROMANTIC REVOLT FROM 1800 TO 1833[2]

(i) *Discontent with existing literary conditions*

As we have seen, the origins of the Romantic revolt against neo-classicism date from the mid-eighteenth century, and it had long since declared itself when the Liberal exiles returned in 1834. But before that year it was no more than an undercurrent in an outwardly placid neo-Classical river : not until some years later did it begin to dominate literary life and only for a very short time did this domination continue. Our first task is to note the various forms which it took and to trace its slow emergence.

During the first third of the nineteenth century there was widespread discontent with existing literary conditions, and in particular with the state of the drama, the maximum impatience being with the dominance of the Unities. Durán's *Discurso* (1828), though in the main constructive, may be cited as evidence here. It declaims against the " attempt to imprison national talent," the " persecution of creative genius," the " ruin of our ancient drama " by Spanish critics and the " ridiculous mania " for trying to span the sublime dramatic creations of the seventeenth century with the rule and measure that fitted the drama of Greece, Rome and France.[3] Durán had no quarrel with classicism and would never have called himself a Romantic : his quarrel was with those who forced his country into imitation of " an exotic drama, foreign to its character, which has neither prospered

---

[1] *H.R.M.S.*, I, 205-349.   [3] *M.A.E.*, II, 301, 317, 280, 281.
[2] *H.R.M.S.*, I, 205-232.

61

on our soil nor can prosper for so long as we are Spaniards and not Frenchmen."[1] Classicism and romanticism, he says, should be recognized as distinct *genres* requiring different modes of expression. We should no more ask Calderón to follow the dramatic rules applicable to Racine than to write in French.[2]

This is the eminently sane position of a man who declares " I belong to no party." Those unacquainted with contemporary preceptists might not describe it as a position of revolt at all. But, though Durán has no objection to rules as such, and indeed believes that Golden Age drama would have been the better for more of them,[3] he makes it clear that he himself attaches little importance to precept. The " sublime and ideal beauty " of Romantic poetry, he declares with unwontedly florid eloquence, " is nourished and sustained in the boundless spaces of eternity " and " the greater or lesser enthusiasm " which inspires the poet is " the only limit which he imposes upon his audacious metaphors and upon his great and sublime thoughts."[4] From this Durán infers the impossibility of imprisoning Romantic drama within the bounds set by the three Unities and insists upon the need for variety and contrast in tone and expression, verisimilitude in language and the "admission and amalgamation " of tragedy, comedy, satire, the lyric and the bucolic within Romantic drama.[5] The pages from which these arguments are taken might almost have come from the *Préface de Cromwell*.

Another cause of discontent was the gallicized character of the Spanish language—a dead language, exclaimed Bartolomé José Gallardo, with a satirist's licence, lying in bondage to France :

> .... La lengua castellana murió y es fuerza estudiarla ya como lengua muerta .... En efecto el francés manda al español. La lengua castellana se aprende por la francesa .... No tienen por de buen cuño la frase que no se ajusta a la galicana.[6]

[1] *Op. cit.*, II, 287.
[2] *Op. cit.*, II, 295.
[3] *Op. cit.*, II, 316-17.
[4] *Op. cit.*, II, 315.
[5] *Op. cit.*, II, 315-16.
[6] *Obras escogidas*, ed. P. Sainz y Rodríguez, Madrid, 1928, I, 48-50.

One of the services which the Spanish Romantics were to attempt to render to literature was the re-enrichment of their language with the wealth of the past. They did not de-gallicize it, for many of them had lived long in France and some moved almost as easily in French as in Spanish. But they created more alternative forms, restored forgotten expressions and substituted simple, direct and telling words for the phrases weakened by convention and insincerity to which they took such strong exception. Here, as in certain other aspects of the Spanish Romantic movement, Revival is indistinguishable from Revolt.

Again, there was great dissatisfaction with the miserable conditions under which writers had to work. Some of them were in exile abroad ; others were in disfavour at home. Almost all, except those who had additional occupations or private means, were compelled to live on the border-line of poverty. " El día que no imprimimos," as Larra put it, " no comemos."[1] Hack-work and ill-paid journalism kept alive some who later were to be in the foremost rank of literature. Conditions, in short, were at their lowest level, even " in a country where literature has almost invariably been the resource of the author who has no other."[2]

(ii)   *Discontent with the state of the drama.*

All this was particularly true of the stage, dissatisfaction with the state of which was now growing apace. The cause of the dissatisfaction seems to have lain partly in the type of play produced and partly in the conditions of production.

As to the type of play, the determining factor was generally the insatiable eagerness of the lower and middle classes for novelty and excitement, which ran away with any critical standards that they might have possessed and accounted for the great vogue of pseudo-historical melodrama and for the fantastic popularity of such plays as Grimaldi's three-act " melo-mimo-drama mitológico-burlesco de magia y de

[1] " Fígaro de vuelta."

[2] *El Pobrecito Hablador :* " Reflexiones acerca del modo de resucitar el teatro español."

grande espectáculo," *La Pata de cabra*. Larra's article, "Una primera representación," gives an interesting conspectus of the stage productions of a single year (1835) summarized under eight heads : [1]

- (i) "Lo que se llama comedia antigua "—i.e., anything earlier than about 1770 ;
- (ii) "Drama, dicho melodrama," translated from the French ;
- (iii) "Drama sentimental y terrorífico," also translated;
- (iv) "Comedia dicha clásica de Molière y Moratín " ;
- (v) "Tragedia clásica, ora traducción, ora original " ;
- (vi) "Piececita de costumbres, sin costumbres, traducción de Scribe " ;
- (vii) "Drama histórico, crónica puesta en verso, o prosa poética " ;
- (viii) "Drama romántico, nuevo, original . . . el único verdadero." [2]

Translations, it will be noted, comprise at least four classes out of these eight, a proportion which seems approximately to represent their frequency. They were the merest hack-work, Larra tells us—the kind of thing for which, to quote his inimitable phrase, " no se necesita más que atrevimiento y diccionario." [3] As the remuneration for a translated play was the same as for an original one, and translations were often preferred to original dramas, the author could hardly be blamed for spending a week in translating a play rather than six months in writing one.

Some of the translations given were, as we shall later see, from Hugo, Dumas, Alfieri and other dramatists of merit, nor were the versions always unworthy of their originals. But the popularity of these was eclipsed by that of writers whose appeal bordered on the meretricious and many of whom are now entirely forgotten. The phenomenal vogue of Scribe is described and satirized again and again. His name is " ya una verdadera pesadilla, pues apenas hay día en que

---

[1] The list is not complete, for it omits the extremely popular *comedia de magia*.

[2] " Una primera representación."

[3] " De las traducciones."

no le veamos estampado en los carteles del teatro."[1] Hardly less popular was the melodramatic Victor Ducange, that " dramatist of the boulevard " whose most famous drama Larra made the theme for a savage piece of anti-Gallic satire.[2] Others were the novelist-playwright, Frédéric Soulié, and a pre-Romantic, Casimir Delavigne. These, it will be noted, were all French. The one Englishman whose vogue on the stage rivalled theirs was Shakespeare, and so frequently was he translated into Spanish from French adaptations that he might almost have been thought of as a Frenchman. Even where a translation appears to have been made direct from the original, the recasting process is suggestive of the French neo-Classicists. Nevertheless, such mutilated versions were quite popular.

So much for the type of play being produced in the Madrid theatres and for the discontent with which authors in general regarded it. Discontent with the conditions of dramatic production was even more understandable. The management of a theatre was seldom a success. The two Madrid houses, the Príncipe and the Cruz, were small and comfortless : the upper classes seldom visited them, except to see operas ;[3] the lower classes would have only sensation, " magic " and farce. There was no cultured middle-class audience to save the situation. Except by translating, dramatists could hardly live, and in exchange for the little they did earn they usually had to surrender their rights to a manager. Censors arbitrarily condemned or mutilated manuscripts sent to them—or occasionally lost them. Actors took a low place in the social scale and were given more frequent changes of part than they could possibly undertake without detriment to their efficiency.

(iii)   The slow emergence of the Revolt

It is clear enough from this evidence—and much more could be cited—that a many-sided literary revolt was needed

---

[1] *Boletín de Comercio*, September 10, 1833.
[2] See *H.R.M.S.*, I, 218, nn. 5-6.   [3] Cf. *H.R.M.S.*, I, 212-13.

in the eighteen-thirties. But, except as regards drama, the ideas which the prevalent dissatisfaction evolved were not at once translated into practice in the sphere of creative literature. Prose fiction was so quiescent that it may almost be left out of consideration, while in lyric poetry, as will later be seen, both Revival and Revolt were delayed longer than in the other *genres*. But in drama many indications appeared of what in a later day were to be recognized as the elements of romanticism.

An apt illustration of this is furnished by the evolution of the dramatic principles of the poet and critic Quintana. Here was a neo-Classic who began writing in his teens, lived to be eighty-five, and, though he never joined the Romantics, showed a growing sympathy with them which they fully appreciated. At the age of nineteen he published an ultra-conservative didactic poem, *Las Reglas del drama*, and at thirty-three a play, *Pelayo* (1805)—an uninspired product of pseudo-classicism for all the mediaevalism of its theme. An earlier play, however, *El Duque de Viseo* (1801), clearly foreshadows the far-off revolt in drama. Deriving partly from English sources, it has a prologue describing the " greater extravagances " to be found in the " wild and sublime works of the extraordinary Shakespeare." To Monk Lewis's *Castle Spectre* (1798), which gave him his subject, Quintana was probably indebted for his attempts to create dramatic atmosphere. He takes some liberties with the Unities and occasionally breaks into language of Romantic extravagance. There is even a ghost in the play, though it is not brought on to the stage : that would be too much to expect from the first year of the nineteenth century.

Thirty years after writing the *Reglas del drama*, Quintana revised it for a new edition and greatly modified its severity. His earlier judgment, he now implies, was influenced by the unhappy state of the theatre, which, thanks partly to the satire of Leandro Moratín's *Comedia nueva*, has at last improved. He insists less rigorously on the observance of the Unities of time and place : " if there are striking reasons in their favour, there are also striking examples on the other side." Everybody makes exceptions to the Rules and those who defend them sometimes create as much inverisimilitude as do their opponents. The question (he concludes), which is being hotly debated by Classicists and Romanticists, may be left undecided.

Another characteristic of the Romantic revolt which began to make its appearance about this time in drama, as in lyric poetry, was a growing discontent with the traditional metres. Occasionally this discontent declared itself in the most unlikely places : even Luzán had used several measures in translating a play by La Chaussée ; Iriarte had introduced some *redondillas* into his earliest comedy ; and García de la Huerta, in versifying Pérez de Oliva's *Agamenón vengado*, had varied his hendecasyllabics with *silvas*, *liras* and *octavas reales*. Of more modern writers, Manuel Eduardo de Gorostiza, a pronounced Moratinian, varied the *romances* of his first play, *Indulgencia para todos* (1818), with *redondillas*, *quintillas* and *décimas*—an innovation which would hardly have been approved by Moratín. Other and later metrical experiments will be described in a later chapter, but we may refer here to one of them which drew a comment from Juan Eugenio Hartzenbusch, a dramatist who was later to excel in the art of metrical variety.

The author of it was a youth of nineteen, a pupil of Lista, Mariano Roca de Togores, afterwards Marqués de Molíns. In 1831, inspired by contemporary French drama, and " the new school, called ' Romantic '," he attempted, in his biographer's words, " to introduce romanticism to the Spanish stage," by writing a verse drama in varied metres entitled *El Duque de Alba, drama romántico*.[1] As for some reason it was neither published nor publicly acted until it appeared in a revised form and under a new title (*La Espada de un caballero*), in 1846, it is impossible to say how Romantic it originally was. But its author's own memoirs inform us that it contained numerous " innovaciones y . . . escándalos," one of which was its mingling of tragedy and comedy. They add that the literary group which discussed the play debated two important questions :

---

[1] Cf. Hartzenbusch's preface to Molíns' *Obras poéticas*, Madrid, 1857, p. xii.

1. Si la varia versificación es conveniente al drama ;
2. Si los principios literarios, que se designan con el
nombre de romanticismo, pueden revestirse en el teatro
moderno español con un atavío puramente nacional.[1]
It is the first of these questions that interests us here, and
Hartzenbusch, in his preface to the works of Molíns, declares
that, though " more warmth than it merited " went into its
discussion, it was "in reality practically settled" all the time.[2]

(iv) *The Coteries*

Towards the end of the period under survey an important
influence upon the Romantic revolt was exercised by the
well patronized, though short-lived, literary coteries.   In
those days, Spain had no literary societies of high standing.
The Madrid Ateneo, now well over a century old, was closed
during the last ten years of Ferdinand VII's reign, and was
re-opened, or, more exactly, re-founded, in 1835.   A new
and ephemeral literary influence in Madrid, the Liceo, was
not founded until 1837.   With no such clearing-house for
literary ideas in existence, and many of Spain's best writers
in exile, such ephemeral literary societies as were formed had
an added significance.

The first in date of the coteries met on Sunday mornings in
1827 at the house of the translator of Bouterwek's history of
Spanish literature, José Gómez de la Cortina.   All its members—about a dozen—were writers exasperated at the
sterility which political conditions were imposing upon
literature and at the servility to French pseudo-classicism
which marked the literary work of the day.   The best known
of them were Mariano José de Larra, then a boy of eighteen;
Serafín Estébanez Calderón, ten years his senior ;   Manuel
Bretón de los Herreros, already the author of some popular
comedies ;   a rather older man, Antonio Gil y Zárate, who
was also writing, and translating, light comedies with great
rapidity ;   Lista's young Argentine-born pupil, Ventura de
la Vega ;   and Patricio de la Escosura, Vega's schoolfellow
and close companion.   This we learn from Mesonero

[1] *Op. cit.*, II, 277-80, and *H.R.M.S.*, II, 396.
[2] *Op. cit.*, I, xiii.

Romanos, another member of the group, who became its chronicler. Full of enthusiasm and energy, these young writers delighted in destructive criticism and attacked pedants like Gómez Hermosilla freely. But they were also eager for knowledge, devoting themselves to original writing or to browsing in libraries and archives. Some of them had not inconsiderable ambitions, which were destined to be fulfilled.[1]

A second coterie (1829-30), of which Mesonero Romanos was also a member, was a somewhat more turbulent and less studious one, centring round the attractive personality of Salustiano Olózaga. The twelve members of this circle won less fame than did their predecessors : only Mesonero and Gil y Zárate made any considerable contribution to literature. After meeting for almost two complete years, the circle was broken up by the arrest of some of its members on political charges.[2]

But scarcely had Olózaga's circle died when a new and much more important one sprang up—a circle which for a time was to become the centre of the slowly maturing Movement. This was the Parnasillo, inaugurated at the end of 1830 in the " reducido, puerco y opaco café del Príncipe."[3] The founders were José María de Carnerero, Juan de Grimaldi, Manuel Bretón de los Herreros, Antonio Gil y Zárate, Serafín Estébanez Calderón and Mesonero Romanos. These were joined in due course by a large number of rising young writers—notably Larra, Escosura, Vega, Espronceda, Miguel de los Santos Álvarez, Antonio María Segovia, Eugenio de Ochoa and Jacinto Salas y Quiroga. The group was thus a large one, which met in sections— lyrical, dramatic, critical, etc.—and it has sometimes been spoken of as though it were the centre of a literary revolution.[4] But this it was not : it represented nothing very definite, had little cohesiveness, dwindled quickly in numbers and within four years was dead. Whatever influence it

---

[1] R. de Mesonero Romanos : *Memorias de un setentón*, Madrid, 1881, II, 21-7, *passim*.

[2] *Op. cit.*, II, 29-31.   [3] Larra : *El Pobrecito Hablador*, No. 1.

[4] Cf. *H.R.M.S.*, II, 396.

wielded came through the individuals who composed it. These individuals had great gifts of expression, but they used them in wrangling and attacking others rather than in laying the foundations of a new and stable literature. They formulated no creed, they contemplated no constructive action and they founded no school. Therein lay their weakness, and from it, as we shall see, springs the weakness of the Romantic revolt as a whole.

II. FOREIGN INFLUENCES UPON THE ROMANTIC REVOLT[1]

One of the most widely held fallacies about the Spanish Romantic movement is that it came from abroad. The " new literary school," the germ of which, as Mesonero Romanos said, was within the nation, and had been " so ably developed in the immortal creations of Calderón and Rojas, of Lope, Tirso and Alarcón,"[2] has been spoken of by some critics as though it were a foreign importation. Others describe the revolt-element in the Movement as exotic, while conceding that the revival-element was largely native. If, however, we examine the specific foreign influences which affected the Revolt, we shall find them to be less extensive than those connected with the Revival. Foreign influences upon the Revival came from England, France, Germany and Italy. The Revolt, on the other hand, was hardly influenced from abroad at all except by two first-rank writers in France and one (or at most two) in England, though there was also a kind of collective " atmospheric " influence of England and France upon the Spanish *emigrados* which no doubt intensified the violence of the Revolt but is extremely elusive of assessment.

(i) *French Influences : Hugo and Dumas*

The two first-rank French authors alluded to were Hugo and Dumas. Hugo's influence was much the wider of the

[1] *H.R.M.S.*, I, 232-50.
[2] *Memorias de un setentón, ed. cit.*, II, 145.

two, ranging over drama, lyric poetry, fiction, criticism and literary theory. It was, however, less profound than has been supposed—often amounting to no more than a vogue. This began only in 1834 and was largely confined to drama. Hugo's lyrics were but little known and the direct influence of his literary theory was surprisingly small. But from 1835 to 1838 his plays were translated and performed continually, not only in Madrid, but in the provinces. During those few years he was eulogized to the point of literary apotheosis. *Lucrèce Borgia*, the first of his plays to be given in Spanish, was described as " the great colossal Romantic drama " of the " incomparable Victor Hugo,"[1] and this type of eulogy is not exceptional, but almost the rule.

Dumas, strange though it may seem, was, if anything, esteemed even more highly than Hugo. The two were often bracketed by the critics : it was Larra who referred to their " colosal y desnuda escuela."[2]   And Larra, who had a large following, by no means put Hugo before Dumas. Hugo, he said, was " más osado, más colosal que Dumas " : he had more novelty, audacity, extravagance, imagination and poetry ; Dumas, a better knowledge of stagecraft, a stronger emotional appeal, more passion, more realism, greater truth to life.[3]

First represented in Spain two months later than Hugo, Dumas soon began to gain upon him. From 1834 to 1838 his plays were performed much more frequently, and if his vogue, like Hugo's, was short, and challenged by fierce opposition, the public paid willingly to see his plays and kept asking for more. His influence upon individuals, too, was greater than Hugo's, which can be seen, and somewhat faintly, only in García Gutiérrez, Gil y Zárate and Escosura. Dumas, on the other hand, had a very strong influence on García Gutiérrez, as well as on Larra, Rivas and Bretón de los Herreros—a considerable achievement.

---

[1] The quotations are from press announcements of the Barcelona performances.

[2] Larra : *Macías,* " Dos Palabras."

[3] Critiques of *Teresa, Catalina Howard, Hernani.*

(ii) *English Influences : Shakespeare and Byron*

Of English authors, Shakespeare would no doubt have
stimulated the Revolt had Spain been permitted to appreciate him, but it was not until the Romantic movement had
passed its zenith that he became known otherwise than in
diluted translations and adaptations made through the
French. The only English writer who can be said to have
fed the spirit of the Revolt is Lord Byron, the extent of
whose influence can be gathered from the abuse which was
heaped upon him by the anti-Romantics. He was, at best,
a " frenzied and sublime genius," the " father of exaggerated
romanticism "—at worst, " a braggart about crime," the
man who " to a certain degree inaugurated the poetic
immorality which was to dominate the literature of his
century." [1]

Byronism, beginning much later in Spain than in France
or Germany, made itself felt only about 1826, but gained
ground steadily till 1830. During these years, translations,
often through the French, came thick and fast. Then, for
seven years, they dropped off, but on the other hand the
periodical press took Byron up and published innumerable
short versions, critical studies and imitations of his works
until about 1842. Investigations have shown that Byronism
in Spain was at its height between about 1828 and 1837—
i.e., during the most important of the formative years of the
Romantic revolt.

Of Byron's individual followers the most important by
far was Espronceda, whose debts to him may be deduced
from concrete borrowings. *Sardanapalus, Sun of the sleepless,
The Corsair* and *Don Juan* influence Espronceda's minor
poems, while between *Don Juan* and *El Diablo Mundo* there
are constant parallelisms both of theme and of technique.
These borrowings, too, are not mere unintelligent plagiar-
isms, like Espronceda's borrowings from Scott, but treat-
ments showing real originality. Espronceda's religious
scepticism, his often incoherent philosophy, his habit of
irreverent mockery, his political radicalism, his *desengaño*,

[1] Cf. *H.R.M.S.*, I, 245, nn. 1-5.

his defence of the despised and outcast, his railing against society and authority—all these traits, when they do not derive from Byron or testify to his influence, make Espronceda an ideal interpreter of Byron's character and an able champion of the Romantic revolt.

(iii)   *An Italian Influence : Alfieri*

It will be appropriate here to discuss the vogue of Alfieri in Spain, for, although his plays are not the products of literary revolution, there is a close connection between their popularity in Spain and the development of the Romantic revolt.

The Spanish vogue of Alfieri begins near the end of the eighteenth century and reaches its height during the second and third decades of the nineteenth.   Several of his plays were represented in Madrid between 1805 and 1815.   In 1812, Antonio Saviñón's translation of *Bruto primo*, as *Roma libre*, was performed, and published, at Cádiz, " to celebrate the publication of the new Constitution of the Spanish monarchy."   Saviñón also translated *Polinice* as *Los Hijos de Edipo* (1814) ; Dionisio Solís published versions of *Oreste* (1807) and *Virginia* (1813) ; and *Oreste* inspired one of Ángel de Saavedra's early plays, *El Duque de Aquitania* (1817).

If it be asked what a neo-Classicist can have to do with Romantic revolt, the answer is not hard to find.   Though Alfieri's early plays are as gallicized as was eighteenth-century Spain, he veered sharply round, much as Spain was to do later.   It was during the years 1808-14, when liberalism was finding expression in Spain, that his plays were first given there.   Blanco García observes that, just as the vigour and the independence of the Romantic lyric were foreshadowed by the anti-Napoleonic odes of 1808-14, so the Alfierine translations and original plays of the type of *Pelayo* and *Numancia* " initiate the emancipation of the stage." [1]   It was not the form or the style of Alfieri's plays

[1] F. Blanco García : *La Literatura española en el siglo XIX*, 3rd ed., Madrid, 1909-12, I, 111.

that attracted Spain, but their themes, directed against tyrants and oppressors. And, when the War of Independence was over, he remained popular both for the liberalism of his ideas and because of his predilection for themes of violent passion, unrestrained desire and strenuous inward conflict.

III. THE REVOLT IN DRAMA, 1834-1837[1]

Ample evidence exists that, when Ferdinand VII died, in 1833, a literary revolution was generally believed to be imminent. The belief is perfectly understandable. Gradually, and over a long period, both authors and public had been prepared for the outbreak of a revolt in drama. Everywhere independence from French pseudo-classicism was being claimed. Liberalism was invading both politics and literature. The melodrama of the late eighteenth century was leading the way to the Romantic drama of the nineteenth. The fact that many authors were still observing the Unities and other Classical conventions is of less importance than might appear : they were often nearer to the Revolt than they knew.

Nevertheless, although the careful student of literary history can appreciate the gradualness of the development of Spanish Romantic drama, it seemed to the critics of the thirties that something in the nature of a sudden explosion had taken place. The phenomenon which they had themselves predicted for the immediate future had come upon them with the rapidity of a comet—" cometa que aparece por primera vez en el sistema literario, con su cola y sus colas de sangre y de mortandad."[2] " In a single year," wrote Larra, in his critique of the Spanish *estreno* of Dumas' *Catherine Howard*, " we have passed in literature from Moratín to Alexandre Dumas." He exaggerated ; but his exaggeration is more illuminating than many a truism.

---

[1] *H.R.M.S.*, I, 250-300.
[2] Larra : " Una primera representación."

The revolt in drama, following hard upon the return of the exiles, declared itself openly in 1834, and for about three years maintained its success, though only at a moderate level. Hardly one of the new plays carried all before it and some were almost complete failures. Still, their total effect was such that, from 1834 to 1837, Romantic drama was the dominant force upon the Spanish stage, though it never took entire possession of it.

It should be noted that such success as it achieved was almost wholly confined to native Spanish products. However limited and brief the popularity of these, that of translations from the French was more limited still. The principal service rendered by these translations was to stimulate the taste for native drama of similar pattern.

A brief account of the principal plays performed in Madrid during these three years will give some idea of the tastes and tendencies of that period and of the state of the theatre.

(i) *Madrid Drama :* 1834

Three plays of 1834 stand out as representative of the Romantic revolt in drama : Martínez de la Rosa's *Conjuración de Venecia*, Larra's *Macías* and Bretón de los Herreros' *Elena*.

La Conjuración de Venecia (April 23, 1834) had nearly thirty performances in twelve months—a striking testimony, for those days, to the popularity of a mildly audacious drama. Unusual interest was aroused by its innovations : a picturesque Venetian setting ; a skilful mingling of passion, emotionalism and gentle sentiment ; a combination of prose with verse ; a disregard for the Unities of time and place ; the multiplication of characters ; carefully worked up effects, enhanced by some degree of truth in characterization ; the introduction of elements of mystery ; and the creation of the first " Romantic hero." Its hideous sacrifice of propriety and probability in the second act was not felt in 1834 to be unjustifiable. Larra, at least, saw no objection to the unnatural use made of the pantheon. The antithesis which this involved he thought tragically splendid, " terrible," " sublime," while the dramatic irony inherent in the situation " supone el mayor conocimiento dramático."[1]

Larra's *Macías* (September 24, 1834), withdrawn after five performances, but well reviewed and twice revived later in the season, was preceded by a curiously self-conscious prologue disclaiming for it the title " Romantic " in the modern French sense. True, it attempts to observe the Unities of time and place ; its metres, like its characters, incline to the conventional ; it has little local colour. Yet, on the other hand, its plot is dominated by unbridled passion ; it protests against the tyranny of moral law and social convention ; and it makes frequent use of Romantic devices. In brief, *Macías* is much the kind of play that we should expect to find in 1834 : it has neither completely thrown off pseudo-classicism nor completely put on neo-romanticism ; it belongs to an advanced stage of the transition from one vogue to the other.

More significant than *Macías* is Bretón de los Herreros' *Elena* (October 23, 1834), for Bretón was a Classicist, an imitator of Moratín and a translator of Scribe, who had developed a highly individualized manner and found his *métier* in a type of play the very reverse of Romantic. *Elena* seems at first to be built according to a Moratinian formula : the charming young heroine, the lover of her heart, and her importunate suitor-uncle, together with a Sevilian lady, her titled gallant and the normal complement of servants. But the play soon deviates from character-comedy and by the third act has become melodrama. Elena proves to be a lachrymose creature, swooning at convenient dramatic moments and by the fifth act in a state verging on frenzy. The uncle, victim of a vehement and unbridled passion, storms through four acts, and in the fifth appears with a dagger and two pistols, shooting himself (off-stage) at the precise moment when the true lovers unite in an indissoluble embrace. His valet, beginning quite conventionally, assumes

---

[1] Larra : **Critique** of *La Conjuración de Venecia*.

the rôle of assistant villain and is pitched by his runaway mount down a precipice.

(ii) *Madrid Drama :* 1835

Except in these three plays, the Romantic revolt in 1834 seems to have accomplished little. French dramatists, notably Scribe, were drawn upon freely ; while *Macías* was opening the autumn season at the Príncipe, its rival, the Cruz, rallied the opposing party with a week of Moratín, and at both theatres, throughout the year, there was much Classical comedy and *comedia de magia.* The same is true of 1835. Rivas' highly Romantic *Don Álvaro* was given seventeen performances, but Larra's translation from Scribe, *El Arte de conspirar,* had twenty-six. Pacheco's Romantic *Alfredo* was played on three nights ; Gil y Zárate's Classical *Blanca de Borbón* on seven. Most of the Romantic pieces given in 1835 came from France—from Hugo, Dumas and Ducange. Between them, however, native Romantic dramas and foreign translations gained greatly during 1835 over dramas of the Classical type. Well established plays such as the comedies of Moratín were revived from time to time but scarcely ever for more than one or two performances. There was also a marked falling-off in the popularity of Scribe, as well as in the number of Golden Age plays, which in 1834 had been comparatively large. The names of Lope de Vega, Tirso de Molina and Calderón figure on the programmes but little. Temporarily, at least, the seventeenth century gives place to the nineteenth : the Revival yields to the Revolt.

The Romantic play of the year was *Don Álvaro, o la Fuerza del Sino* (March 22, 1835). Announced before its *estreno* as " románticamente romántico," [1] it fully justified the description, not so much by its reminiscences of Golden Age drama as by the boldness with which it flung off

---

[1] *Correo de las damas,* March 21, 1835.

Classical tradition. " If anyone denies or doubts that we are witnessing a revolution," wrote a critic shortly after the *estreno*, " let him go to the Teatro del Príncipe and see this drama." [1] Its mingling, in the same scene, of different metres, and of prose with verse, was striking enough, but, to nineteenth-century Spain, its linking of comedy with tragedy, humour with pathos, vulgarity with sublimity, farce with eloquence was something entirely new. The personality of Don Álvaro—the Romantic hero *par excellence*—the exuberance of local colour, the use made of the themes of fatality and melancholy, the bold handling of coincidence : all these traits stamp the play as super-Romantic. But most striking of all is the vastness of its conception. " Inmenso como la vida humana, rompe los moldes comunes de nuestro teatro, aun en la época de su mayor esplendor." [2] Passion strides through it, controlled only by the mystery of fate, and the amazing catastrophe is felt to be as magnificent as it is impossible.

Yet this super-Romantic play had by no means a good press and only a very moderate reception on the stage. [3] Eleven performances in Madrid for a first run, and thirty-seven, in Madrid and Barcelona combined, during three years, is hardly a triumph. Both *La Conjuración de Venecia* of 1834 [4] and *El Trovador* of 1836 [5] outclassed it completely. The nature of its reception augured poorly for the future in Spain of ultra-Romantic drama, but the " tremebunda algazara " [6] between Classicists and Romanticists to which it led gave it an importance to which we shall shortly return.

Its success was considerable, however, compared with that of Joaquín Francisco Pacheco's prose drama, *Alfredo* (May 23, 1835). Following a successful short run of Bretón's *Todo*

[1] *Revista española*, March 25, 1835.

[2] Menéndez y Pelayo : Additions to Otto von Leixner : *Nuestro Siglo : Reseña histórica, etc.*, Barcelona, 1883, p. 293.

[3] *Ángel de Saavedra*, etc., pp. 70-80 ; *H.R.*, 1934, II, 69-70.

[4] 55 performances in 4 years and a far better press.

[5] 61 performances in 2 years ; and cf. pp. 80-1, below.

[6] *El Observador*, April 13, 1835.

es farsa en este mundo, which ridicules an exaggerated Romantic, this play was given at the Príncipe for three nights to half-empty houses, whereupon the management, deciding that romanticism satirized was more profitable than romanticism in practice, took it off and put on *Todo es farsa* again. The press was somewhat kinder to it : one review eulogized it, another paid it the compliment of treating it seriously and the rest criticized it not more severely than they had criticized *Don Álvaro*. The historian of to-day regards it as one of the most puerile of Romantic exaggerations and marvels that it could ever have been staged at all.

(iii)   *Madrid Drama :* 1836

The years 1836 and 1837 mark the crest of the Romantic revolt in drama. Most of the plays produced during those years are more or less Romantic. It is now no longer a daring innovation to present a play which rejects the Unities of time and place and either rejects or puts a very liberal interpretation upon the Unity of action. Plays abound which introduce mediaeval local colour with great freedom. Four-act and five-act plays grow common ; verse not infrequently mingles with prose ; and verse-measures are often varied according to the emotional tone aimed at.

Neither now nor later did the Classical tradition entirely disappear. Bretón alone, who seldom deviated from it and remained popular throughout, would account for its continuance. The Scribe play maintained a certain level of popularity, but a lower one than before. No author other than a Romantic could count on runs of more than five or six nights during 1836. The dominant note of the Madrid stage was variety. Within the ample repertoire of the theatres, of which there were now three, there was room for Classical and Romantic, native and foreign alike. Little more interest, however, was shown in Golden Age drama : an occasional *refundición* was still given, but stronger meat was being demanded by those who liked all-Spanish menus and some of it at least was of home production.

Three original plays—all Romantic in type—are the out-standing features of the year 1836. Antonio García Gutiérrez's *El Trovador* had twenty-five performances in the year ; Martínez de la Rosa's *Aben Humeya*, ten ; and José María Díaz's *Elvira de Albornoz*, three.

El Trovador (March 1, 1836) was the only Romantic play to take Madrid by storm. Its author, a poverty-stricken youth of twenty-four, made his name in a night. " El autor del *Trovador*," commented Larra, in his critique of the play,

> se ha presentado en la arena, nuevo lidiador, sin títulos literarios, sin antecedentes políticos : solo y desconocido, la ha recorrido bizarramente al son de las preguntas multiplicadas : " ¿ Quién es el nuevo ? " " ¿ Quién es el atrevido ? " Y la ha recorrido para salir de ella victorioso.

By the next morning the reputation of the drama and of its author was made, and for the next fortnight little else in the dramatic world was spoken of.

> Al día siguiente no se hablaba en Madrid de otra cosa que del *drama caballeresco :* desde muy temprano asediaban el despacho de billetes ayudas de cámara y revendedores : los padres de familia más metódicos prometían a sus hijos llevarles al teatro, como si se tratara de una comedia de magia : la primera edición del *Trovador* se vendía en dos semanas ; se oían de boca en boca sus fáciles versos ; se repetía su representación muchas noches ; al autor se le concedía por la empresa un beneficio.[1]

Two months after its *estreno* in Madrid, it was being played with equal success in the provinces—in Barcelona, in Valencia and even in remoter parts :

> Se representó en pueblos donde no se conocían antes las representaciones escénicas, sirviendo de teatro un desván destinado a pajar, y vistiendo un protagonista el traje de miliciano nacional, a falta de otro más apropiado.[2]

The critics lauded the play to the skies. It heralded " the dawn of a new age of splendour for drama."[3] Its " triumph "

[1] A. Ferrer del Río : *Galería de la literatura española*, Madrid, 1846, pp. 257-8.
[2] R. de Mesonero Romanos : *Memorias de un setentón*, Madrid, 1881, II, 254.
[3] *Eco del Comercio*, December 26, 1837.

would " long remain in the memory of the Madrid public." [1] It " merited unstinted praise." [2] Even after six years, during which many rapid changes had come over Spanish drama, it could still be described by a critic as " the most popular play in Spain." [3]

With its double plot, its defiance of precept and all the external characteristics of romanticism, *El Trovador* flung itself, at its very outset, into the now generally accepted fashion. Dominated, like *Macías* and *Don Álvaro*, by wild love and unbridled impulse, it implies, and even proclaims, revolt against convention and law. Its picturesque characters stand out against a background of unrest, rebellion and mystery. In its first lines we breathe the atmosphere of the supernatural. Its first scene foreshadows the Romantic hero. Fully revealed, the nameless troubadour-warrior with the heart of a king and dreams loftier than the Biscay mountains is as attractive a figure as Spanish romanticism has given us. Mystery continues to characterize the play, its dramatic value enhanced by touches of symbolism. Antithesis, in character and in situation, attracts the spectator, without being too crudely forced upon him. Melancholy is introduced with artistic effect, untouched by gloom, and mingling picturesqueness with sentimentality. Probability is to some extent sacrificed to horror, but there is much less of this than in most contemporary Romantic plays. For all these reasons, it may be said that, in merit as well as in popularity, *El Trovador* represents the crest of the Romantic revolt in drama.

As *Don Álvaro* had done in the preceding year, *El Trovador* stood a head and shoulders above the other original plays of 1836. Martínez de la Rosa's *Aben Humeya* (February 14, 1836) had been played in French, at Paris, in 1830 and Madrid spectators must have thought it retrogressive. Its affiliations with pseudo-classicism are evident. The Unity of

---

[1] *El Artista*, 1836, III, 119.
[2] This was Larra's verdict. Cf. *El Español*, March 4-5, 1836.
[3] *Eco del Comercio*, September 22, 1842.

place is stretched slightly, but rigid adherence to the Unity of time destroys every vestige of probability. The medium is prose and the style somewhat prosaic. Passion for effect obliterates any remaining traces of verisimilitude and incipient tragedy degenerates into melodrama. The most attractive feature of the play is its apt use of local colour : Martínez de la Rosa knew his history and applied it with dramatic skill.

Of much less merit was José María Díaz's historical drama *Elvira de Albornoz* (May 23, 1836), a weak play, poor in characterization, artificial as to plot and highly exaggerated in expression. Not yet had a drama appeared so full of Romantic devices. Antitheses, dramatic surprises and psychological improbabilities abound. Great metrical variety and a sprinkling of lyrics diversify the form of the play and the language vacillates between a clumsy pseudo-classicism and the most hyperbolical expressions of Romantic passion. It is not surprising that, like *Alfredo* in 1835, it was withdrawn after three performances.[1]

(iv)   *Madrid Drama :* 1837

The year 1837 shares with the year 1836 the fullest success of Romantic drama in Spain, and far surpasses it as regards the predominance of native drama over foreign. Of the original Spanish plays produced in 1837, at least eleven, either wholly or very largely Romantic, are of more than average merit, and one is outstanding.

This last is Juan Eugenio Hartzenbusch's *Los Amantes de Teruel* (January 19, 1837). Given during the year fifteen times in Madrid, and six times in Barcelona, it had neither the fire of *Don Álvaro* nor the irresistible picturesqueness of *El Trovador*. Its author struck out in a third direction, weaving the threads of a well-known mediaeval love-story into a drama instinct with emotion. The success and popularity of play derive less from its flavour of adventure, its Moorish

---

[1] It was given at the Príncipe on May 23, 24 and 25. Curious to relate, *Alfredo* had been performed at the same theatre on the same three days of 1835.

scenes or its effective technical devices than from its many-sided emotionalism. There is, first, the central true-love *motif*, running right through the plot and expressing itself continually in outbursts of lyricism. There is the attractive theme of reconciliation after chivalrous strife. There is the emotional tension attributable largely to the time-element, and, by means of secondary incidents, spread over two acts of skilfully protracted conflict. There are lachrymose passages of a kind in keeping with the taste of the day, and there is a mingling of the serious, the humorous and the pathetic, less boldly but no less acceptably effected than in *Don Álvaro*, by means of a particularly delightful character, the servant Teresa. All this more than compensated for inexactitudes and anachronisms, for a feeble catastrophe, for improbabilities of characterization, and for weakness of versification and phraseology. In Isabel, Hartzenbusch created a thoroughly sympathetic Romantic heroine, though Marsilla and several of the other characters are somewhat disappointing. The fact is that Hartzenbusch, though conscientiously adopting the devices of the day, and doing his best with its extravagant diction, was only a half-hearted Romantic.

The numerous other successful plays of 1837 must be described more briefly. Bretón, with his semi-Romantic *Muérete y verás* (April 27, 1837), achieved a run equal to Hartzenbusch's. Four crisply drawn Bretonian comedy characters are making conventional love when they find themselves faced with a highly dramatic situation of which the *dénouement* is predictable with ease. The interest of the play lies in the working out of a plot which a less placid and balanced dramatist would have turned intò melodrama. Bretón pays his tribute to the prevailing fashion in an exceptionally well constructed play with a striking title. It is instructive to note its relations with Dumas' *Catherine Howard*.[1]

García Gutiérrez made a sorry attempt to repeat his early triumph in *El Paje* (May 22, 1837). All the faults of third-

[1] Cf. Piñeyro-Peers, pp. 144-5.

rate Romantic drama can be found here : unrestrained horror, misdirected emotion, glaring improbabilities of plot and character, false psychology and the usual exaggerated language. Ferrando, the " page," supposed to be a youth of fifteen, rants like a pre-Shakespearian villain and none of the other personages is much more human. We reach here the farthest limit of the Romantic revolt and a standard of drama which no country could long tolerate.

Much better, though less successful, than *El Paje* was Escosura's first play, *La Corte del Buen Retiro* (June 3, 1837), an attempt to " amalgamate the romanticism of Calderón with that of Dumas and Victor Hugo."[1] Specifically, the author works on a Hugoesque formula in depicting the deformed fool's passion for Philip IV's Queen, and on the other hand sprinkles the play with historical allusions and brings Calderón, Velázquez, Góngora and Quevedo on to the stage in turn, like the organizer of an amateur pageant. Unfortunately the public found the play incredibly dull and it had only four performances.

Roca de Togores, Marqués de Molíns, did better with *Doña María de Molina* (July 24, 1837), given thirteen performances, well received by critics as knowledgeable as Hartzenbusch and Donoso Cortés[2] and eulogized by the leading review of the day as " a masterpiece at the first attempt."[3] Except in its careful reconstruction of mediaeval history and the conscientiousness with which the author avows his departures from it, the play is entirely in consonance with the prevailing mode. One notes the large number of characters and the groups of non-speaking characters ; the metrical variety, including the somewhat arbitrary introduction of prose ; poetical disregard of the Unities ; scenes contrived to convey the maximum dramatic effect and subordination to such effect of character-development. Not that the characterization is at all despicable :   the

---

[1] Escosura's own statement : Preface to *Don Jaime el Conquistador*, Madrid, 1838.

[2] Hartzenbusch in Molíns' *Obras poéticas*, Madrid, 1857, p. xix. Donoso Cortés in *El.Porvenir*, July 28, 1837.

[3] *Semanario pintoresco español*, July 30, 1837, II, 236.

Queen, save in her " Romantic " poses, is a convincing figure ; Alfonso Martínez, the good *procurador*, is a noble creation ; and a number of the secondary characters are at their best more than credible. We can overlook the weaknesses of plot and the superabundance of wearisome talking in favour of the author's *aciertos* in characterization and regard for historical truth.

There is none of this last in José Castro y Orozco's *Fray Luis de León* (August 15, 1837), a " melodrama in four acts and in different metres " given only six performances. Never were more scandalous liberties taken with a historical figure than in this caricature of the Augustinian poet, turned into a Romantic hero with a " perenne melancolía " and a " pasión fatal,"[1] both of which he develops against the picturesque background of Granada. The violence of the play is chiefly confined to plot and language. Castro had no great skill in the Romantic modes, nor does he seem to have been at heart a convinced Romantic.

José Muñoz Maldonado's *Antonio Pérez y Felipe II* (October 20, 1837) was lucky to have eight performances, for it combines Hugoesque antithesis, illustrated, in the character of Philip, with a melodramatic bathos typical of Hugo's third-rate imitators, a violent or a grisly episode being introduced at intervals to sustain the spectator's probably flagging attention. In the fifth act reason appears to depart from the play entirely.

In *Carlos II el Hechizado* (November 1, 1837), Gil y Zárate, an apparent—but only an apparent—convert to the new mode, tried to appeal both to the Romantic ardour of young Madrid and to the anti-traditionalist spirit which had been growing up since the death of Ferdinand VII, four years earlier. The play ran for twelve consecutive nights, and the historical interest of its production lies in the difficulty of determining the precise nature of the reception which it received. On the one hand it had a good first run, a eulogistic press and an early revival ; on the other, it was freely condemned as anachronistic, exaggerated, unoriginal, irreligious

[1] *Op. cit.*, I, vi, viii.

and immoral. Though the violence of these criticisms is largely attributable to religious passion, we may detect, in their number as well as in their severity, a sign that the vogue of pure romanticism was ending.

To-day the drama stands out, even from the extravagance of its contemporaries, as an uncouth mixture of the fantastic, the horrible and the ridiculous. The character of Charles II had considerable dramatic possibilities, and even in a play where psychology is overlaid by a craving for meretricious effect, it is not lacking in pathos. But the scandal of the play is Froilán, the King's fawning and hypocritical confessor, a parody of Hugo's Frollo, whose unbridled, illegitimate passion for Charles's daughter Inés was presumably intended to attract both anti-clericals and Romantics. Other Romantic traits—the conglomeration of *dramatis personae*, the disregard of the Unities, the use made of the grotesque and the contrast between grave and gay—are obscured almost completely by exaggerated language and by scenes alternately ludicrous and repulsive. The melodrama has constructional merits and variety both in characterization and in metre, but the irrational eulogies it received would, but for the extraneous issues involved, be suggestive of frank decadence.

Two other Romantic dramas appeared in November. Escosura's *Bárbara Blomberg* (November 19, 1837) was given six times, but its determination to avoid the exaggerations criticized in *La Corte del Buen Retiro* must have made it intolerably dull and artificial. Bretón achieved eight performances for the second attempt at Romantic drama which he made during the year, *Don Fernando el Emplazado*. Considering that history had provided him with a naturally dramatic plot, complete with exposition, climax and catastrophe, and already treated by Lope de Vega, the play cannot be called successful. The mode of the day is served by the crude antitheses of characterization and the highly melodramatic ending ; the real Bretón appears in thumbnail character sketches, in occasional irony and in the easy flow of the verse, which he could produce with equal skill in comedy and in drama.

Finally, in *El Rey Monje* (December 18, 1837), García Gutiérrez advanced greatly upon *El Paje*, without, however, recovering either the charm of *El Trovador* or its dramatic merit. The improvement is due partly to a very considerable beauty in language and versification and partly to a great increase in dramatic power, as distinct from dramatic violence. A number of dramatically effective, if artificial, scenes are thrown into strong relief. Antithesis and coincidence play an important part in the plot, as do the themes of passion, melancholy and disillusion. But, while these qualities principally suggest the " new " romanticism, the prominence of the themes of honour and vengeance, together with many isolated passages, recall the drama of the Golden Age. With its mediaeval theme and its Calderonian language, *El Rey Monje* is as much a drama of the Revival as of the Revolt.

This was by far the best total of creditable plays produced by the Romantic movement in any one year, and its effect was enhanced by a number of successful revivals. The eleven plays just reviewed account for over one hundred performances ; another thirty-five were occupied with five of those previously described. These Spanish plays almost entirely ousted Romantic dramas translated from the French. Only four performances were given in Madrid of plays by Hugo ; only nine of plays by Dumas. Translations of French comedy, however, prospered, as did the Classical plays of Moratín and Bretón, though the evidence is too slender for us to decide if this is an indication of an anti-Romantic reaction.

One other characteristic of this year is a revival in the popularity of Golden Age drama. For several seasons no more than occasional performances from that source had been given. Now we suddenly find about thirty, including some well supported revivals. Coupled with the decline in French Romantic drama, this suggests that preferences are veering back from the Revolt to the Revival.

From the plays of 1837, then, we can learn something of the climax of the success of the Romantic revolt and of the

7

beginning and the nature of its decline. When, in a later chapter, we survey the plays of the years immediately following, we shall see that decline becoming more evident.

(v) *Provincial Drama :* 1834—1837

Neither in Barcelona nor in Valencia did the dramatic revolt achieve more than a fraction of its success in Madrid. In 1835, Barcelona saw no Dumas, no Delavigne, no Soulié and no *estreno* of *Don Álvaro* ; it had only four performances of any play by Hugo, three of *La Conjuración de Venecia* and six of *Macías*. Ducange was but slightly more popular than Hugo and the dominating figures are Scribe and Bretón ; there are also occasional excursions into patriotism. During 1836 and 1837, attempts were made to popularize Romantic drama, but with a success far behind that reached in Madrid.

The Romantic revolt, however, did have some echo in Barcelona. In Valencia it was hardly known at all. Even the Revival had little effect on the stage : Golden Age plays, which were fairly popular between 1825 and 1830, almost disappeared. The city which wept for Desdemona and sighed with Paul and Virginia had little to say to Delavigne, Ducange and Soulié. Dumas and Hugo were rather more popular, but their vogue on the stage began only in 1836 and was much slighter than in Barcelona. The native expression of the Revolt was almost completely neglected. In 1835, *Aben Humeya*, *Macías* and *Don Álvaro* between them totalled but nine performances. Only *El Trovador*, with five performances, had any success in 1836, and in 1837, though *Don Álvaro* and *El Trovador* had short revivals, *Los Amantes de Teruel* was the only new Romantic drama to be performed more than once.

IV. The Revolt in Lyric and Narrative Poetry, 1834—1837[1]

It is impossible, for historical reasons, to treat the other literary *genres* precisely as we have treated drama. The history of the novel belongs, not to the Revolt, but to the

[1] *H.R.M.S.*, I, 301-25.

Revival. In the lyric and narrative poetry of the period there is also, at first sight, more of revival than of revolt. Some critics, therefore, mistakenly assert that the Revolt was confined to drama. In fact, however, much of its force, as regards both content and form, was felt by lyric poetry, while even narrative poetry, in which there was more scope for revival than for revolt, was not unaffected by it. But the rapid growth and climax of the revolt in poetry came, not in 1834-7, as in drama, but in about 1839-40. We can therefore carry its history only a short distance in this chapter.

(i) *Slow growth and late fruition*

Luzán, whose *Poética* was first published exactly one hundred years before the date which closes this part of our survey, had believed that he was not merely leading poetry back to the ordered paths from which it had strayed, but was also revivifying it. His numerous admirers united in subscribing to that belief, and from the beginning of the last third of the eighteenth century it was widely believed that a great poetic revival was at hand, and that to Luzán was due a large share of the credit for it. " La restauración de las letras," wrote López de Sedano in 1768, " ha empezado siempre por la poesía . . . Por eso debemos lisonjearnos de no estar ya muy lejos aquellos tiempos felices, en que vuelvan a verse una y otra en el aumento, y auge a que los condúzca el restablecimiento del *buen gusto* en todas las artes y ciencias."[1]

When the Salamancans began to write, their contemporaries saw in them the heralds of the renaissance, and the herald-in-chief was Meléndez Valdés. To us that poet is a writer of the second rank, whose importance is mainly historical, but to the pre-Romantics, and even to many of the Romantics, he was the leader of a great poetic revival— " restaurador del Parnaso español,"[2] " el poeta de más fama del siglo XVIII, el que restituyó la poesía a su antiguo

---

[1] *Parnaso español, etc.*, Madrid, 1768, I, vii.

[2] Wolf : *Floresta de rimas modernas castellanas*, Paris, 1837, I, 364.

esplendor".[1] " ¡ Gloria al grande escritor," Quintana had written of him, in 1797,

> a quien fué dado
> romper el sueño y vergonzoso olvido
> en que yace sumido
> el ingenio español. . . . ! [2]

Even López Soler, whose articles in the *Europeo* show that he knew what poetry was, wrote that " en él (Meléndez Valdés) . . . empieza la época moderna de las musas castellanas."[3]

This belief in an eighteenth-century poetic revival explains why the climax of the Romantic revolt in poetry was delayed even longer than in drama. It was generally agreed that nothing but a revolution could save the theatre, but, strange to say, the condition of non-dramatic verse was regarded with quite fair satisfaction. Though in fact it was only rarely that even a gleam of true poetry shone out from the masses of verbiage that went by that name, it was equally rarely that the need was felt for anything better.

Even as late as 1837, the emancipatory movement in poetry had hardly established itself. Cabanyes, one of the first innovators, had died without becoming known outside Barcelona. Rivas had produced little verse suggestive even of the possibility of revolution. Espronceda had not yet published his *Estudiante de Salamanca* or his *Diablo Mundo*, nor had he collected his shorter poems. Salvador Bermúdez de Castro, who in 1840 was to produce a volume of the most Romantic poetry that Spain had seen, was only just beginning to write at all. Zorrilla was still a boy : it was in this very year of 1837 that he read those verses by Larra's grave which made him famous :

> Entonces, de en medio de nosotros, ... vimos brotar y aparecer un joven, casi un niño, para todos desconocido. Alzó su pálido semblante, clavó en aquella tumba y en el cielo una mirada sublime, y . . . . leyó en cortados y trémulos acentos los versos . . . . que el Sr. Roca tuvo que arrancar de

---

[1] Gil y Zárate : *Resumen histórico de la literatura española*, Madrid, 1943 (quoted from 6th ed., Madrid, 1874, p. 631).

[2] B.A.E., XIX, 9.

[3] *El Europeo*, December 27, 1823.

su mano, porque, desfallecido a la fuerza de su emoción, el mismo autor no pudo concluirlos.   Nuestro asombro fué igual a nuestro entusiasmo . . . . y los mismos que en fúnebre pompa habíamos conducido al ilustre Larra a la mansión de los muertos, salimos de aquel recinto llevando en triunfo a otro poeta al mundo de los vivos y proclamando con entusiasmo el nombre de Zorrilla.[1]

Once the taste for such revolutionary poetry as Zorrilla's had begun to spread, there was no further chance for the so-called renaissance associated with Meléndez Valdés. These verses read at Larra's grave were Romantic in form : their forty-nine lines are arranged in eight stanzas of six distinct patterns and of four, five, six and eight lines. They were Romantic in content : in their idealization of the young suicide, their Vigny-like insistence on the " mission " of the poet and his essential unhappiness on earth, and the vigorous metaphors with which these ideas were driven home. The lines had done for lyric poetry something of what *El Trovador*, the year before, had done for drama.   Only three years earlier, in 1834, Alcalá Galiano had declared that " la escuela de Meléndez, o la de Luzán más españolizada, es hoy día la dominante en nuestra literatura " ;[2] Mármol, invoking the " restoration " of Spanish poetry by Cadalso and Meléndez, had printed over one hundred pages of " pastoriles " in the purest eighteenth-century style ;[3] and Larra had complained that in poetry

> Estamos aún a la altura de los arroyuelos murmuradores, de la tórtola triste, de la palomita de Filis, de Batilo y Menalcas, de las delicias de la vida pastoril, del caramillo y del recental, de la leche y de la miel, y otras fantasmagorías por este estilo.[4]

" Ningún rumbo nuevo," he had sighed, " ningún resorte no usado."[5] But in the year of his own death the new direction was to make itself evident.

[1] *Obras de Nicomedes Pastor Díaz*, Madrid, 1866-7, III, 44-5.

[2] Preface to *El Moro expósito*.

[3] *Romancero*, Seville, 1834, 2 vols.

[4] " Literatura.   Poesías de D. Juan Bautista Alonso."

[5] *Ibid.*

(ii)   *The Revolt in its relation to poetic form :   versification and diction*

We may first consider the Romantic revolt as it affected poetic form—in particular, versification and diction. Freedom to use verse-forms of the past had long been demanded. At the very beginning of the century, Quintana, in the main a conservative, pleaded for rhymeless verse. Let the French have their rhymes, is his argument ; their inharmonious, monotonous language needs them. But we Spaniards,

> con un idioma tan rico, tan vario en sus terminaciones, tan sonoro en sus sílabas y tan majestuoso en su dicción, nosotros hacemos una injuria a nuestra bella versificación y a nuestra lengua si reputamos la rima como de absoluta necesidad en poesía.[1]

Juan Bautista Arriaza, though he eulogized and translated Boileau's *Art poétique*, commented upon the superiority of Spanish verse over French in the matter of variety[2] and used blank verse for his translation. Francisco Sánchez Barbero used metres in 1805 as varied as those that Espronceda was to use in 1840. Manuel María de Arjona, who died in 1820, was a bold innovator, as was Cabanyes, who died in 1833. Bretón both defended and indulged in metrical innovations in drama. And, in the year after Cabanyes' death, Jacinto Salas y Quiroga flung himself resolutely into revolution.[3] But the greatest and the most determined of the innovators in form was Espronceda.

The whole story of Espronceda's life reveals a "Romantic hero," with all the characteristics of the Romantic temperament : a passion for freedom, a life ruled by impulse, a tendency to rebellion for rebellion's sake. His life was a Romantic poem,

> un poema
> con lances raros y revuelto asunto,[4]

[1] *Variedades de ciencias, literatura y artes,* 1804, IV, 355.

[2] *Arte poética,* Madrid, 1807, p. 66.

[3] *Poesías,* Madrid, 1834. The preface to this volume is a Romantic manifesto.

[4] *El Diablo Mundo,* Canto I.

and his description of himself uses the very figure of speech
under which Larra had described neo-Romantic drama :

> Yo me arrojé cual rápido cometa
> en alas de mi ardiente fantasía.[1]

When his life flickered out before it had burned at its
strongest, his friend Ros de Olano applied to the tragedy
its victim's own words and called him

> el cometa sin medida
> que se apagó en mitad de la carrera.[2]

One feels that his untimely death was entirely in keeping
with his turbulent career and his impulsive character.

His themes, again, have all the inconsequence and variety
of romanticism :

> Batallas, tempestades, amoríos,
> por mar y tierra, lances, descripciones
> de campos y ciudades, desafíos,
> y el desastre y furor de las pasiones,
> goces, dichas, aciertos, desvaríos,
> con algunas morales reflexiones
> acerca de la vida y de la muerte,
> de mi propia cosecha, que es mi fuerte.[3]

He writes, as he puts it,

> sin ton ni son, y para gusto mío . . . .
> Sin regla ni compás canta mi lira :
> ¡ Sólo mi ardiente corazón me inspira ![4]
>
> .   .   .   .
>
> En varias formas, con diverso estilo,
> en diferentes géneros, calzando
> ora el coturno trágico de Esquilo,
> ora la trompa épica sonando :
> ora cantando plácido y tranquilo,
> ora en trivial lenguaje, ora burlando
> conforme esté mi humor, porque a él me ajusto,
> y allá van versos donde va mi gusto.[5] .

Even within a single poem, *El Diablo Mundo*, he veers
suddenly from the sublime to the grotesque, from ugly

---

[1] " A Jarifa en una orgía."

[2] *Poesías de D. Antonio Ros de Olano*, Madrid, 1886, p. 46.

[3] *El Diablo Mundo*, Canto I.

[4] *Ibid.*   [5] *Ibid.*

cynicism to passionate sincerity, from pondering the eternal
verities to trifling with childish rhyme and futile phraseology.
One never knows what the turning of a page will reveal in
Espronceda.

In no respect, however, is he more typically the Spanish
Romantic than in his metrical innovations. " He has
revolutionized versification," declared Ros de Olano in the
preface to Cantos I and II of *El Diablo Mundo*, and, though
such a claim takes no account of the work of his predecessors,
it is not greatly exaggerated. In his shorter lyrics he uses
familiar metres, but generally varies them ; more frequently
still he experiments with bold alternations and variants and
also with inventions of his own. The " Canción del Pirata,"
only 90 lines long, is built on a triple scheme, varied so as to
echo the sense. " El Mendigo," of 118 lines, is constructed
on a quadruple pattern, with even subtler variations. " El
Reo de Muerte" has a very marked change of metre corresponding to the change of tone from despair to serenity and
two further changes of the same type which foreshadow the
art of *El Estudiante de Salamanca*. " El Verdugo," in places, is
suggestive of the florid ode, but, in the striking pattern of its
metre alone, and still more markedly in its diction, it has
enough of Espronceda to be recognizable as his. "¡ Guerra !"
opens in the purest eighteenth-century style, but more
modern stanzas follow, and three distinct movements corres-
pond to three fairly well marked divisions of thought. This
triple division is more clearly marked still in " A una estrella,"
the construction of which may be represented by the figures
1, 2, 3, 1 ; and also in " A Jarifa, en una orgía," with a
formula 1, 2, 1 + 2 + 1. These indications will give some idea
of how far Espronceda outstrips his predecessors as a modern
poet and how industriously he is preparing those metrical
effects which he developed later.

Rivas, in his early poems, is metrically unadventurous,
and he uses a single loose and easy hendecasyllabic measure
throughout the *Moro expósito*. His prologist describes him as
employing a metre which, although, " through its asson-
ance, the peculiarity of our language, it is pure (*castizo*) and
exclusively Castilian," has " rarely if ever been used in works

of this length." While this is true enough, it in no way stamps the metre as revolutionary ; and actually, in versification as in other matters, Rivas was primarily a revivalist. When not wishing to use Classical metres, he goes back for his models to mediaeval poetry or to the Golden Age. Only in his *Leyendas* (1854) does he indulge in metrical variety, and that only to a mild degree.

Next to Espronceda, the Romantic of greatest metrical originality during this period is Salvador Bermúdez de Castro, whose so-called *estrofa bermudina* (eight hendeca-syllables, rhyming *abbc decc*, the fourth and the eighth line lacking the final syllable) expresses the predilection of many Romantics for the *agudo*. The long quatrains of his "Toledo," written on the theme

> Duerme, Toledo, duerme, y en tu almohadón de piedra
> reclina descuidada tu polvorosa sien,[1]

contrast strikingly with the short lines of " El Harén " :

> Era noche ;
> la sultana
> su persiana
> levantó .... [2]

or with the light tripping stanzas of " La Barquilla " :

> Así el hombre entretanto
> corre tras un encanto ;
> se afana, sin saber
> que es llanto
> lo que pensaba ser
> placer.[3]

A second manifestation of the Romantic revolt in poetic form lies in the sphere of diction. To some extent this was stimulated by the Revival, but many of the Romantics were content to take over the clichés and clumsy periphrases of their precursors. Rivas' diction, for example, shows only a gradual advance from his earliest poems to the *Moro expósito* (1834) and indeed to the *Romances históricos* of 1841. The old conventional epithets and allusions, the meaningless images,

---

[1] *Ensayos poéticos*, Madrid, 1840, pp. 169-84.
[2] *Op. cit.*, pp. 91-5.   [3] *Op. cit.*, pp. 253-6.

die away little by little ; brief, telling descriptions become more numerous ; and the use of Rivas' favourite medium of colour increases. His growing addiction to narrative poetry made his vision clearer and his expression more forceful. The same may be said of several of his contemporaries : when they wrote narrative poetry, they were clear, effective, even impressive and brilliant ; but as soon as they returned to the lyrical they found themselves wading in a sea of words. As a result, reform in diction lagged some way behind reform in metre.

Espronceda furnishes the best early example of the revolt in relation to diction. By 1837 he was writing a poetical language at once forceful and vivid. In the " Canción del Pirata " his economy of words permits hardly a synonymous epithet. He has discovered the force of stark antithesis :

> ¡ Sentenciado estoy a muerte !
> Yo me río,

and of monosyllabic emphasis :

> Que yo soy el rey del mar.

" El Reo de Muerte " begins to seek out epithets deliberately for their effect ; and, if with them we occasionally find more conventional phrases, that is only because their author has not completely learned his lesson. When his subject lends itself to conventionalism, as in the last two stanzas of " El Reo de Muerte," here and there in " El Verdugo " and in the opening lines of " ¡ Guerra ! ", he cannot always resist it. But it is clear that, long before he had written his chief poems, he was a Romantic in diction.

(iii)   *The Revolt in its relation to poetic content*

From form we pass to content. The recovery of freedom in choice of theme was brought about chiefly through the Romantic revival : this is, indeed, one of the best examples of the way in which Revival and Revolt are indistinguishably fused. Freedom in this respect came as a gradual growth rather than as a sudden reaction from the past. Many of the themes of pseudo-Classical poetry had always been artificial and were now outworn. Many others, though intrinsically of perennial interest and universal appeal, had fallen into disfavour because artificiality in the treatment of them had become a tradition. How attractive by contrast were mediaeval themes, which had been treated simply and humanly, if sometimes crudely, in a distant past !

Still, even the immense outburst of lyricism associated with the years 1839-40, to be described in a later chapter, did not bring complete emancipation from the old artificial forms and the old themes. But it was in those years that the full extent of the invasion of poetry by the new themes began to be realized. These, since they were not confined to either lyric or narrative poetry, it will be convenient to study, together with the other elements which make up Spanish romanticism, separately.[1] But we may enumerate here the fresh subjects which entered poetry before 1837. Of individual types, nearly all the most popular have a clearly sentimental appeal. The " Romantic hero " of drama is less popular in lyric and narrative poetry than the rebel-criminal type on the one hand and the orphan-foundling or hermit-pilgrim type on the other. The first of these three types exercised much the same attraction in poetry as did the " Romantic hero," in his active aspect, in drama ; the two last responded to the same emotional need as did the " Romantic hero " in his passive or sentimental aspect, which was rather the more characteristic of the two.

Except with regard to individual types, the thematic peculiarities of the Romantic lyric in this period differ but slightly from those of Romantic drama. The element of vagueness and mystery, often allied to the horrible and the grotesque, is a constant in Romantic literature. So, too, is the element of melancholy in its various forms, ranging from an objective philosophical pessimism to a fiercely rebellious discontent arising largely from individual disillusion. Sensibility, especially to the influences of Nature, is less prominent in the lyric poetry of Spanish romanticism,

[1] Cf. pp. 192-9, below.

whether early or late, than in that of other countries. Various forms of sentimentality are observable in this period, notably the humanitarianism so typical of the pre-Romantics. The peculiar Romantic pose which represents the poet as divinely inspired to fulfil a " mission " developed in Spain after 1837. To all these subjects we shall return in our penultimate chapter.

V. The Climax of the Revolt : Classicists versus Romanticists[1]

By the year 1837, as we have now seen, the Romantic revolt had, except in prose fiction, made considerable progress. In narrative poetry, it had lent a great impetus to the Revival. It was preparing the way for the emergence of a new and distinctive type of lyric poetry. In drama, it had enjoyed more resounding successes than in any other *genre* and a far-seeing critic might well have prophesied that its greatest days were over. The climax of the Revolt, however, which had come with the triumph of *El Trovador*, was quite remarkable enough to inhibit any misgivings.

(i)   *General satisfaction of the Romanticists with the results of the Revolt*

The dominant note of Romantic comments on the progress of the Revolt in the years immediately preceding 1837 is one of vast satisfaction. Its most ardent supporters evidently believed that an extreme form of romanticism had come to Spain to stay : " un romanticismo español, enteramente nuestro, el del pueblo donde todo lleva el carácter del romanticismo."[2] " Romántica es nuestra historia," added the critic who wrote those words in 1835, " romántico nuestro cielo . . . romantícese también nuestra escena."[3] " Esperemos," wrote Larra, early in 1836,

[1] *H.R.M.S.*, I, 325-49.
[2] *Revista española*, August 27, 1835.   [3] *Ibid.*

Esperemos que dentro de poco podamos echar los cimientos de una literatura *nueva*, expresión de la sociedad *nueva* que componemos ; toda de *verdad*, como es de *verdad* nuestra sociedad : sin más reglas que esa *verdad* misma, sin más maestro que la *naturaleza, joven*, en fin, como la España que constituimos.[1]

How different was this language from that of 1834—only two years earlier ! In that year Alcalá Galiano had described his countrymen as " fettered with the shackles of French classicism (and) almost alone, among the moderns of Europe, in not daring to trespass beyond the limits laid down by foreign critics of the seventeenth and eighteenth centuries."[2] Larra, in the *Revista española*, had stigmatized Spanish literature as " a great extinguished *brasero*, with an occasional pale and flickering spark gleaming amid the ashes." " Our Golden Age," he had added, " has long since passed away and our nineteenth century has not yet arrived."[3] Then came the change. In the next year, and in the same review, the arrival of romanticism in drama was hailed by Larra as something " new, original . . . never before produced or heard of."[4] Eugenio de Ochoa, writing retrospectively in 1836 in a review, *El Artista*, which had been born with the " new era,"[5] saw the history of the past two years as a "most brilliant triumph " for the Romantics. " Ya es evidente," he had written in the preceding summer, " que el romanticismo, bueno o malo, existe ; y no es poco haber logrado tamaño triunfo."[6] But now romanticism does more than exist—it dominates. " La revolución literaria que empezaba a formarse cuando salió a luz este periódico, y que nosotros abrazamos con entusiasmo y convicción, ha sido ya coronada por el más brillante triunfo."[7] Quotations could be multiplied to illustrate the exuberant

[1] " Literatura. Rápida ojeada sobre la historia e índole de la nuestra, etc." *El Español*, January 18, 1836.

[2] Preface to *El Moro expósito* (Rivas : *Obras, ed. cit.*, III, xxviii).

[3] " Literatura. Poesías de D. Juan Bautista Alonso."

[4] " Una primera representación."

[5] Cf. p. 101, below.   [6] *El Artista*, 1835, II, 47.

[7] *El Artista*, 1836, III, 1.

delight with which the out-and-out Romantics greeted this apparent victory. But the partial establishment of Romantic ideals also stirred up the Classicists afresh to do battle. The conflict was short, hardly exceeding the limits of date (1834-7) with which we have been dealing. It is possible, therefore, to describe its main course quite briefly, leaving certain particular aspects of it to be treated in a later chapter.

(ii)   *The Conflict between Classicists and Romanticists*

The conflict, beginning abroad, made itself felt in Spain only about 1832, gathered force during 1833, and became violent only some time after the return of the exiled Liberals. In 1834, for example, the two parties were fighting " con la tolerancia debida en semejantes creencias."[1] But the fight had begun in earnest, and every new work of any substance ran the risk of being drawn into the dispute by the one party or the other. Alcalá Galiano refused to admit that the *Moro expósito* was either Classical or Romantic, adding that this distinction was an arbitrary one which he did not recognize.[2] But he admitted it by implication and the poem could not escape being used in party warfare. The same is true of Larra's drama *Macías*. The author might hope to keep the goodwill of both parties by asking " Is it a Romantic drama?" and declaring that anyone who attempted to stamp it or to classify it as such was deluded ; but it was in fact so stamped and so classified—and Larra himself, rightly or wrongly, was straightway labelled a Romantic,[3] a title which he has never lost.

(iii)   *The Conflict in the periodical press*

Soon both parties were well entrenched behind their respective periodicals, for it was in the press that they fought their chief engagements.

[1] P. A. de la Avecilla : *Poética trágica*, Madrid, 1834, *cit. H.R.M.S.*, I, 329, n. 4.
[2] Rivas : *Obras, ed. cit.*, III, xxxi.
[3] Cf. pp. 146-7, below.

The Romantics' principal organ was *El Artista* (1835-6), founded by Eugenio de Ochoa, who was well known as a translator of Victor Hugo. He described it as a review intended for idealists in art and literature, contributed to it various Romantic tales and poems, and took an important share in the polemic of the day, resolved to wrest the victory from his equally determined opponents. In a slightly ridiculous panegyric, accompanied by considerable abuse of the other side, he seized upon three outstanding authors of the past—Homer, Dante and Calderón—claiming them as the " true apostles of romanticism." The " simple dogmas of this school," he asserted, had been " maliciously " misinterpreted by its detractors—the " partisans of routine," of whom, to their " inestimable happiness," the Romantics had made " mortal enemies."

Ochoa was seconded by a greater man than himself : Espronceda. The most entertaining piece of prose that that not very inspired prose-writer ever published was a short and witty satire of the pastoral poem, entitled " El Pastor Clasiquino," which carried the war into the Classicists' own territory. Clasiquino, a Treasury office clerk by profession, lived in a drab street in Madrid, and his Clori was only his housekeeper : " de genio pertinaz y rabioso . . . le llenaba de apodos y vituperios a todas horas." But his soul was the soul of a shepherd of neo-Classic pastoral poetry.

> " *Nada como las reglas de Aristóteles*," solía también decir Clasiquino a veces, que, aunque pastor, había leído más de una vez las reglas del estagirita. " ¡ La naturaleza ! La naturaleza es menester hermosearla. Nada debe ser lo que es, sino lo que debiera ser." [1]

The rest of the criticism of the *Artista* follows the lead given by Ochoa and Espronceda. Evocations of the Middle Ages, laudatory biographies of the literary and artistic leaders of the Golden Age and cordial notices of the historical novels of Trueba y Cosío and Escosura help the Romantic revival, while critiques of current plays lend support to the Revolt. The principal significance of the *Artista*, however, like nearly all the best work it produced, was not critical, but

---

[1] *El Artista*, 1835, I, 251.

creative.   Ochoa himself, though no great creative artist, contributed a continuous stream of tales and verses, all of either the chivalric, the lachrymose or the sepulchral type, and sometimes blending all three.   It is easy to poke fun at such things, but even a glance at the review will show what a service Ochoa did to his time by encouraging hidden talent. Very few youths of the day who became well-known writers are unrepresented in its few issues.   It published a story and three poems by Zorrilla, when he was only eighteen, a year before he appeared at Larra's funeral.[1]   Espronceda contributed two poems and some fragments of his " El Pelayo."[2]   Other contributors were Ventura de la Vega, Salvador Bermúdez de Castro, Gabriel García Tassara, Castro y Orozco, Pacheco, Trueba y Cosío, Roca de Togores and Nicomedes Pastor Díaz.   And all this published work appeared within the space of hardly more than a year.   One can imagine what the influence of the *Artista* might have been had it lived longer.

Several other Madrid reviews, though not avowedly Romantic, were favourably inclined to the new movement. *Cartas españolas* (1831-2) allowed it a fair hearing.   Its successor, the *Revista española* (1833-6), famous for its articles by Larra, stood for liberalism, both in politics and in literature, and became more progressive as it grew older.   *El Siglo* (1834) was more definitely Romantic, replying to readers who thought it too advanced that " the hour for reform had struck," both " in politics and in poetry."[3]   *No me olvides* (1837-8), edited by Salas y Quiroga, was the *Artista's* lineal descendant.   Its contemporary, *El Siglo XIX* (1837-8), was also Romantic in sympathies, though less concerned with the Revolt than with the Revival.

The anti-Romantic journals were equally active.   The *Estrella* (1833-4) fulminates against the Romantics' " infirm imagination " and " monstrous literature."   The *Eco de Comercio* (1834-48) fulminates less, but is coldly critical or blandly unaware of such events as the *estreno* of *Don Álvaro*

[1] *Op. cit.*, II, 103-7, 112-13, 155-6, 185-7.
[2] *Op. cit.*, I, 43-4, 137-8, 183-4 ; III, 159.
[3] *El Siglo*, January 24, 1834.

or even of the *Trovador*. The *Abeja* (1834-6), in theory impartial and eclectic, is generally critical of the Romantic movement and often hostile to it. In these periodicals, and outside them, die-hard Classicists, most of them elderly, inveighed against those " hediondos y abominables . . . ingeniazos modernos,"[1] the Romantics, while younger men fought more good-humouredly and with greater effect. Estébanez Calderón, for example, stood up gaily to Espronceda ; and " Abenámar " (Santos López Pelegrín), with an eye on *Don Álvaro*, poked fun at the Romantic *cliché* and at the *fuerza del sino :*

¡ Maldición ! Horrible suerte
tuviste, Paca, al nacer . . . .[2]

(iv)   *The Conflict in Barcelona*

Only in Barcelona, of the provincial cities of Spain, do we catch any echo of the Classical-Romantic battle. The greater preoccupation of the Catalonians with the Revival than with the Revolt made of itself for the rejection of much that was felt to be exotic. Thus the conflict, where it developed, was not so much between Classicists and Romanticists as between Scott and Byron, Chateaubriand and Hugo, the adherents of López Soler and the followers of Ochoa. So completely were Catalonians won over to the Romantic revival that they say little about classicism, or the Classical-Romantic conflict, at all.

The periodicals of Barcelona at this time, some of which have as much literary value as their Madrid contemporaries, are neither anti-Romantic nor even as eclectic as the *Europeo*. The *Diario de Barcelona* was catholic in its comprehensiveness and was often strongly influenced by native aspects of romanticism. The *Vapor* (1833-8), having López Soler as its first editor and Aribau on its staff, naturally maintained the traditions of the *Europeo :* its dominating ideas were cosmopolitanism, mediaevalism, patriotism and chivalry ; its dominating influence was that of Sir Walter Scott. It was

---

[1] José Mor de Fuentes : *Vida y escritos, etc.*, Barcelona, 1836, p. 171.

[2] *H.R.M.S.*, I, 340.

particularly hospitable to young writers, of whom it had quite
a galaxy. Many of its contributors eulogized the poetry of
the Spanish Romantics and even their mediocre historical
novels ; far fewer made themselves the fervid apologists of
Romantic drama. The *Guardia nacional* (1835-41), a daily
paper with literary leanings and pre-eminently Liberal in
its policy, is of the first importance for an understanding of
the Romantic movement, both in Barcelona and in Spain as
a whole. It is here that the revolt-aspect of Catalonian
romanticism is chiefly seen, though the revival-aspect is also
well represented, and the general tone of the paper, which
occasionally prints anti-Romantic articles, is one of moderation.

(v) *Atmosphere of the Conflict*

To catch something of the atmosphere of the Romantic
conflict is not easy, but contemporary testimony frequently
reminds us that it was waged over a far wider front than that
of pure literature. Here, for example, is an illustration, in a
popular periodical, entitled " Un clásico y un romántico
cuando llueve." [1] The Classicist is well protected from the
rain by a stout umbrella and has all the appearance of solid
comfort. The Romantic walks along in a despondent and
absent-minded attitude, drenched through and through.
Here, again, is a pen-picture contrasting a highly respected
Classicist, Don Deogracias, who lives in a floridly decorated
house and consumes hearty breakfasts of *torreznos, tortas*, rolls
and chocolate, and Don Teodoro, a pale-faced young
Romantic, who lives in a remote attic and breakfasts upon
tea. [2] Such skits as this, of quite general application, played
leading parts in the Romantic battle, which extended even
to women's journals and the intimacy of the home. Girls of
the early nineteenth century were as apt to develop a passion
for Dumas and Hugo as girls of the sixteenth had been for
" books of chivalry." Their most susceptible age, one
satirist avers, was from nineteen to twenty-one, after which

---

[1] *Semanario pintoresco español*, June 1, 1837, II, 174.
[2] *Leyendas y novelas jerezanas*, Ronda, Madrid, 1838, p. ix.

they " begin gradually to recover their commonsense."[1]
But by no means always. Manuela, the Romantic sister in
Bretón's *Me voy de Madrid*, raves about the heroine in Hugo's
Lucrèce Borgia :

> ¡ Aquélla sí que es mujer . . . . !
> . . . . ¡ Qué alma tan hidrópica
> de agitaciones sublimes ! [2]

and the Classically-minded Tomasa speculates on that
lady's abilities in the domestic arts of knitting and making
jam, to be told that Classicists have neither nerves nor
feelings. A dialogue in a contemporary review takes us into
the region of dress :

> " ¿ . . . . No habéis visto ese traje *tan romántico* que lleva ? "
> " Yo," le repliqué, " he visto un traje con mangas
> estrechas y con adornos, que, lejos de recordarme los de la
> *edad de los romances* (los cuales creo deban ser los únicos que el
> nombre de *romántico* merezcan) me ha parecido un remedo
> de los tiempos de Luis XIV o de Luis XV de Francia,
> que por cierto fué una época bien contraria a todo lo
> romántico." [3]

Needless to say, there was a " Romantic " type of features,
especially common in young men. The haggard cheeks, the
pale complexion, the haunted look or the flashing eye, and
the ubiquitous *melena* were as unmistakable as the black coat,
cherry-coloured doublet and pale green trousers which we
associate with Théophile Gautier. And there are several
typically Romantic poses—the lyric fervour which inspires
serenades to the moon, or, equally readily, dirges in chance
graveyards ; the amorous melancholy which prompts the
fruitless search for the sympathetic heart ; the excitability of
a " Don Fogoso Cuchillada " and a wildness of demeanour
which one contemporary *costumbrista* derives from—the
Spaniard's Gothic ancestry ! [4]

> Su imaginación se exalta, sus facciones se alteran y su
> traje exterior sufre una gran variación ; el Hernani de
> Victor Hugo es su héroe, se propone imitarle al menos en
> su larga barba y gran perilla y su objeto es buscar una

---

[1] *La Paz*, Barcelona, August 26, 1838.
[2] *Me voy de Madrid*, I, ix. Cf. *H.R.M.S.*, II, 402-5.
[3] " Romanticismo en las modas." *No me olvides*, June 4, 1837.
[4] " Romanticismo." *Guardia nacional*, April 12, 1836.

joven que sienta y le haga sentir las pasiones vivas de su héroe.[1]

Un calavera se llama " romántico," y toma igual título el furioso que le planta a Vd. una estocada y aquel a quien sus vicios han aburrido, y llevado hasta el borde del precipicio, se sonríe al suicidarse con la persuasión de que muere " románticamente."[2]

Nor can we leave the type without recalling Mesonero Romanos' mythical nephew, to be described hereafter, who, having arranged to his satisfaction a mode of attire which made him " the most Romantic picture in the whole of Madrid," turned his attention to his character, " asegurándome que encontraba en su corazón algo de volcánico y sublime."[3]

These absurdities of the " melenudos semidioses "[4] all entered into the Romantic conflict which raged during the years 1834-7. When, however, at the end of 1837, we read such phrases as

Ya que no somos románticos en el sentido que dan a esta voz los clásicos ; ya que no somos clásicos en la acepción en que toman la palabra los románticos, evitemos disputas y denominaciones de partidos,[5]

we realize that some new spirit is abroad which we may vaguely believe we have encountered already. When, no later than 1839, we find Zorrilla, the Romantic youth who had made his *début* two years earlier, at Larra's grave, begging his readers " que no se cansen en volver a sacar a plaza la ya mohosa cuestión de *clasicismo y romanticismo*,[6] we suspect a sudden and overwhelming revulsion of opinion from all kinds of conflict. That something of this kind did take place we shall presently see, but first we must follow the fortunes of the Romantic movement a little farther.

[1] *Correo de las damas*, April 10, 1834.

[2] *El Vapor*, January 3, 1836 ; *Guardia nacional*, January 19, 1836.

[3] R. de Mesonero Romanos : *El Romanticismo y los románticos*, Liverpool, 1933, pp. 15-16.

[4] P. A. de Alarcón, in his preface to A. Ros de Olano : *Poesías*, Madrid, 1886, p. 10.

[5] *Semanario pintoresco español*, December 10, 1837, II, 388.

[6] Preparatory note to *Cada cual con su razón* (Madrid, 1839), dated August 27, 1839.

CHAPTER IV

THE FAILURE OF THE ROMANTIC MOVEMENT [1]

I. THE ROMANTIC "TRIUMPH" [2]

Until the history of the Romantic movement came to be systematically studied, it was the custom of historians of Spanish literature to follow the example of Ochoa and describe it as having achieved a "triumph." "Romanticism", says one, " which had triumphed in France with the staging of *Hernani* (1830), was destined to triumph in Spain some five years later." [3] " Some years had still to pass," writes another, " before the new movement was assured of its definite and indisputable triumph." [4] And these two twentieth-century historians are merely echoing Valera, who was a friend of the Duque de Rivas, and wrote at a time when some of the later Romantics were still living. " On the appearance of romanticism," says Valera, " it strove with the school called Classical and in the end overcame it . . . The end of the war was the triumph of romanticism." [5]

That the Romantic movement, far from being a "triumph" in Spain, was to all appearances a failure is a proposition which needs some explanation. It is not that it left no traces —on the contrary, as later chapters will show, its influence was felt throughout the nineteenth century. Romanticism is too deeply engrained in the Spanish temperament for any Romantic movement, however slight, to disappear entirely. What happened was that the Movement, as such, collapsed,

[1] *H.R.M.S.*, II, 1-57.   [2] *H.R.M.S.*, II, 1-2.

[3] J. Fitzmaurice-Kelly : *A New History of Spanish Literature*, Oxford, 1926, p. 438.

[4] M. de Montoliu : *Manual d'història crítica de la literatura catalana moderna*, Barcelona, 1922, p. 66.

[5] J. Valera : *Florilegio de poesias castellanas del siglo xix*, Madrid, 1902-3, I, 46, 48.

before an ideal to be described in the next chapter ; that it
never had any unity or any cohesion at all ; and that, as a
constructive and militant force, a " school " or a self-
conscious entity, it never existed. The freedom it brought
was accepted ; the patriotic impetus partly responsible for
its introduction continued. But the Movement itself was so
devoid of solidarity that men who in 1835 identified themselves with the Romantics are to be found, five or ten years
later, pathetically pointing out the virtues of the other side.
The individualistic tendency of the Spanish genius, which
always militates against co-operative enterprise, has seldom
been more strikingly illustrated than in this movement, so
long and so confidently awaited, which, when at last it
declared itself, so quickly lost its hold.

II. FAILURE IN MADRID [1]

Since none of the historians who label the Romantic
movement a triumph offers evidence in support of this
generalization, let us examine the history of the Movement
after 1837 and see if any can be discovered.

(i) *Disappearance of the Coteries*

First, it will be noticed that after 1835 there were no more
coteries like those of Cortina and Olózaga—above all, no
Parnasillo. Had the exiles returned to Spain imbued with a
desire to disseminate the principles of romanticism there,
one would have expected a foregathering of leaders, a
publication of manifestos, a plan of attack to be directed
against those who still championed the opposing cause.
None of these things happened. There were various clubs,
casinos and circles, whose interests were chiefly political.
There were Ateneos and Liceos which were founded, or re-
founded, after 1833, both in Madrid and in the provinces ;
these were centres for the exchange of any kind of idea, and,
in so far as their interests were literary, were often less

[1] *H.R.M.S.*, II, 3-16.

Romantic in fact even than in conception. Nor was there apparently any great demand for Romantic *cénacles*. Larra, Espronceda and Zorrilla were Romantics both by temperament and by achievement, but neither they nor, after 1834, the Duque de Rivas, showed any desire to lead others into the same path as they had followed themselves. Apparently the mission of the Romantic poet, on which they lavished so much sentiment, did not extend to the making of conversions.

(ii) *Failure of the principal Romantic reviews*

It may be replied that the true coteries and *cénacles* of Spanish romanticism were the literary reviews, which formed the natural means for the dissemination of modern ideas. There is no single year, however, in which even a bare majority of the contributions to those reviews were of a Romantic character. The number of anti-Romantic contributions was frequently greater and that of neutral contributions was always greater. Nowhere, in fact, does the weakness of the Movement stand out more clearly than here.

Let us consider, furthermore, the history of those reviews which were founded to give expression to Romantic ideals or which at some stage associated themselves with romanticism. The *Artista*, established in 1835 with such high hopes and so distinguished a list of contributors, came to an end in the following year after a life of only fifteen months, for want of subscribers. Those " quince meses de azarosa existencia," to quote its gloomy *despedida*, show clearly that romanticism in Spain could count on little support.

Other Romantically inclined periodicals shared the *Artista's* fate. The *Revista española*, with its Liberal principles, had the good fortune to survive through the period of Romantic expectation, but the same year of 1836 was fatal to it. The *Siglo* lasted only for six weeks. *No me olvides* and *El Siglo XIX* lived for a few months. No successor appeared that could maintain a whole-heartedly Romantic policy and yet attract sufficient subscribers to pay its expenses. A few periodicals,

like *El Entreacto* (1839-40) and *El Iris* (1841), accepted contributions from Romantics, among others, but aimed
principally at being as informative and comprehensive as
possible. One pathetic attempt—the last—to provide an
all-Romantic review was made by the founders of *El
Pensamiento* (1841). The regular contributors to this were,
almost without exception, Romantics—Espronceda, Enrique
Gil y Carrasco, Miguel de los Santos Álvarez, García
Tassara, Ros de Olano. Its tone, though never extravagant,
is definitely Romantic, as anti-Eclectic as anti-Classic. Yet
El Pensamiento, born early in May 1841, was dead in
October.

(iii)   *Decline of Romantic drama*

Turning to literary productions less ephemeral than
contributions to reviews, we observe a general falling-off,
after 1837, in both the popularity and the quality of Romantic
drama. We may or may not accept Hartzenbusch's statement that Romantic drama was still dominating the stage in
July 1837,[1] but it certainly cannot be maintained that there
was any such domination twelve or eighteen months later.
It will shortly be seen that, on the one hand, the vogue of
foreign Romantic drama declined rapidly, while on the other,
with the exception of Zorrilla, no author at home produced
Romantic plays of the merit of *Don Álvaro* and *El Trovador*,
and comparatively few produced Romantic plays at all.

The two chief branches of non-dramatic poetry, as we
have seen, developed quite diversely. In narrative poetry,
which matured early, the Romantic strain went deeper than
in drama, and thus kept its popularity longer. Lyric poetry,
on the other hand, was slow, from the Romantic standpoint,
in reaching its full growth. Romanticism in the lyric was on
the up-grade until 1840, in which year every collection of
verse that appeared was wholly or largely Romantic. Yet
almost immediately afterwards it began to decline, until
Ramón de Campoamor, an author who had started life as a

[1] In the preface to Molíns : *Obras poéticas*, Madrid, 1837, pp. xviii-xix.

Romantic, led the reaction, publishing his anti-Romantic *Doloras*, with marked success, in 1846.

Romantic fiction, which, until about 1837, can hardly be said to have had a separate existence from Sir Walter Scott, won recognition only through two or three novels, of which the latest and the best was Enrique Gil y Carrasco's *El Señor de Bembibre* (1844). But, though mediocre semi-Romantic novels were abundant at this time, realism had already begun to mingle with romanticism, attracting a considerable public with La Avellaneda's *Sab* (1841) and *Espatolino* (1843) and strengthening its appeal upon the appearance of Fernán Caballero. The novel is the last of the *genres* which anyone would cite who wished to contest the fact that the Romantic movement was a failure.

(iv)   *Growing number and success of satires on the Romantic Movement*

Another sign of the impotence of the Romantic movement is the growing success that was achieved by satires upon it. That a skit should have been popular is, of course, no proof that it hit its mark ; but, if we bear in mind the weakness and the insecurity of the position of the object satirized, the presumption of success becomes a very strong one. Even to-day one can smile at the shrewd hits of " Abenámar," whose photograph-like caricatures were all the more effective with the air so full of exaggeration.[1] Those who preferred more extravagance in their satires could read such fantastic skits as Eugenio de Tapia's " Las visiones de un patriota somnámbulo " and " Miserere del dramaturgo romántico"[2] or his novel, *Los Cortesanos y la Revolución* (Madrid, 1838), which poked fun at all kinds of Romantic excesses. Better known than either Tapia or " Abenámar " was Serafín Estébanez Calderón (" El Solitario "), an anti-Romantic who was skilful in his ridicule of the absurdities of the new movement if he could not, or did not, combat its theories.[3]

[1] *El Porvenir* : cf. *H.R.M.S.*, II, 7, n. 1.

[2] *Juguetes satíricos en prosa y verso*, Madrid, 1839, pp. 14-15 (quoted in *H.R.M.S.*, II, 7), 16-19 (reproduced *H.R.M.S.*, II, 406-7).

[3] Cf. A. Cánovas del Castillo : " *El Solitario* " *y su tiempo*, Madrid, 1883, I, 114-15.

There were also anonymous satires, such as " La Derrota de los Románticos " (1837)—a pamphlet written with tremendous zest, negligible as literature, but interesting for its conception of Romantic art, and for its concluding lines, which are no doubt meant to be topical and may be thought by some to approach actual fact. A great Classical-Romantic battle, held outside the palace of Apollo, ends in the rout of the Romantics :

> Los románticos, en cuanto sintieron dentro de sí la cuadrilla infernal, se dispersaron en el instante, retirándose cada uno a su hogar, pero sin dejar por eso de escribir. De aquí resultó que si hasta este día habían sido horrorosas sus composiciones, en lo sucesivo han sido más horrendas todavía.[1]

But the most deadly of all the satires on romanticism in Spain—the more so for being entirely good-tempered—was Ramón de Mesonero Romanos' famous " El Romanticismo y los Románticos," [2] which was read at the newly founded Madrid Liceo and bears the date September 1837. He himself considered that the chief merit was due to him, not so much for writing it as for having dared to make it public, " at a time when the new sect of Hugolaters dominated the whole line, from one end of the republic of letters to the other." Though, as we can now see, the position of the innovators had already begun slightly to weaken, this was barely perceptible at the time and the loss of ground was not yet important. So it was a bold stroke to deliver himself of this satire in the Madrid Liceo—" the centre of the new opinions," as he calls it, and the " lists in which their most ardent champions did battle," [3] though it was also a haunt of those who subjected the new opinions to gentle satire. But so evident to all was the good humour lying beneath the irony that no offence was taken, either by the Liceo itself or

---

[1] Cf. *H.R.M.S.*, II, 10.

[2] Published in the *Semanario pintoresco español*, September 17, 1837 (II, 281-5) and reprinted in *Escenas matritenses*, 2ª Serie, Madrid, 1862, pp. 115-33. Published separately in *El Romanticismo y los Románticos, y otras escenas matritenses*, Liverpool, 1933, pp. 11-31.

[3] *Memorias de un setentón*, Madrid, 1881, II, 153.

by the majority of those who heard the address or read it on its publication.

The narrative of the satire is concerned with its author's fictitious nephew, who has been converted to an extreme form of romanticism. He first attempts to make his personal appearance conform to his newly-embraced creed ; and his success in this respect is described with much wealth of detail. He then proceeds to " romanticize his ideas as he had romanticized his person," and decides to embrace the career, or rather the " mission,"[1] of poetry. Next he writes a drama, which, after some amusing parodies of Romantic epithets and other literary mannerisms, Mesonero describes as follows :

¡¡ ELLA . . . . !!! Y ¡¡ ÉL . . . . !!!

Drama Romántico Natural,

EMBLEMÁTICO-SUBLIME, ANÓNIMO, SINÓNIMO, TÉTRICO Y
ESPASMÓDICO ;

Original, en Diferentes Prosas y Versos
En seis Actos y Catorce Cuadros

Los títulos de las jornadas (porque cada una llevaba el suyo a manera de código) eran, si mal no me acuerdo, los siguientes : 1ª. Un crimen. 2ª. El veneno. 3ª. Ya es tarde. 4ª. El panteón. 5ª. ¡ Ella ! 6ª. ¡ Él ! y las decoraciones eran las seis obligadas en todos los dramas románticos, a saber : Salón de baile ; Bosque ; La capilla ; Un subterráneo ; La alcoba ; y El cementerio.

The characters include the Dux of Venice, the Tyrant of Syracuse and the Archduchess of Austria ; a spy, a favourite, an apothecary, a ghost, a Jew, four grave-diggers, a chorus of Carmelite Nuns and another of " PP. Agonizantes," " un hombre del pueblo " and " un pueblo de hombres." The epoch is the " fourth and fifth centuries." The " scene is Europe, and the duration of the play, a hundred years."

The remainder of the narrative describes the nephew's romantic love-affair, which comes to an equally romantic end. Eventually the uncle takes the situation in hand and

[1] Cf. p. 191, below.

sends the boy into the army ; in a year's time he returns, a complete cure.

Mesonero himself, in a note appended to the essay as published in its later form, gives an account of the reception of his satire which, if contemporary testimony can be trusted, errs on the side of modesty. A few people, he says, accused him of indulging personal enmities, but in general he was credited with " good intentions " and " uprightness of literary judgment."[1] He then, after forty years have passed, attempts an estimate of the satire's influence :

> Algo cree haber contribuído a fijar la opinión hacia un término justo entre ambas exageraciones clásica y romántica ; por lo menos coincidió su sátira con el apogeo de la última de éstas, y desde entonces fué retrocediendo sensiblemente hacia un punto racional y admisible para todos los hombres de conciencia y de estudio. Dió además la señal de otros ataques semejantes, en el teatro y en la prensa, que minando sucesivamente aquel ridículo de secta, acabó por hacerle desaparecer.[2]

(v) *Early descriptions of the Movement as a failure*

Very soon after the date at which the Romantic movement used to be spoken of by historians as having established itself, it was generally acknowledged to have failed, or, at all events, to have come to an end. As early as 1840, candid critics are asserting this quite freely ; ten years later it has become a commonplace. Even a fervid Romantic like Nicomedes Pastor Díaz could describe his typically Romantic poems as " hijos de esta triste edad," with its " estéril y anárquica literatura."[3]

> En esta época desventurada, las facultades poéticas se extinguen pronto, la imaginación se desencanta, el corazón se hiela, el gusto en vez de perfeccionarse se corrompe, las ilusiones se disipan y la región poética del mundo se eclipsa.[4]

[1] *Op. cit.*, II, 154.   [2] *Ibid.*
[3] *Poesías*, Madrid, 1840, p. 4.   [4] *Ibid.*

In 1841, another Romantic, Salvador Bermúdez de Castro,[1] reports that Romantic dramatists " are no longer, as they were, the idols of modern opinion. The reaction against them . . . is becoming stronger and stronger. . . . The days of battle have passed." [2] Romantic devices—" enamoured troubadours, tourneys . . . dark towers and dwarfs "—no longer hold the public, which is sated with adulteries and murders. The vogue of such themes (continues Bermúdez de Castro) was simply a protest against eighteenth-century dullness. The need for that protest is now over. Romanticism, like classicism, has spent itself, and " all sensible men " follow the middle path.

> Ya es ridículo distinguir en dos sectas a los clásicos y a los románticos : ha habido entre todos los hombres sensatos un concilio literario aconsejado por el buen sentido, en que se han transigido los opuestos intereses . . . . El tiempo y el juicio público han verificado paulatinamente esta fusión.[3]

In 1846, Manuel Cañete, then a young man just becoming known as an acute critic, wrote an article on " the present state of lyric poetry in Spain." His estimate of the condition of Spanish literature is not flattering to the Romantic revolt. The " few literary beliefs which still exist in our country," he says, are revolving in a " chaos," and literature, like politics, is a prey to " the most anarchical and contradictory ideas." Lyric poetry—" el inmenso fárrago de malos versos que se publican diariamente "—has been ruined by a false conception of art. Only Zorrilla enjoys real popularity— and (says Cañete) it is by no means certain whether that is good for literature or bad. Rivas, in his *Moro expósito*, had pointed the way to a finer ideal of poetry, but his "bellísimos Romances históricos " are too full of beauty to be enjoyed by a degenerate public.[4]

Both in Madrid and in the provinces, the Revolt collapsed more markedly than the Revival. The latter suffered less

---

[1] " Movimiento dramático." In *El Iris*, 1841, I, 77-82, 93-8, 109-14.

[2] *Op. cit.*, I, 111.   [3] *Op. cit.*, I, 112.

[4] " Estado actual de la poesía lírica en España." In *El Fénix*, June 28, 1846.

from the defection of its exponents or the attacks of its adversaries than from loss of cohesion and from disorganization consequent upon the invasion of foreign ultra-Romantic drama and prose fiction and the association of mediaeval and Golden Age themes with Romantic exaggerations. Accordingly, it not only avoided complete failure, but in an indirect fashion continued its good work, which indeed has never ceased down to this day.

The Revolt, on the other hand, having effected a few reforms and convinced men of letters of the need for them, and for others, died out almost entirely. The contemporary description of it as a *llamarada*—a flash in the pan[1]—was a most apt one. Once the brief glamour of a few eventful years was over, men saw that the exaggerations of French romanticism were quite out of place in Spanish literature, and that the Revolt, which at first had aimed at freeing literature from the servitude of France, had ended by threatening it with a new servitude as demoralizing as the last.

III   FAILURE IN THE PROVINCES[2]

We have already seen that the interest shown by the provinces in the Romantic movement was almost entirely limited to the Revival. The Revolt, though occasionally referred to in provincial periodicals, had no independent existence outside Madrid, except in Barcelona, where for some years there was a certain degree of conflict between those who conceived romanticism as being wholly, or largely, a revival of literature—mainly native literature— and those who gave that name only to that " ridícula fantasmagoría de espectros y cadalsos . . . violenta exaltación de todos los sentimientos . . . inmoral parodia del crimen y (de) la iniquidad "[3] with which, even as he defended the Movement, Salas y Quiroga disclaimed all connection.

---

[1] Cf. *H.R.M.S.*, II, 15, n. 2.   [3] *H.R.M.S.*, II, 16-27.
[2] *No me olvides*, May 7, 1837.

In one sense, therefore, it is true to say that, as there was hardly any " movement " in the provinces, the question of the success or failure of the Romantic movement there hardly arises. It is possible, however, to show that such activity as there was, and the interest taken in the activity of Madrid, had hardly reached their height when they began to decline. We shall therefore briefly review the situation in the four chief provincial centres—Barcelona, Valencia, Seville, Granada : Cádiz, the fifth centre previously surveyed, had long before 1837 lost most of the importance which its political prominence had given it earlier in the century.

(i)   *Barcelona*

In Barcelona, the position is complicated by the Catalan Renaissance, which from about 1840 became so increasingly important that at last only literature written in the Catalan language came to hold much interest for Catalonians. Since the Catalan Renaissance gradually absorbed the Romantic revival, it is impossible to make an accurate survey of the position of " Spanish " romanticism in Barcelona after its very earliest years. Here, alone in Spain, there continued to be coteries, leaders, meetings for action, concerted efforts— all, broadly speaking, connected with the furtherance of romanticism. But not of " Spanish " romanticism. As many of the writers of the day used Spanish as well as Catalan, it might be maintained that the Romantic revival enjoyed an unbroken popularity in Barcelona till, at least, the end of the heroic period of the Jocs Florals in 1877. But this is hardly a fair contention, since the motive force behind this form of the Revival was a desire for the restoration of the Catalan language.

The controversies alluded to in the last chapter soon subsided, partly, perhaps, through the influence of the literary historian Manuel Milá y Fontanals, who began to write in the *Vapor* in 1836 and rapidly gained a public for his articles written in defence of what he called romanticism, but of what was, in fact, only the Romantic revival, considered chiefly in its mediaeval aspect.[1] These articles show how little there was in common between the mediaevalism in favour of which, said Milá, " Europe has decided," and the revolutionary romanticism of an Espronceda. Soon after this, Mesonero Romanos' famous satire on romanticism and the Romantics was reprinted in the *Guardia nacional*,[2] which gave Milá an opportunity to make explicit the difference between the form of romanticism attacked in it and that in which he believed. To the latter he boldly maintained that there was now no alternative, except in comedy.[3]

Milá, whose influence grew rapidly, stood for a historical form of romanticism—the romanticism of the Revival, with only so much of the Revolt as was necessary to give the Revival confidence and power. The finest achievements of the Romantic movement, in Europe as a whole, were to him the historical novel and historical drama, though he strongly censured the revolutionary type of historical drama,

> el que . . . . se complace en acumular escenas escandalosas, diviniza las más viles pasiones, predica las funestas doctrinas del fatalismo, forma una ciencia y un código de la desesperación y se empeña en desterrar dos virtudes sin las cuales no puede existir felicidad entre los hombres : el arrepentimiento y la resignación.[4]

Others followed Milá's lead ; and when, in 1838, the *Vapor*, for some time the chief vehicle of advanced literary ideas, came to an end, most of the exaggerations of romanticism disappeared with it. Both in the thirties and in the forties there were smoulderings of revolutionary ardour, but the chief exponents of the Revolt in Catalonia—authors forgotten to-day—were not men of the calibre of Rivas, Espronceda and Zorrilla, or even of Ochoa, who had at

---

[1] *E.g.*, " Clásicos y románticos," August 7, 1836 (reprinted in *Obras completas*, Barcelona, 1888-96, IV, 1-5) ; " Primer período de la poesía dramática española," October 5, 1836 ; critiques of plays, October 24 and November 19, 1836.

[2] October 1-2, 1837.   Milá's reply is in the issue dated October 5.

[3] Quoted in *H.R.M.S.*, II, 18.

[4] M. Milá y Fontanals, *Compendio del arte poética*, Barcelona, 1844, p. 112.

least talent, energy and acquaintance with writers abler than himself. They were mainly journalists, having little contact with Madrid. Cabanyes, a better man than any of them, died young, as did Semís, Carbó and Piferrer, three Catalonians who might have formed a true " Catalan school " of romanticism. It seems more likely, nevertheless, that they would have swelled the ranks of the revivalists, among whom lies all the genius of the early nineteenth century in Catalonia.

What is true of individual writers applies also to the favourite *genre* of the revolutionaries—drama. With insignificant exceptions, no new ultra-Romantic play had any vogue in Barcelona after 1837. Nor were the old favourites to any great extent remembered. We may appropriately sum up the situation in the words of a contemporary, Joaquín Rubió y Ors :

> Del romanticismo quedó, pasados algunos años, lo que . . . . en él estaba cimentado en las leyes del buen gusto y en los principios fundamentales e invariables de la ciencia de lo bello : lo que en él se introdujo de exagerado, de convencional . . . . , ya al pasar por Francia, ora al desbordarse entre nosotros al salvar los Pirineos . . . . continuó siendo . . . . comida predilecta de estómagos estragados, y objeto preferente de la admiración del vulgo.[1]

(ii) *Valencia*

In Valencia, the Spanish home of Chateaubriand, lachrymose romanticism and the *mal du siècle*, there was no more interest in revolutionary romanticism than in Barcelona. Both the earlier and the later periodicals dissociate themselves from the Revolt : their romanticism is that of Arolas. If we could define romanticism as a combination of patriotism, melancholy, religiosity and picturesqueness, a case might even be made out for the existence in Valencia of a Romantic " school." But investigation shows that this combination alone appealed to the Valencians. True, the energetic little group of publishers referred to above had

---

[1] J. Rubió y Ors : *Noticia de la vida . . . de . . . Roca y Cornet*, Barcelona, 1876, p. 32.

9

contrived to foster a taste for such fiction as that of Mrs. Radcliffe and Eugène Sue, but this was short-lived. It is on the stage that the Valencians' indifference to advanced Romantic art is most clearly manifested. Hugo practically disappears after 1838 and Dumas maintains his vogue very little longer. Native Romantic plays achieve only occasional performances. Moratín and Bretón are much preferred to them, as they have been all the time.

(iii) *Seville*

In Seville, one of the principal foci of literary interest during the latter part of the eighteenth century, literature had fallen upon evil days and revived only about the year 1860. The Sevilian Academy was suspended early in the reign of Ferdinand VII ; its archives were destroyed during the French invasion ; and, though an attempt was made to revive it in 1820, it lapsed again soon afterwards and no more is heard of it until the late thirties. Its first volume of *Memorias literarias* appeared in 1773 ; its second, exactly seventy years later.

Nor is there much evidence of sympathy with the Romantic movement even then. The 1843 volume contains a violent attack upon it[1] and a "historical eulogy" of the neo-Classic Montiano. The poems which it prints, though occasionally built around Romantic themes and showing some influence of the Revival, are in the main solid edifices of good Classical architecture. If romanticism was to reach Seville, it was unlikely to come through Academic channels.

As no other channel existed, Romantic ideals filtered through gradually, rather than entered boldly ; and they were prevalent chiefly in the small literary circle of which the patron was the Duque de Rivas. The interests of this group centred in the works of its own members. The slight and ephemeral periodicals which they published down to about 1845 occasionally defended romanticism, but little interest appears to have been taken at Seville in Madrid Romantic drama, and in one of these reviews (1841) Escosura asks if

[1] Cf. *H.R.M.S.*, I, 328-9, II, 25.

there is any real dramatic literature at all in Spain and answers his question in terms of Bretón de los Herreros.[1]

(iv) *Granada*

Provincial indifference to the Romantic movement is more marked in Granada even than in Seville. In the *Alhambra*, a literary review published there from 1839 to 1841, there are clear signs of this. Manuel Cañete, for example, then a very young man, writes on " Our Dramatic Literature."[2] There was a time, he says, when Spain was famous for her drama and Lope de Vega was known throughout Europe. Now our stage is " inundated with imitations" ; our national drama is nothing but a copy of that of France. Nicolás de Roda, writing, about the same time, on the " influence of the theatre on manners and of manners on the theatre,"[3] has no better idea of Spanish drama. After praising in turn the national dramas of England and France, and comparing them both with that of Germany, he proceeds to examine the drama of Spain, which, though by nature " energetic, natural and often original," is, at the time at which he writes, merely exaggerated and servile. More extraordinary still is an earlier review in the *Alhambra*,[4] the writer of which roundly declares :

> El movimiento literario de Europa apenas tiene representación en nuestra patria.

Where, we may permit ourselves to enquire, is the Romantic " triumph " ?

IV REASONS FOR ITS FAILURE[5]

The reasons for the failure of the Romantic movement to establish itself in Spain have very little to do with the strength or weakness of the Romantic traits in Spanish literature,

---

[1] " Observaciones sobre la literatura dramática en España." *Revista andaluza*, 1841, I, 453-61.

[2] *La Alhambra*, 1840, III, 40-1.

[3] *Op. cit.*, 1839, II, 191-2.

[4] *Op. cit.*, 1840, III, 125-7.

H.R.M.S., II, 27-57.

still less with the Spanish character. The Romantic revival, which had been going on for nearly a century, was fully strong enough during the period 1834-7 to carry the whole country. And, we may ask, if the Romantic revolt in France, with its appeal to the Middle Ages in Spain, to Spain's Golden Age and in particular to Spain's Lope de Vega, could achieve success, how could a movement with similar inspiration fail to do so in Spain itself?

Two causes jointly account for this failure. First, no general agreement was ever reached in Spain as to what romanticism was; its full possibilities, except perhaps by an insignificant minority, were never realized. Secondly, this movement, which lacked the solidarity generally resulting from a clearly envisaged ideal and a definite programme, lacked also any form of leadership.

(i) *Currency of differing conceptions of the nature of romanticism*

That the opponents of romanticism should misrepresent its doctrines is not surprising : so much is common to all controversy. They attacked the most vulnerable points in the Romantics' writings mercilessly—*viz.*, (1) their impatience with restrictions like those of the Unities, which it was easy to interpret as rebellion against every kind of rule and an ideal of complete lawlessness; and (2) the exaggerations of modern Romantics, especially those of England and France. It is surprising to find how ceaselessly the anti-Romantics harped on these themes, as though they scarcely realized that there was anything in romanticism beyond them.

These, for example, are the themes which continually recur in an early series of attacks (1814, 1817-20) made by Böhl von Faber's adversary, Mora. Romanticism, to Mora, is " detestable " ; it " discredits the eternal rules of taste and shakes off the yoke of the precepts." [1] Its innovations are " Ossianic vaporosities " [2] or " vaporous irregularities " [3] ;

---

[1] *Mercurio gaditano*, Cádiz, No. 127, September 22, 1814.

[2] *Crónica científica y literaria de Madrid*, 1817, No. 11.

[3] *Op. cit.*, 1818, No. 126.

its works are nothing but " irruptions of our modern van-
dals,"[1] who sup full of horrors, their heroes being "assassins,
bandits, witches, magicians, corsairs, devils and even
vampires."[2] As Mora is writing solely of foreign romanticism—in particular, it seems, of Byron—his violence is
perhaps understandable. It is harder to excuse the critic
who in 1828 describes Durán's idea of romanticism, ex-
pounded in the *Discurso*, as " nothing but an admixture of
tragedy and comedy, subjected to no other rules than those
indicated by the author's wish or fancy."[3]

During the years of the Classical-Romantic conflict,
definitions of this type abound, which reduce themselves to
the single idea of lawlessness :

> . . . . romanticism, that is to say rebellion against all
> principles and laws which experience and the study of
> antiquity have dictated in matters of literary composition.
> (1834)[4]
>
> . . . . an innovation dating from the end of the eighteenth
> century and contemporary with the development of the
> germ of the great revolution which changed the face of the
> universe. (1834)[5]
>
> . . . . romanticism, or the rule of the absence of rules.
> (1835)[6]
>
> The Romantics, without defining their doctrines, " attempt
> to found a new school based upon the breaking of all the
> rules, and admitting neither principles nor models." (1836)[7]

" Down with tyrannical laws ! " the Romantics are
represented as saying. " Let there be freedom in the realm
of poetry ! Let every poet write henceforth without any kind
of impediment or restriction ! Let it be understood that he
who writes the most will be the most learned ! . . . Henceforth to be poets we need only pen, ink and paper."[8]

---

[1] *Op. cit.*, 1820, No. 306.   [2] *Op. cit.*, 1819, No. 275.

[3] *Correo literario y mercantil*, 1828, p. 72.

[4] *La Estrella*, 1834, Vol. II, No. 52. The reference is primarily to France.

[5] *Boletín de Comercio*, No. 27, May 27, 1834.

[6] *Revista española*, April 12, 1835.

[7] *Diario de Barcelona*, December 9, 1836.

[8] *La Derrota de los Románticos* (cf. p. 112, above).

Few of the anti-Romantics' variants of this definition show
any greater comprehension of their opponents' ideals. Sometimes they are flippant, describing the *Hernani*-worshipper
who models his costume on his hero's and travels to Italy to
indulge his passion for melancholy.[1] More commonly they
ridicule the exaggerations in the Romantics' writings. A
" never-ending tissue of horrible events piled one upon
another in the greatest possible confusion" is given the name
of the Romantic novel.[2] Romantic drama "presents vice and
crime, the consequences of violent and undisciplined
passions, and presents them as they are in all their hideous-
ness and horror."[3] In much the same strain Tapia, in a
witty verse epistle of two hundred lines, each ending—a
common Romantic habit—in an *esdrújulo*, describes the
alacrity with which he goes to the theatre,

> en especial si el drama es de los hórridos
> que docta multitud llama románticos,
> compuesto por autor, cual Dumas célebre,
> a quien sueles llamar galo-vandálico,

and relates the detail of a typical performance :

> Hubo decoraciones muy exóticas,
> noche de tempestad, truenos, relámpagos,
> convento, panteón, ruinas y cárceles,
> guerreros, brujas, capuchinos, cuákeros.[4]

Mora never succeeded in understanding what romanticism
meant. As late as 1847 he sees it as a combination of rebel-
liousness and a love of the horrible. Romantic doctrines,
he tells us, are those to which

> toda regla es traba ignominiosa,
> que la pedantería al genio impuso.

And again :

> El romancesco es por esencia triste ;
> el horror es el mote de su secta ;
> horror es a sus ojos cuanto existe.[5]

---

[1] *Correo de las damas*, April 10, 1834.

[2] *Op. cit.*, March 20, 1834.

[3] *Revista española*, July 20, 1835.

[4] " El Teatro." B.A.E., LXVII, 680-2.

[5] " Mis opiniones." In *Revista de España y del extranjero*, 1847. Cit.
M.L.R., 1923, XVIII, 46.

Lista, making a real effort, as it would seem, to understand and define romanticism, thought of it as completely negative and as none of the things it pretended to be : " anti-monarchical, anti-religious and anti-moral "—just " literary freedom."[1]

The foregoing conceptions of romanticism emanate from writers who are either wholly or in large measure its opponents. The presentation of it by the neutrals is equally incomplete. Martínez de la Rosa, to whom any extreme party seemed " intolerant and unreasonable,"[2] and who was " disinclined to enlist under the banner either of the Classics or of the Romantics,"[3] had had ample opportunity, before 1833, to inform himself on the tenets of the Romantics, and sufficient had been written in Spain to leave no doubt as to the breadth of their ideals. Yet he can see little difference between the two parties except as regards freedom from, or submission to, rules.[4] Gil y Zárate, who, like Martínez de la Rosa, wrote both Classical and Romantic plays, thinks of Classical literature as that of the ancients and of Romantic literature as that of the moderns.[5] And Mesonero Romanos, in 1837, observed that this word " romanticism," which was on everybody's lips, meant something different to each :

> ¡ Cuántos discursos, cuántas controversias han prodigado los sabios para resolver acertadamente esta cuestión ! y en ellos ¡ qué contradicción de opiniones ! ¡ qué extravagancia singular de sistemas . . . ! ¿ Qué cosa es romanticismo . . . ? les ha preguntado el público ; y los sabios le han contestado cada cual a su manera. Unos le han dicho que era todo lo ideal y romanesco ; otros, por el contrario, que no podía ser sino lo escrupulosamente histórico ; cuales han creído ver en él la naturaleza en toda su verdad ; cuales la imaginación en toda su mentira ; algunos han asegurado que solo era propio a describir la edad media ; otros le han hallado aplicable también a la moderna ; aquéllos le han querido hermanar con la religión y con la moral ; éstos le

[1] *Ensayos literarios y críticos*, Seville, 1844, II, 39.

[2] *Poesías*, Madrid, 1833, Advertencia, p. ii.

[3] *Ibid.*

[4] *Op. cit.*, pp. iii-iv.

[5] *Manual de Literatura*, Madrid, 1844, p. 138.

han echado a reñir con ambas ; hay quien pretende dictarle reglas ; hay, por último, quien sostiene que su condición es la de no guardar ninguna.

A few months previously, the same sentiments had been more tersely summarized by a Barcelona newspaper in the following definition :

Romántico—otra de las palabras más gastadas y menos comprendidas por los que más la gastan.[1]

But the key to the failure of the Romantic movement is to be found not in the misrepresentation of it by opponents or by neutrals, but in the confused ideas of its nature and aims which were held by the Romantics themselves. Only a survey of their writings can give any adequate idea of how much they differed. This survey may well start in 1823, with the *Europeo*.

Monteggia develops a threefold ideal of romanticism, constructive in type, relating to style, argument and execution, and embodying the positive elements of sensibility, melancholy, mediaevalism, freedom in choice of subject, freedom in execution, subordination of form to inspiration, and the maintenance, in every work of art, of a " unity of interest."[2] This is an unusually comprehensive conception of romanticism, and it should be observed that it emanates from a foreigner.

López Soler, also writing in the *Europeo*, stresses the importance of originality, but concentrates on mediaevalism and Christianity. To him the " origin of romanticism," on the poetical side, is to be found in " the splendid ostentation of the Crusades, the knightly virtues and code of honour," and, on the " sublime and metaphysical side," in a " color lúgubre y sentimental " which derives from religion and imparts to Romantic compositions a high degree of interest. The other " sources " of romanticism are the dress which Nature wears in the countries that have given it birth, and feudal life, the customs of which (says López Soler) are much more " poetic " than those of antiquity.[3]

---

[1] *El Vapor*, March 21, 1837.

[2] *El Europeo*, October 25, 1823.

[3] *Op. cit.*, November 22, 29, 1823.

Durán is another mediaevalist who lays the greatest stress on the place of Christianity in literature. In several ways he recalls Monteggia and López Soler, but his ideas add something to theirs, and to the widening concept of romanticism he adds the ideals of Golden Age drama. His views on the nature of romanticism are more complex than those held by most of his contemporaries. He distinguishes two types of literature : " the Classical, which proceeds from the political and religious life of ancient peoples, and the Romantic, whose creations belong to modern life, emanating from the spirituality of Christendom, the heroic customs of the Middle Ages and a different way of considering humanity." [1] Christianity, to Durán, is the principal element separating Romantic literature from Classical, and throughout his pamphlet he gives a religious bias to the matter under discussion.

Closely connected with this is another distinction. The Classical writer " considers only the external actions of man, and his virtues and vices in the abstract," [2] the result being that the protagonist of Classical drama " is wholly lacking in that individuality which characterizes him and distinguishes him essentially from other men dominated by (the same) passion." [3] The Romantic describes the " interior man," the individual, delving into " the recesses and most secret places of his conscience and seeking there the merit and motive of his actions." A corollary of this is that the Classicist writes with a " definite and fixed moral purpose," which, with the Romantic, is subordinated to the presentation of individual characters. [4]

Different, too, are the Classical and the Romantic writer in their treatment of a theme. Inspiration, to the Romantic, is supreme. It is no arbitrary or petulant desire for freedom that makes it impossible for the Romantic dramatist to submit to the three Unities, but the very nature of his art. He must also be free to use such language as suits his plot and characters, amalgamating on occasion such diverse styles as

[1] " Discurso, etc.", *M.A.E.*, II, 307.   [3] *Ibid.*
[2] *Op. cit.*, *M.A.E.*, II, 313.   [4] *Ibid.*

the "tragic, lyric, bucolic, satiric and comic."[1] In short, he must use as many forms of expression as he finds in life itself.

Elsewhere in his *Discurso*, Durán likens romanticism to the return to Nature. Classical dramas he describes as " gardens adorned with care," " inspiring ideas of order, symmetry and taste " ; Romantic literature, to a " rude and magnificent " landscape, to " uncultivated nature seen from the lofty peaks of the Apennines," " enrapturing the soul " and inspiring unanalysable emotions.[2] The purpose of these comparisons is to reinforce the argument that there is good both in classicism and in romanticism, but the use of the metaphors, which amount to an implicit definition of romanticism, is important to our subject as a whole.

This composite ideal resembles that of Milá y Fontanals, from whose somewhat florid description of romanticism (1836)[3] can be distilled a number of its component elements —mediaevalism, regionalism, popular literature ; the Orient, the North, the Gothic ; Christianity, mystery, melancholy ; picturesqueness, imagination, colour. In the following year Milá specifically examines the various current conceptions of romanticism and decides that their number and diversity are of little moment.[4]

Here, however, we are anticipating by a year or two, for, on the approach of the brief period of the Romantic battle, the conceptions of romanticism held by most of its defenders had begun to simplify. Though the ideals of the Romantics at this time were seldom as negative and destructive as their opponents pretended, they had lost the breadth which one finds in Monteggia and Durán and many of them could identify the Movement with only one idea—freedom. The most distinguished of these was Larra, to whom, in 1835, Romantic drama meant " naturalness on the stage, light, truth, liberty in literature, recognition of the right of man, law without law (*la ley sin ley*)."[5] The conceptions of Milá and Larra meet

---

[1] *Op. cit., M.A.E.*, II, 315-16.

[2] *Op. cit., M.A.E.*, II, 293-4.

[3] Cf. p. 118, above.

[4] *Guardia nacional*, October 5, 1837. Cf. p. 118, above.

[5] " Una primera representación." *Revista española*, April 3, 1835.

in Alcalá Galiano's preface to Saavedra's *Moro expósito*, where romanticism in drama means disregard of the Unities, the mingling of tragedy and comedy, mediaevalism, Christianity and a certain " modern " and chivalric colour. To Ochoa, on the other hand, Spanish romanticism was a " literary revolution," a deposition of French dramatists who " formerly reigned despotically on our stage."[1]

Many more examples, of which these are representative, might be given of the differing conceptions of romanticism held by its exponents.[2] It can hardly be wondered at if there was confused and loose thinking about it when not only adversaries and neutrals, but its very protagonists, differed in their interpretation of its principles. The contemporary critic could never have been sure if his friendly or even flattering articles would be approved by more than a small proportion of the men whose work they praised ; and this not merely in the formative years of the Movement but in the period of its " triumph." If romanticism were established in Spain, one would naturally expect to meet no more confusion or vagueness as to its aims. Opposition to it there might still be, but both the conflicting parties would presumably know what they were fighting about.

On the contrary, there is ample evidence to the confusion on the subject which existed both in the popular and in the critical mind. In 1833, just as the Romantic battle in Spain was about to begin, a critic complained that romanticism had not yet defined itself :

> Todavía no nos han dado los románticos idea exacta de lo que ellos llaman su escuela. Apoderados de un sobrenombre . . . . , han comprendido bajo su acepción no sólo lo perteneciente a los antiguos romances caballerescos, sino también todo aquello en que las pasiones y el sentimiento se esfuerzan de una manera patética y exagerada, único blanco de su incierta doctrina. Ésta no se halla a nuestro alcance ; ellos ni la entienden, ni se entienden a sí mismos.[3]

---

[1] *El Artista*, 1836, III, 1.

[2] A further selection, taking the survey down to 1854, will be found in *H.R.M.S.*, II, 41-6.

[3] José de la Revilla : " Disertación, etc." In *Memorias literarias de la Real Academia Sevillana de Buenas Letras*, Seville, 1843, II, 3. The " Disertación " is dated December 1833.

The last statement is downright enough, but in 1833, after all, the Movement had hardly declared itself. It was no longer in its infancy, however, in 1837. With one exception (*Don Juan Tenorio*) the whole of the plays chiefly associated with it had appeared. Its champions were nearly all in full vigour, and its position was as well established as it was ever to be in the future. One would assume that the Movement was now understood and defined to everyone's satisfaction. Yet it was in this year that, in words already quoted,[1] Mesonero Romanos testified to the disunion prevalent among the Romantics and the vagueness of their ideal.

> ¿ Qué cosa es romanticismo . . . . ? les ha preguntado el público ; y los sabios le han contestado cada cual a su manera. . . .

In the next year (1838) we find uncertainty in the mind of so acute and experienced a critic as Alcalá Galiano. This is a surprising discovery, for Alcalá Galiano was a convert from classicism and a close friend of more than one of the leading Romantics. He had fled from the name of romanticism in 1834, and now he shows signs of fleeing from the reality. He not only comments on the confused state of opinion with regard to Romantic drama, but confesses himself unable to see any difference between it and Classical drama, except in such matters of form as the observance of the Unities.[2] In 1839, the historian Pedro José Pidal wrote of romanticism : " Ni sus preceptos ni sus modelos están aún bien determinados,"[3] and a Sevilian review underscored this same vagueness :

> . . . . la palabra *romanticismo* . . . . palabra vaga y dudosa por su extensión, oscura por su significado, e incierta por sus diversas aplicaciones . . . . Defínala el que la comprenda con distinción, si es que puede comprenderse hasta no ver más fijo su significado.[4]

[1] P. 125, above.

[2] *Revista de Madrid*, 1838, I, 51.

[3] *Estudios literarios*, Madrid, 1890, II, 208.

[4] Diego Herrero in *Nuevo Paraíso*, Seville, 1839. Cit. E. Allison Peers : *El Romanticismo en España*, Santander, 1924, pp. 63-4.

Finally, in 1847, Hartzenbusch, who ten years previously had been in the front rank of the Romantics, discussed contemporary literature in a lecture given to the Madrid Ateneo, without saying a word on romanticism. What he emphasizes is the very unsettled condition of literature and the inability of his contemporaries to say what it betokens. Their opinions fall into two classes :

> Por la una se establece que la literatura contemporánea carece de carácter propio o tiene por distintivo la confusión y la anarquía ; por la otra, se le atribuye un carácter formado ya, o por lo menos en camino para formarse.[1]

An astonishing description, this, by a Romantic, of the effects of a movement so recently at its height. Is not the satirical definition of the European movement given by Pérez de Camino as early as 1829 essentially true of the Spanish movement throughout its course :

> La secta literaria llamada romántica . . . . que se distingue sobre todo por la incoherencia de las ideas y por la falta de plan . . . .?[2]

(ii) *Lack of a leader*

The second reason for the failure of the Romantic movement seems to have been its lack of a leader. Given the right man for that *rôle* at the right moment, it might have developed as much individuality in Spain as it did in France. A distinctively Spanish form of romanticism might have carried the whole of young Spain had it been propounded by someone outstanding both as critic and as creative artist. In the months immediately following the publication of Mesonero Romanos' satire, when the successes of Romantic drama were fresh in men's minds, and yet when it must have been plain that the country would never accept a romanticism either destructively revolutionary or satanically melodramatic, such a leader might have turned the whole course of Spanish literary history.

But the men who troubled least about theories of literary

---

[1] *Siglo pintoresco*, Madrid, 1847, III, 149-52.

[2] *Poética y sátiras*, Bordeaux, 1829, quoted from the edition of Santander, 1876, p. 264.

art were the literary artists and hardly one of the chief Spanish writers of the early nineteenth century could muster even as much interest in the subject as did Lope de Vega. The constructive critics and the theorists of the age were almost without exception men of low grade as regards creative literature : they were read with tolerance but they had no great following and their work was soon forgotten.

The man who might most easily have become the leader of the Spanish Romantics was the Duque de Rivas, and there were three points in his life when it must have seemed that he would. The first was upon the publication of the *Moro expósito* in 1834—a poem of monumental size, hailed as " unprecedented " in Spanish literature.[1] The second was in 1835, at the time of the *estreno* of the " románticamente romántico " *Don Álvaro*. The third was in 1841, after the publication of the *Romances históricos*, a work which, as many realized, was much more in harmony with the Spanish temperament than *Don Álvaro*. Enrique Gil's enthusiastic review of the *Romances* shows how Rivas was regarded by those who hoped for most from him. " Hace tiempo," wrote Gil, " que su huella ha quedado profundamente grabada en el campo de nuestra regeneración poética, *cuyo primer adalid es*."[2]

But the genial Duke did not take the hint. After succeeding to his title, he re-entered politics, and, while continuing to write, alternated reactionary work so exasperatingly with progressive that to literature the last twenty years of his life are almost negligible. The fact is that he never again took himself seriously as a writer. His later dramas, with the single exception of *El Desengaño en un sueño*, go back completely on the Romantic movement. His pronouncements on romanticism were few and disappointing. His one late excursion into narrative poetry—the *Leyendas* (1854)— represents an interesting, but quite isolated, example of what he might have excelled in. From every point of view Rivas is a lost leader.

[1] Cf. p. 45, above.

[2] E. Gil y Carrasco : *Obras en prosa, etc.*, Madrid, 1883, II, 146-7. The italics in the quotation are mine.

Who else might have led a national Romantic movement? Let us consider the possibilities.

Larra, perhaps, might have done so had he lived ; but his true genius lay, not in construction, but in criticism, and half a dozen of his best critical essays are worth his one novel and all his dramas, both original and translated. Nor had he any great interest in literary theory. If he can be called a Romantic,[1] it is not because he formulated, or subscribed to, Romantic tenets, but because he looked forward to the new movement, appreciated and shared many of its ideals and welcomed it as something that would rekindle literature.

García Gutiér.ez brought to the beginning of his Romantic career very little of such pseudo-Classical baggage as might compromise a reformer. But very soon after the production of *El Trovador* it became clear that he had few literary ideals and was temperamentally unfit to be a leader.

Espronceda, from first to last, was a thorough-going individualist. Brought up under the influence of Lista, it was natural that, when he reacted against it, he should do so strongly. But, though he lived in the Paris of 1830, and, on returning to Spain, met in the Parnasillo nearly all the great Romantics of the decade to come, he had no idea of a constructive school or of Romantic solidarity. Mesonero Romanos once described him as "lanzando epigramas contra todo lo existente, lo pasado y lo futuro."[2] The picture is significant. He could launch epigrams, but he could not lay down principles ; he could satirize but not organize ; he could have declaimed against a school, but he could not have founded one.

Zorrilla, born in 1817, grew up with the Romantic movement and inherited from Rivas and his contemporaries a carefully prepared public. Coming to manhood just as the movement of 1833-7 was hovering between success and failure, he might well have stabilized it and given it self-consciousness, though never the good sense which, among other qualities, was essential to it, if it was to establish itself

[1] Cf. p. 146, below.
[2] *Memorias de un setentón*, Madrid, 1881, II, 59.

as the national type of drama. A Romantic by temperament, as well as by the accident of the age in which he lived, he never became a Romantic by conviction. Indeed, though he described the Movement as "spontaneous" and "necessary,"[1] and though it gave him the freedom to write as his fancy dictated and to follow his own inspiration, he bestowed on it all kinds of uncomplimentary epithets. It was that " descabellada escuela de los espectros y asesinatos históricos, bautizados con el nombre de dramas románticos,"[2] that " infierno insondable y nuevamente abierto."[3] Zorrilla was certainly no Romantic leader.

The remaining men who might have filled the rôle lacked genius for it rather than inclination. Ochoa, a dilettante and a critic, certainly no creative genius, strove valiantly for a few years on the Romantic side, though later his profession of romanticism became lukewarm. Salas y Quiroga, whose preface to his *Poesías* of 1834 was perhaps the boldest and clearest of all Romantic manifestos, and made a definite appeal for literary cohesion and progress, was not of a type to inspire for long, and soon he, too, was dabbling in other fields. So with all the rest. The opportunity was a great one. Had the right man come forward at the right moment, the Romantic movement might have developed as much individuality in Spain as it did in France. But the moment passed, the man failed to appear and the Romantic movement disintegrated into a phase and a tendency.

(iii) *Other alleged reasons for the failure of the Movement*

The foregoing seem to be the chief reasons for the failure of romanticism to persist for many years even as a loosely defined movement, and still more to form itself into a school. Other reasons which have been alleged are more debatable. It has been said that it wore itself out by its own

[1] José Zorrilla : *Recuerdos del tiempo viejo*, Barcelona-Madrid, 1880-2, II, 33.
[2] *Op. cit.*, I, 59.
[3] *Op. cit.*, I, 48.

violence—but the French movement, which was far more violent, lasted much longer. It has been alleged that it failed because it was bankrupt of ideas—but romanticism lives, not by ideas, but by feeling and inspiration. A more plausible view is that the Romantic movement ended with the first half of the century, being unable to stand against the invasion of realism because it had itself never kept any contact with real life. Actually, however, the Romantic movement had lost its force long before the mid-century, while even the first tricklings of realism had hardly begun. Further, there is every reason to suppose that, had a Spanish Victor Hugo arisen, Spanish literature would have followed him gladly, for decades, into an existence completely removed from real life, rejoicing in its chimeras, dreams and visions. The reaction, in such a case, would have been a marked one, but it would have been a reaction from something more definite than the Spanish Romantic movement in fact ever possessed. As it was, the very vagueness of the Movement inhibited reaction ; it may even be that its very failure was responsible for its ultimate success.

Chapter V

THE RISE AND TRIUMPH OF ECLECTICISM[1]

I. The Position of Classicism after 1837[2]

So the Romantic " movement " or " school " in Spain
came to an end—the " movement " that had no programme
and no single ideal, the " school " that had no meeting-
place, no pupils and no master. That romanticism itself did
not come to an end, but continued, and has continued to the
present day, we shall show in our final chapter. For the
present, we are concerned with the fact that, a few years
after the alleged " triumph " of Romantic drama, the self-
conscious Romantic movement which had announced itself
with such *éclat* was widely discredited in Spain and literature
was in a hopeless state of conflicting tendencies and a confusion that has never since been wholly resolved.

Into the midst of this confusion there entered, about
1837, a strong if also somewhat formless movement which
found more general acceptance than either classicism or
romanticism, and achieved a genuine triumph which was
denied to both. It was strong in that, from the beginning,
it appealed to a large and growing number of Spaniards,
and was subscribed to, in theory or in practice, by nearly all
the leading authors in the country from 1840 onwards.
Though, like the Romantic movement, it had no single
leader, half-a-dozen prominent writers were recognized as
its foremost exponents. A programme it certainly had—a
sufficiently definite one to unite its adherents, yet a sufficiently elastic one to command a large following at a time of
widespread indecision. This new movement was a literary
eclecticism, which aimed at establishing a *justo medio* between

Classical and Romantic ideals, at adopting from each party what it judged to be the elements of the greatest stability and the most enduring value, and at recognizing no distinctions other than between art and non-art, genius and absence of genius, good and bad.

But it must not be supposed that the Eclectic movement was merely a compromise. Its most significant features are the early date at which it began to manifest itself and the sureness and gradualness of its growth. We shall see that the rise of the Eclectic movement is almost contemporary with that of the Romantic movement ; that the slogan of *justo medio* was heard in Spain some years before that of "liberalism in literature " or any other trans-Pyrenean catchword ; and that many authors and documents popularly considered Romantic were in fact Eclectic. Thus the movement, which had been gaining strength during the whole of the period between the *Europeo* and the *Artista*, was no hastily conceived compromise between two ideals with each of which it had something in common, but a slow and a native growth—an influence, long present in literature, which came to the front when it was needed, and, once there, carried all before it.

(i) *Pseudo-Classicism*

Before surveying the rise, invasion and triumph of eclecticism in Spain, we may cast one final glance at the position of pseudo-classicism. It so happened that a number of the eighteenth-century exponents of this waning mode— Gallardo, Gallego and Quintana, for example—lived on till half-way or more through the nineteenth century. Mora, indeed, continued his opposition to romanticism for almost fifty years after the controversy with Böhl von Faber, outlived Larra, Espronceda and Rivas and died only in 1864. But neither they, nor the younger anti-Romantics, attempted to lead a neo-Classical counter-reaction : so incurably romantic a people was not likely to accept a return to classicism so soon after escaping from it. The majority of the leading Classicists, old and young, adapted themselves to eclecticism sufficiently well to be numbered by their contemporaries among its adherents. The public was in no mood for any form of exclusiveness in literature, and, with few exceptions, authors wrote, of necessity, for their public. But we may also suppose that the foremost writers of the day were themselves temperamentally inclined in the same direction. Most of them had been reasonably mature even when eclecticism was being preached in the *Europeo*, and, having witnessed its gradual rise, were at least as likely to develop sympathy for it as for romanticism. Though they reacted to it somewhat diversely, the general position of each of them with regard to it was much the same.

(ii) *The Survivors of Pseudo-Classicism*

Let us now look at the chief survivors of eighteenth-century pseudo-classicism. The most reactionary of the conservatives were Gómez Hermosilla, a pure pedant, and Mor de Fuentes, who seems to have had a constitutional apathy to everything not completely antiquated. The former, in a so-called critical account of recent Spanish poetry written about 1837 and published in 1840,[1] practically confines himself to the works of the Salamancans and the Sevilians ; his very publisher, in a preface, protests against the " impassioned eulogies " which he heaps upon the younger Moratín.

Reinoso, Arjona and several of their fellow-Sevilians stood in the main by the Classical position but could appreciate what was best in the newer movements. Because they sided with the Eclectics against the Romantics they have sometimes been erroneously classed with them : in reality, they were pseudo-Classics forced into eclecticism by the impracticability of a Classical reaction.

Gallardo, Gallego, Arriaza and Quintana are in a somewhat different position. Attached though they remain to pseudo-classicism, their love of independence, liberty and sometimes liberalism prevents them from being completely

---

[1] *Juicio crítico de los principales poetas españoles de la última era*, Paris, 1840, 2 vols.

antagonistic to the Romantics, whose merits they are both too shrewd and too honest not to recognize. With them may be contrasted the Duque de Frías, who, finding romanticism merely " absurd,"[1] maintained an aristocratic aloofness from it, but forbore to attack it.

Three other conservatives went over to the Eclectics more completely. Javier de Burgos, often incorrectly classed as a die-hard Classicist, was director of three literary periodicals, from a study of which it may be deduced that he inclined to follow the *justo medio*.[2] Lista, as we have seen, did his best to understand the new movement : torn between the classicism of his respected contemporaries and the romanticism of his most brilliant pupils, he admired Shakespeare, Calderón and Scott, though not Dumas and Hugo. Mora, too, must be classed as an Eclectic. Desiring that his poems should be judged " no . . . como clásicas, ni como románticas, sino como suyas,"[3] he found " the Classic who disdains, despises or ridicules the new artistic elements introduced into literature" and "the Romantic who treats the models of perfection abounding in the opposing ranks with such disrespect and hostility "[4] equally incomprehensible. With these may be included Eugenio de Tapia, an almost exact contemporary of Quintana and an effective satirist of the Romantics who had never been a Classicist as much in theory as in practice. His novel *Los Cortesanos y la Revolución* (1838), which had more in common with Romantic fiction than he thought, makes a comparison between the two ideals which is by no means unfair to either.[5]

(iii) *The Development of Realism*

These were the chief survivors of pseudo-classicism. Learning nothing and forgetting nothing, they lived on in their loneliness until a more liberal generation succeeded them. Nowhere, in the purest form, did Classical ideals persist

[1] Cf. *H.R.M.S.*, I, 339. [2] *Op. cit.*, II, 64.
[3] *Leyendas españolas*, Paris, 1840, p. xiv.
[4] *Op. cit.*, p. xii. [5] *Cit. H.R.M.S.*, II, 8-9.

after the failure of the Romantic movement to establish itself. It was only in the closely related form of realism that they gained any popularity, and even here they mingled with the remnants of Romantic idealism and so formed an eclecticism of another kind. This is exemplified, from 1849 onwards, in the works of Böhl von Faber's daughter, " Fernán Caballero," whose semi-realistic novel, *La Gaviota*, appeared in that year ; in the easy-going story-teller, Antonio de Trueba ; and in the versatile Andalusian, Pedro Antonio de Alarcón. In drama this type of realism develops rather later, but in narrative poetry it is older than in the novel, for there is a strong admixture of realism, not only in the *leyendas* of Rivas and Zorrilla, published in the fifties, but even in the *Romances históricos* (1841) of Rivas, and in his *Moro expósito* (1834).

The realism that entered Spain in the thirties, however, was of a different kind. Defined by one of its chief exponents, Mesonero Romanos, as the " pintura filosófica, o festiva y satírica, de las costumbres populares,"[1] it was known then, and has always been designated since, as *costumbrismo*. It was in this *genre* that such classicism as had any vitality established itself ; and though, by the mid-century, it had begun to prejudice itself by its exaggerations, the first few years of its popularity carried it to great heights. It was a welcome refuge for many who were repelled by Romantic absurdities and desired a literature which should reflect contemporary society. *Costumbrismo*, however, was not easy. It demanded stylistic skill, observation, reflection, objectivity of outlook, calm judgment. " Retrata más que pinta," wrote Larra of Mesonero Romanos,[2] in whom he found too little animation. We may use the phrase in a more modern sense to describe the fundamental difference between *costumbristas* and Romantics: the former were photographers ; the latter, painters. And photography proved a solace to those who disliked contemporary painting for its excessive crudity.

Of the three chief *costumbristas* of this early period,

[1] *Panorama matritense*, Madrid, 1862, p. xvii.
[2] Larra : *Obras*, Madrid, 1855, III, 151.

Estébanez Calderón ("El Solitario"), an Andalusian, and Mesonero Romanos ("El Curioso Parlante"), a Madrileño, belong to the Classic-Eclectic reaction ; Larra ("Fígaro"), from whose studies of contemporary society subjectivity and passion are never for long absent, must be considered as *sui generis*. The three began this type of work at almost exactly the same time, but Larra died just as the fashion for *costumbrismo* was becoming general, so that the other two are more representative of its maturity. Differing in style and in manner of presentation as markedly as Andalusia differs from Castile, they both reveal a *casticismo* only slightly diluted by their circumstances and temperaments and they both commend their art by the effectiveness of their execution.

Mesonero Romanos, by nature observant and detached, excelled in the *genre* as though he had invented it. For thirty years (1831-60) he contributed articles to periodicals, chiefly on *costumbres* ; his heart and soul were in his native Madrid, and it can be imagined how much he tells us of life in the capital at a time when it was undergoing a series of rapid transformations. His collected sketches—*Panorama matritense* (1835-8), *Escenas matritenses* (1842) and *Tipos, grupos y bocetos de cuadros de costumbres* (1862)—as well as his later *Memorias de un setentón* (1881) are justly famous. Superficially, his sketches are often personal, but in essence they are highly objective : he has no axe to grind, no grievance to ventilate and no thesis to expound. If his placid manner and uniformity of style sometimes tend to monotony, this is generally dispelled by the engaging anecdotes and picturesque details in which all his work abounds.

Estébanez Calderón is known chiefly by his *Escenas andaluzas*, published as articles during the thirties and collected only in 1847. Far removed from 'Mesonero's Castilian sobriety are their rich colouring, their versatile character-sketches and their sprightly dialogue, not to mention their frequently affected style and recondite vocabulary. It is unfortunate that allusions in them are apt to recall the immeasurably superior *Novelas ejemplares*. But if one compares these Classical-Eclectic products with the contemporary pseudo-historical novels of the Romantics, it is very clear on which group the mantle of Cervantes has descended.

II The Rise of the Eclectic Ideal [1]

(i) *Eclecticism in theory*

It is in no way irrelevant, in this chapter on the Eclectic movement, to discuss the beginnings of nineteenth-century realism, since both its principal representatives were Eclectics. Estébanez Calderón passed from the incurable conventionality of his pseudo-Classical poems (1831) to the sentimental mediaeval romanticism of his novel *Cristianos y Moriscos* (1838) and thence to the mild realism of *Escenas andaluzas* (1847). Mesonero Romanos could, in practice, embody both the conflicting ideals in one short article ; in theory, he upheld the principle of indifference to both in the interests of artistic excellence.

We have now to show that the general acceptance of Eclectic principles was not the result of a hastily formed desire for compromise in the middle of a literary conflict, and this we can best do by sketching their gradual development during the early years of the nineteenth century.

It ought first to be made clear that the sense in which the word " eclecticism " is here used denotes a self-conscious movement and must not be taken as covering the gradual appearance of Romantic tendencies in eighteenth-century neo-Classical poetry or drama, or the gradual incorporation of Romantic elements in the novels and dramas of the reign of Ferdinand VII. We shall not, for example, describe Cadalso as an Eclectic, for, though traces of both the Classical and the Romantic can be found in his work, there is no proof, or even indication, that he was conscious of the duality. Cabanyes, on the other hand, finds a place in this chapter because he deliberately chose certain Classical themes and forms, and yet in certain respects rebelled against

[1] *H.R.M.S.*, II, 73-89.

Classical formality and claimed freedom for the Romantic side of his temperament.

Bearing this distinction in mind, we may look for the far-away origins of the Eclectic movement in the critical habits implanted by Erauso y Zavaleta, Estala, Nipho and other eighteenth-century apologists for the Golden Age. While never unreservedly praising Lope de Vega or Calderón, they placated the stricter Classicists by admitting, and perhaps exaggerating, the defects which they found in them, and at the same time emphasizing those of their merits which the Romantics were later to magnify. These authors, like the anthologists who set Romantic ballads beside Classical eclogues as typical of the best Spanish poetry, were doing, more or less consciously, what the Eclectic theorists began loudly to recommend in the nineteenth century. In them, therefore, the movement may be said to have its origin.

(ii) *Development of Eclecticism, c.* 1820-1836

It was not until about 1820 that the existence of eclecticism as a movement began to be recognized. Javier de Burgos' *Miscelánea de comercio, artes y literatura* (1819-21) placed itself half-way between the " enthusiast for the culture of the ancients " and the " enemy of antiquity."[1]   The *Censor* (1820-22) defended the Unities, expressed general appreciation of the Golden Age, attacked melodrama, emotional drama and *comedias de santos* and accorded sober commendation to any *refundiciones* which respected their originals.   In 1819, Leandro Moratín's friend and biographer Manuel Silvela went farther.   The " desarreglo y descabellada licencia " of the *romanescos*, he declared, could not be met by the " rigidez más escrupulosa " of classicism.   " Entre estos dos extremos puede haber un justo medio."[2]   In poetry, at least, he contemplates a kind of Eclectic renaissance :

> Nuestra poesía en estos últimos tiempos empieza a presentar un aspecto que parece conciliarlo todo, y en que ni la imaginación es frenética, ni el genio esclavo de una servil imitación.[3]

[1] Cf. *H.R.M.S.*, II, 64, n. 7.

[2] *Obras póstumas*, Madrid, 1845, I, 181.   [3] *Ibid.*

Even so early as this, then, we have Burgos and his colleagues endeavouring to combine what was best in native romanticism with what as neo-Classics they believed essential to literature, and Silvela, on the other hand, opposing foreign romanticism, but realizing that only the pursuit of a middle course could conciliate revolutionaries and conservatives.

The *Europeo* carried the Eclectic ideal one step farther. López Soler, not yet the full-fledged Romantic that he was to become by 1830, shows a distinct tendency to reconciliation. There is excellence, he contends, in the work of the *homéridas* as in that of the *osiánicos*, so why should each party attempt to depreciate the other ? Classicism and romanticism are two distinct modes : the latter, though more recent, has not done away with the former. [1]

To pick up all the threads of Eclectic theory left by writers between 1823 and 1837 would be to repeat much that has been said in the foregoing chapters. In Durán's *Discurso*, in Alcalá Galiano's preface to the *Moro expósito*, and in innumerable articles, and even books, by less known writers, will be found indications of the influence being exerted by this growing ideal. Not only was no serious opposition offered to it during this period, but even writers of whom we think as completely Romantic looked upon it with favour. Espronceda, comparing the progress of poetry with that of politics, thought that " perfection lies in the reconciliation of the greatest possible degree of liberty with the greatest possible degree of orderliness." [2] Salas y Quiroga, though attacking the ideal of the *justo medio* in so far as it encouraged restrictions of the imagination and pedestrianism in style, agreed entirely with the Eclectics that both classicism and romanticism had contributions to make to literature. [3] Avecilla, after painting a vivid picture of the strife between the two parties, reflects upon the possibility of reconciling them. [4] Probably every Romanticist, he remarks, dislikes

[1] *El Europeo*, December 6, 1823.
[2] *El Siglo*, January 24, 1834.
[3] Preface to his *Poesías*, Madrid, 1834.
[4] *Poética trágica*, Madrid, 1834, p. 57.

Romantic aberrations, while no Classicist would really subject all creative writing to one set of rules. Both would give a certain freedom to the imagination, would imitate nature and would avoid aridity without falling into a frenzy. Why, then, can they not be reconciled ?

> Clásicos y románticos escritores, todos nos presentan bellezas que estudiar y defectos en que aprender. Recurramos a ellos, meditémoslos con desvelo infatigable.[1]

All the three foregoing examples belong to the year 1834. By 1836—the year of *El Trovador*—the issue between Romantics and Eclectics was clear-cut, decisively expressed and, in the literary world at least, generally understood. Lista, lecturing at the Madrid Ateneo, used words which might have been the slogan of the Eclectic party :

> Las escuelas denominadas clásicas y románticas pueden ser buenas a la vez, pero nunca los extremos de ambas.[2]

Milá y Fontanals expressed precisely contrary ideas, opposing the very suggestion of reconciliation.[3] A contributor to the *Diario de Barcelona*, however (probably Cabanyes' friend Roca y Cornet), strenuously advocates it. " We cannot imagine," he writes, " what motive has set a dividing barrier between two classes of literature which should be considered as sisters."[4] Romanticism implies a " certain independence " ; but only a few of its " exclusive defenders " have carried this to extremes, and there are laws which great writers will always follow, to whatever school they may belong. The entire series of three articles indicates a detached, moderate and critical attitude towards both parties, and a decided preference for " some of each " over the exclusive productions of either.

In the same year, another Catalan writer, Andrés Fontcuberta, describes eclecticism as a fully formed " school," attacking it as a " sistema bastardo que, como el justo medio

---

[1] *Op. cit.*, p. 74.
[2] *Revista española*, June 16, 1836.
[3] *El Vapor*, August 7, 1836. Cit. *H.R.M.S.*, II, 80-1.
[4] " Clásicos y románticos." In *Diario de Barcelona*, April 25, May 2, May 18, 1836.

en política, nunca producirá nada bueno ni grandioso. El eclecticismo," he adds, "es un viejo decrépito con la máscara de un niño." Of both the Classical and the Romantic " schools " Fontcuberta writes in the past tense : the former was followed only by reactionary slaves of routine ; the latter wrought a revolution, but this is now over and a third " school " holds the field :

> la *escuela ecléctica*, cuyas doctrinas consisten en evitar con igual cuidado la frialdad, la insipidez, la inverosimilitud de los clásicos y la exageración en que incurrieron con frecuencia los románticos.[1]

This description of the three " schools " is perhaps the clearest statement of the position to be found as early as 1836 and it is significant that it should emanate from Barcelona.

(iii) *Eclecticism in practice*

Eclectic practice lagged some way behind Eclectic theory, but even before 1836 a few practitioners of eclecticism can be found. In Cabanyes a mind almost purely Classical, both temperamentally and by education, is combined with a spirit essentially Romantic. The poet works out an Eclectic theory, applies it in his own poetry and dreams of the foundation of a " Catalan school " of like-minded authors. Martínez de la Rosa was an Eclectic—" poco inclinado a alistarme en las banderas de los *clásicos* o de los *románticos*"[2] —who deliberately assumed romanticism at a time when it was becoming popular. Even Larra has been called an Eclectic by some, chiefly on the basis of such personal statements of his own as this from his article on Dumas' *Antony:*[3]

> Sin aceptar la ridícula responsabilidad de un mote de partido, sin declararnos clásicos ni románticos, abrimos la puerta a las reformas, y . . . . nos decidimos a amparar el

---

[1] *El Vapor*, June 20, 1836. On the " harmonic " ideal advocated by Fontcuberta, see *H.R.M.S.*, II, 414-5.

[2] " Advertencia " to *Poesías*, Madrid, 1833.

[3] *El Español*, June 25, 1836. There is much other evidence : the question is discussed in some detail in *H.R.M.S.*, II, 84-8.

nuevo género con la esperanza de que la literatura . . . . tomaría de cada escuela lo que cada escuela poseyese mejor, lo que más en armonía estuviese en todas con la naturaleza, tipo de donde únicamente puede partir lo bueno y lo bello.

It is astonishing to find " how excellently the priests of the old gods and the new got on together "[1] during this time— how readily, for example, journals of the most extreme tendencies accepted contributions from extremists on the other side. The liberal policy, as regards literature, of Burgos' *Miscelánea* and of the reactionary *Censor* is still found in the press some twelve and even fifteen years later. *Cartas españolas*, the *Revista española* and the *Boletín de Comercio* all print Classicists, Romantics and Eclectics indifferently : the last-named comes near to having a definitely Eclectic policy. Even the ultra-Romantic *Artista* was not exclusive. It published eulogistic biographies of Gallego and Lista, the poetry of pseudo-Classicists like Gallardo and Maury and an article by an Eclectic who wrote : " No pretendemos colocarnos exclusivamente en una de las dos bandas en que se halla dividida la literatura. Donde hallemos lo bueno, allí estará nuestra bandera."[2]

III THE TRIUMPH OF THE ECLECTIC IDEAL[3]

(i) *Rapidity of the triumph*

The year 1836 represents the approximate point at which eclecticism may be said to have established itself. Down to that date it had been slowly superseding the moribund mode of the pseudo-Classics, but had been gaining upon the gradually developing romanticism very little. Then suddenly came the invasion of both these fields by the moderate party, the capture of some of their leading combatants, the occupation of journalistic strongholds and the secure

---

[1] A. Cánovas del Castillo : " *El Solitario* " *y su tiempo*, Madrid, 1883, I, 120.

[2] *El Artista*, 1835, I, 40.

[3] *H.R.M.S.*, II, 90-114.

entrenchment of eclecticism in a position quickly seen to be impregnable. From 1836 onwards, while classicism languished, and the Romantic movement, after a further brief flash in the pan, was extinguished, eclecticism advanced rapidly and soon became the most generally held literary doctrine in the country. During the next twenty years continual complaints are made by the Classicists as to the decadence of literature and by the few remaining Romanticists as to its chaotic state. Only the Eclectics are content ; for they feel, rightly or wrongly, that, if all is not yet as it might be, they have at least steered between Scylla and Charybdis and avoided disaster.

The nature of the Eclectic triumph may be illustrated by the conversion from romanticism of two young Andalusians —Juan José Bueno and José Amador de los Ríos. "Formerly," they say in the preface to a collection of their joint poems (1839),[1] " we were fanatically enthusiastic over Hugo and Dumas, we despised Herrera, Garcilaso, León, Rioja and their contemporaries, and we declaimed vehemently against the rules of Aristotle and Horace merely because they were ' Classics.' But now we appreciate beauty wherever we find it, whether in Calderón or in Moratín."[2] The words "Classical" and " Romantic " have lost their meaning for them and they see in the new eclecticism (already adopted, they assert, by the most distinguished writers) the great hope of modern Spanish literature :

> En una palabra, para nosotros han perdido su significación las voces *clásico* y *romántico* y nos hemos acogido a un completo eclecticismo (*sic*), que, adoptado ya por nuestros más distinguidos literatos, reproducirá con el tiempo la escuela original española, que no debe nada a los griegos ni a los franceses.[3]

At this time the Eclectics themselves hardly realized how complete was their victory over the Romantics, for the noisy self-assertiveness of the Romantic extremists was generally taken at more than its face value. But looking back over the conflict to-day we can see that its most striking feature was

---

[1] *Coleccion de poesías escogidas*, Seville, 1839.
[2] *Op. cit.*, p. 4.   [3] *Op. cit.*, pp. 4-5.

the apparent suddenness and the relative completeness of its resolution. All available evidence confirms this : the history of the press, and that of the stage, both in Madrid and in the provinces ; the activities of the Madrid Ateneo and of the provincial Ateneos and Liceos ; the rapidly growing vogue of Eclectic authors and the metamorphic qualities, hitherto unsuspected, which began to be displayed by the Romantics.

For the suddenness of the Eclectic victory there seem to have been several reasons. One was the disillusion caused by the first Romantic dramas which were not translations ; when announced, they had aroused great expectation, but had proved acceptable, neither to the critics, who thought their innovations excessive, nor to the melodramatically minded among the public, who preferred the stronger meat being imported from France. They appealed only to the few who appreciated their freedom, their *españolismo* and their literary merit. When this last was seen to be declining, there was little more chance for Romantic drama, even with a restricted public.

A second reason, probably, was disillusionment with the Romantic novel. Not a single Spanish work coming under this head could compare in merit with the novels of Scott or Hugo, with *Werther, Atala* or *I Promessi Sposi*. Where the Spanish public saw excellence in prose was in the sketches of the *costumbristas*, who increased in number enormously after 1837.

Thirdly, it must have been realized that the Eclectics had greater talent than the Romantics in the important field of satire. The Romantics, unless we count Larra among them, had no satirist at all. No feature of the reviews of the day is more pathetic than the ineffectiveness of their retorts to their opponents' arguments. Excellent though their case was, they continually made it ridiculous by exaggeration ; and, when they attempted burlesque, they failed miserably. The Classicists were in even worse case : they were hopelessly discredited by their literary record, and their polemists, though well stocked with eloquence and abuse, lacked the far more important gifts of wit and humour.

But of both these the Eclectics had plenty, together with descriptive powers unsurpassed in Spanish prose since Cervantes. To the futility of Romantic satire they could oppose the dramatic skits of Bretón, the lively rhymes of Príncipe and Tapia, the merciless sanity and urbane detachment of Mesonero Romanos, the jovial sallies of Abenámar and the more discreet attractions of Segovia. And these satirists made the fullest use of their opportunities : they were active and incisive, sparing none.

Finally, the Eclectics had the advantage of having both a popular case and an easy one to defend, if not theoretically a good one. Romantic periodicals were open to them when they burlesqued the Classicists, and when they portrayed the Romantics almost any journal was glad to print them, for, if classicism was a little *démodé*, romanticism was highly topical. Further, the Eclectics were greatly helped by the re-foundation of the Ateneo of Madrid in 1835 and the foundation of the Liceo in 1837. Had the Romantics been able to assert themselves, it is no doubt they who would have profited, but, though they dominated the Ateneo for a very short time, the foundation of the Liceo found the Eclectics already in the ascendant.

(ii) *Eclectic Periodicals*

The strongholds of eclecticism during the early years of its triumph were the periodicals. In 1836, Mesonero Romanos founded the first, most important and longest-lived of the Eclectic reviews properly so called—the *Semanario pintoresco español*. Nothing could better illustrate the literary tendencies of the time than the fact that, while the Romantic *Artista* survived for only fifteen months, the Eclectic *Semanario* lived on into the next generation.

All its principal contributors were prominent figures in the Eclectic movement : Mesonero Romanos, Gil y Zárate, Segovia and Roca de Togores, Marqués de Molíns. Though it opened its columns to all classes of opinion, most of its essays, reviews and critiques are moderate in tone and it continually preached the doctrine of the happy mean :

Protestamos ante todo con sinceridad, que a ninguna de las dos escuelas pertenecemos exclusivamente. Acérrimos partidarios de la belleza, con igual placer disfrutaremos de sus encantos en las obras de Sófocles que en las de Victor Hugo ; lo mismo en las de Shakespeare que en las de Molière. En donde la veamos la admiraremos, puesto que nunca hemos aplaudido al error ni vituperado el acierto por llegar a nosotros con títulos especiales de escuela.[1]

The growing success of eclecticism, and of the *Semanario*, led to the foundation of a number of other reviews professing a similar literary creed. Two of these, the *Observatorio pintoresco* (1837) and *Nosotros* (1838-9), were short-lived, but the *Correo nacional* (1838-42), described as a " diario ecléctico-romántico,"[2] dispensed small doses of Eclectic theory for over four years, and *El Panorama* (1838-41), a striking monument to the Eclectic ideal, for three. The *Liceo artístico y literario* (1838) stands apart from the rest as being the organ of the Madrid Liceo and committed to the doctrine of the *justo medio*. " The *Liceo*," it announces, " will be neither *Classical* nor *Romantic* in the common sense of these words ; it will combat neither classicism, because it respects the works of Solís, Racine, Tasso and Milton, nor romanticism, because it does not despise Calderón, Shakespeare, Byron or Ariosto."[3]

(iii) *A sign of the times : revival of interest in, and defence of, the Unities*

The revival of interest in the dramatic Unities—in those of time and place no less than in that of action—is another indication that the Romantic movement was on the decline. The resurgence of this question in Spain during the late thirties may have been partly the result of a deliberate attempt to re-establish a measure of classicism, for the most determined of the anti-Romantics had still some fight in them. Or it may merely have been due to a slight exaggeration of the reactionary tendency away from romanticism, by no means surprising in an epoch of such diverse ideals.

[1] J. de la R[evilla] in *Semanario pintoresco español*, 1836, I, 15-16.

[2] *Correo nacional*, March 14, 1839 (Article by Segovia).

[3] Cf. *H.R.M.S.*, II, 105-6.

The principal outward sign of this renewal of interest in the Unities was a thrice-adjourned debate on the subject held at the Madrid Ateneo on February 22, March 1, 8, 1839. Segovia, opening for the pro-Unity party, was opposed, in a lukewarm speech, by Alcalá Galiano. A warm defence of the Unities by Fernando Corradi brought a second contribution from Alcalá Galiano, as well as a mild defence of the Romantics from Hartzenbusch, which was printed verbatim in the *Panorama* and can still be read. It is probably typical of the attitude of the majority of the Romantics of 1835. Hartzenbusch alleges that there are disadvantages alike in complete subjection to the three Unities and in complete emancipation from them. The Unity of action is essential to a play, and the only question admitting of discussion is the permissible degree of latitude of interpretation. The Unities of time and place, if liberally interpreted, can be quite well observed. The golden rule for the dramatist, concludes Hartzenbusch, is to depart from the Rules as little as possible, and for the critic, to be lenient in admitting reasonable licence. A remarkable contribution from the author of the *Amantes de Teruel* ! Had romanticism, and not eclecticism, triumphed in Spain, it would be hard to imagine a debate on the Unities at all, and incredible that the author of a leading Romantic play would defend them.

(iv) *Eclecticism in the Provinces*

Very little need be said about eclecticism in the provinces, for, as we pass into the eighteen-forties, we approach a time when, on the one hand, the regional languages of Catalonia, Valencia and Galicia are becoming more important, and, on the other, provincialism in literature is declining all over Spain. This is due largely to material causes : the improvement made in roads, the building of railways, the general rise in Spain's prosperity, the steady if slow decline of illiteracy and the growth in size and importance of Madrid.

Cádiz, which had long since ceased to have any significance in literary history, came to life again only occasionally, as when Lista published in one of its periodicals (*El Tiempo*) some articles (" De lo que hoy se llama romanticismo ") which aroused great interest in Madrid. Seville, as we have seen, was more interested in its own individual writers than in ideals and movements, while the only literary periodical published during these years in Granada acted mainly as a training-ground for young writers who were to leave it for the capital.

Barcelona, however, retained its importance as a literary centre—partly because of its size, but chiefly because of the intense and ever-increasing activity of the Catalonian Revival. This, besides creating a literature of its own, at first mediaeval in spirit, with a tendency to excessive lyricism and picturesqueness, had also a very definite influence upon Castilian literature in Barcelona, mainly inclining it in the direction of mediaevalism also. Thus Barcelona, which had done so much to foster the growth of the Eclectic ideal in its early stages, now became somewhat indifferent to it, and returned to its first love, the Romantic revival.

Valencia is of rather more interest in this connection, for two of its most characteristic writers, Bonilla and Boix, found eclecticism a considerable attraction. Bonilla, who disliked French Romantic drama, appreciated such a play as *Los Amantes de Teruel*, and even enjoyed so completely Romantic a writer as Byron. Boix, the Chateaubriandesque semi-Romantic, varied lyrical and narrative poetry with an occasional historical drama, eventually turning entirely to history and becoming Cronista of Valencia. Bonilla had turned from romanticism to eclecticism as early as 1837. To oppose romanticism, he wrote in that year, is " a kindness which we owe to society in general," and, although " many recognize two classes of composition, Classical and Romantic, for ourselves we admit under this head only *good* dramas and *bad* ones." [1] Similar ideas are found in many of the reviews of the period, notably in *El Cisne*, which publishes Espronceda, yet satirizes the "Gallo-romantic" conception of love, and declares that it will " never defend either the one movement or the other regarded purely as a system." [2]

[1] *Diario mercantil de Valencia*, February 7, 1837.
[2] Cf. E. Allison Peers : *El Romanticismo en España*, Santander, 1924, pp. 32-4.

IV CHAMPIONS OF THE ECLECTIC IDEAL[1]

(i) *Restatement of the Eclectic ideal*

Our survey of Eclectic theory has taken us from about the year 1820, when it first assumed individuality, down to a point, some twenty years later, at which it had become the literary mode of the day. Its basic principles were adherence to the *justo medio* and the erection of a single standard by which all literature should be judged—that of merit. An almost invariable concomitant of these was the maintenance of a patriotic attitude which led to the continuance of the work of the Revival and also of opposition to foreign importations, notably French Romantic novels and dramas.

We shall now glance at some of the theories of leading Eclectics during the middle decades of the nineteenth century. They diverge very little from the lines we have described, for Eclectic doctrines were few and simple. The value of this survey will lie in its illustration of the solidarity of the Eclectic leaders and in its witness to the substantial nature of their contribution to literary theory.

(ii) *Typical Eclectic theorists : Gil y Zárate, Donoso Cortés, Quadrado*

The only Eclectic theorist who contributed much to creative literature was Gil y Zárate, who began writing comedies in 1816, and, after producing many Classical plays and one notable Romantic play, settled down into an eclecticism which had first attracted him as early as 1832. By 1839 he was completely won to Eclectic theory, and his conversion from a temporary but much publicized adherence to romanticism must have produced a considerable effect. His articles in the *Revista de Madrid* (1839, 1841)[2] are among the best statements of the case for the *justo medio* and his maturer opinions can be studied in a *Manual de literatura*

---

[1] *H.R.M.S.*, II, 114-22.

[2] Notably : "Sobre la poesía dramática" (*Revista de Madrid*, 1ª Serie, III, 156-7) and "Teatro antiguo y teatro moderno" (3ª Serie, pp. 112-24). Cf. *H.R.M.S.*, II, 116-7.

which he wrote in 1842. This is an old-fashioned treatise, in some parts definitely pseudo-Classic and in others inspired by the anti-Romantic reaction. With much of it, however, the Romantics would not have been displeased. It allows the playwright to take liberties with history, recognizes drama as an intermediate *genre* between tragedy and comedy and recommends the use of varied verse-forms, sharply deprecating the limitation of comedy by rule to the *romance*.

A second Eclectic theorist, Donoso Cortés, who later made his name in oratory, social philosophy and religious apologetic, was drawn, as a young man, into the Classical-Romantic controversy. Beginning as a Romanticist, he eulogized Byron and lauded so weak a Romantic drama as Pacheco's *Alfredo ;* but soon his naturally reflective and dispassionate temperament inclined him towards the Eclectic movement and in 1838 he wrote a series of articles conciliatory in tone and to the plain man irresistible.[1] They suggest that, after all, the conflict is a very unreal one and that each party has a completely false idea of the art of the other. Their conclusions are that there exist two " schools," differing profoundly from each other, neither of which must deny the other a place. The controversialists of the day are all perverted extremists.

> Si no hubiera más clásicos que Racine y Molière, ni más románticos que Calderón y Shakspeare, la contienda entre clásicos y románticos no hubiera existido, porque todos los hombres de genio son hermanos.[2]

Romanticism, concludes Donoso Cortés, is the " legitimate and necessary complement " of classicism ;[3] so let us be both Classics and Romantics at once. " La perfección consiste en ser clásico y romántico a un mismo tiempo."[4]

Another Eclectic champion, José María ·Quadrado, one of the founders of a leading Majorcan review, *La Palma*, was very strongly drawn to the Romantic revival but objected to party labels and to the exclusive domination of any

---

[1] Contributed to the *Correo nacional* and reprinted in *Obras*, Madrid, 1903-4, III, 399-437.

[2] *Obras, ed. cit.*, III, 433.

[3] *Op. cit.*, III, 436.   [4] *Op. cit.*, III, 437.

literary system.[1]   Without denying the value of precept,
criticism and respect for the Classics, he refused to let these
things " limit the independence of the imagination."

> En las concepciones literarias no reconocemos más
> reglas que las que sean condiciones de existencia y nazcan
> de las entrañas mismas del asunto.[2]

In another age, Quadrado might have been considered an
almost pure Romantic, but such was his devotion to order—
" the prime constituent of beauty "[3]—that, living when he
did, he readily fell into line with the Eclectics and became
one of their most attractive theorists.

V. ECLECTICISM IN PRACTICE[4]

(i)   *Literature in* 1845 : *Domination of each genre by Eclectic
principles*

Of eclecticism in practice it is difficult to write briefly,
since by 1845 almost all the Romantics and most of the
Classicists had gone over to the third and victorious party.
To survey Eclectic literature, therefore, would be to cover
nearly the whole extent of Spanish literature of the second
third of the century.   It must suffice to demonstrate the
influence of eclecticism on the leading Romantics and then
to describe its dominance over every *genre*.

In 1845, Larra and Espronceda were dead ; Martínez de
la Rosa had abandoned romanticism ; and Rivas had
settled down as an eclectically disposed dilettante. Hartzenbusch, temperamentally inclined to restraint, soon became
an Eclectic in theory, and, later, in practice.   García
Gutiérrez, who had written several Romantic plays, remained nearer to the declining mode than any other dramatist except Zorrilla.   And even Zorrilla was prepared to make
terms with eclecticism.   For some four years, though at the

---

[1] *La Palma*, October 11, 1840.

[2] " Fe literaria." In *Ensayos religiosos, políticos y literarios*, Palma, 1893-6,
I, 37.

[3] *Op. cit.*, I, 33.   [4] *H.R.M.S.*, II, 123-59.

height of his Romantic successes, he experimented in Classical (*e.g.*, *Sofronia*, 1843) and Eclectic (*e.g.*, *La Copa de marfil*, 1844) drama. In theory, too, as well as in practice, he paid homage to the *justo medio*. Neither the " escuela moderna " nor the " escuela antigua " was his exclusive choice.

> . . . . Firme en mi manía
> de andar con entrambas sigo.
>
> . . . .
>
> Mas yo vivo, por fortuna,
> en tal dulce escepticismo,
> que se me importa lo mismo
> por las dos, que por ninguna.[1]

(ii)   *Domination of each genre by Eclectic principles : Drama*

Since the leading Romantics had deserted, it is not surprising that each of the *genres* should have been dominated by Eclectic principles.

On the Madrid stage, eclecticism developed rapidly after 1837. Classical comedy and tragedy were still played ; the vogue of the Classically inclined Bretón and Vega continued; and the historical play, Eclectic in principle, and seldom marked by Romantic extravagances, enjoyed an amazing vogue for several decades. " Ya admitimos como principio literario," wrote a dramatic critic in 1845, " que no hay más géneros que lo bueno y lo malo." And again : " (Estamos) en busca de un equilibrio donde se sostengan mutuamente la libertad y el orden."[2] And those dicta were entirely typical of the epoch.

Of the individuals who dominated the stage, the greatest was Bretón—a Classic by temperament, strongly influenced by Moratín, but later, to a lesser extent, by the Romantic movement also. His best original plays (*e.g.*, *A Madrid me vuelvo*, 1828 ; *Marcela, o ¿ a cuál de los tres?* 1831 ; *Un Tercero en discordia*, 1833) are brilliantly executed upon the Moratinian formula, but he made *refundiciones* of Lope de

---

[1] Cf. *H.R.M.S.*, II, 126-7.

[2] Gavino Tejado, in *El Laberinto*, 1845, II, 202.

Vega and Calderón, translated French melodrama and wrote Romantic (*e.g.*, *Elena*, 1834) and semi-Romantic (*Don Fernando el Emplazado* and *Muérete ; ¡y verás !* : both 1837) plays of his own. But after *Vellido Dolfos* (1839) he never again wrote an original play that even inclined to romanticism. Why should he ? Its day was over.

Ventura de la Vega, often regarded as a belated Classicist, is really an Eclectic. If he extolled Moratín and attacked the Romantics' " furious invasion,"[1] he also eulogized Lope de Vega and Calderón, and his creative work shows a desire to take the best from classicism and from romanticism. Affected for only a short time by the Romantic movement, he followed up his best Classical comedy, *El Hombre de mundo* (1845) with an Eclectic historical drama, *Don Fernando el de Antequera* (1847) and much later (1863) wrote a " tragedy," *La Muerte de César*, which is at least as Romantic as its model, Shakespeare's *Julius Caesar*.

Gil y Zárate, having won success in Classical tragedy and ultra-Romantic drama, spent the rest of his career in writing plays that were indebted to both ideals. Perhaps in his dramatic development, as well as in his merits and failings as a dramatist, he stood for a larger number of contemporary authors than any other. A Romantic—often imitative, declamatory and superficial—in his treatment of history and his choice of metres, and a Classic in his love of order, his preoccupation with form, his characterization and his respect for the Unities, he was nearer still to the Eclectics, and he may have found his way to them by the road of least resistance.

Even Escosura, who in two years made three attempts to create a distinctively Romantic type of play, did not remain a Romantic. Apart from the familiar " Bulto vestido de negro capuz " (1835), all his non-dramatic verse is neo-Classical. In drama (*e.g.*, *Roger de Flor*, 1845) he also turned neo-Classic, going on thence to write Moratinian comedies (*e.g.*, *El Amante universal*, 1847 ; *Las Apariencias*, 1850). Though he occasionally used Romantic licence, drew on the Golden Age, or even referred to himself as a kind of Romantic

---

[1] *Obras poéticas*, Paris, 1866, p. 503.

—Soy romántico, pero romántico español y tradicionalista. Amante de la libertad—la libertad, digo, no la licencia— del ingenio . . . . lo que me parece conveniente y necesario es que seamos, como ellos, españoles.[1]—

he laid down the principle that the best should be accepted from every age and school of thought. The best works of Calderón and Moratín, of Rivas and Vega, appeared to him " igualmente obras maestras."[2]

An Eclectic who achieved a reputation with a single play —*Don Francisco de Quevedo* (1848)—Eulogio Florentino Sanz wrote nothing further but a less successful play and a handful of fragments and translations. His one *acierto* is a historical piece combining Romantic reminiscences and devices with a quite un-Romantic sobriety. The atmosphere he creates is that of Golden Age drama, tinged with a modernity seldom found in his contemporaries.

(iii) *Lyric and Narrative Poetry*

Here eclecticism became the prevailing mode as soon as the romanticism of the poets of 1840 began to weaken. Classicism died hard, and most of the younger poets assumed an attitude of sedate moderation. Two of these stand out : La Avellaneda and Campoamor.

Gertrudis Gómez de Avellaneda, a Cuban who settled in Spain, had acquired all the characteristics of Romantic art before publishing her first collection of verse in 1841, but she had also taken over many habits from pseudo-classicism. Later, her simple manner gave place to the grand manner, but the two modes still influenced her : she retained a predilection for certain Romantic themes and for tricks of Romantic versifying ; but she also clung to antiquated pseudo-Classical language and to eighteenth-century conventional treatment. The Eclectic label may be attached to her novels and dramas, though the former incline to the Romantic and the latter to the Classical. Still, the novels

---

[1] Recuerdos literarios, etc." Cf. *H.R.M.S.*, II, 144-5.
[2] *Ibid.*

have realistic affinities and the dramas range from the Classical tragedy *Alfonso Munio* (1844) to the near-Romantic *Baltasar* (1858). She adheres, in fact, to the time-honoured Eclectic formula, " Some of each."

Her eclecticism differs from that of Campoamor, who, in theory, is equally opposed to extreme objectivity and extreme subjectivity : his ideal is " to attain to art through ideas expressed in common language and to revolutionize poetry both in form and in content."[1] But, in practice, instead of attempting to combine Romantic ideals with Classical, he flings himself from the one ideal to the other— from the almost pure romanticism of *Ternezas y flores* (1840) and *Ayes del alma* (1842) to the almost pure realism of the *Fábulas* (1842) and *Doloras* (1846) ; thence into a semi-Romantic epic *Colón* (1853) and the Romantically inchoate *Drama universal* (1869) ; and finally, in *Pequeños Poemas* (1872 ff.) and *Humoradas* (1886-8), back to realism. Exercising the right to follow whichever literary ideal he chose, he made himself one of the principal Eclectics of the nineteenth century.

(iv) *Prose*

In prose, *costumbristas* abounded, but they are mainly secondary figures. Segovia, with his keen but kindly satire, his nimble dialogue and his real talent for characterization, ranks rather higher than most. López Pelegrín, with whom for some time he collaborated, is fonder of word-play and popular jests. José Somoza, a much older man, is a shrewd observer and a realist in the most literal sense, but lacks imagination. Modesto Lafuente, who wrote as " Fray Gerundio," was the most popular of the *costumbristas*, but an author of little more merit than the journalists whose articles and sketches of this type crowded the papers. For the habit of writing about *costumbres* penetrated everywhere—even to the Romantic *Artista*—though the most congenial soil was to be found in the Eclectic reviews, and particularly in the *Semanario pintoresco español*.

[1] *Obras completas*, Madrid, 1901-3, III, 247.

Costumbrismo perhaps reached its height in Spain in a composite work entitled *Los Españoles pintados por sí mismos* (1843-4), which combined the realistic process of exact observation with that passion for revival which came in with the pre-Romantics. It aimed at preserving, by methods of photographic accuracy, the principal Spanish types, which otherwise might be forgotten. Most of the sketches are polished and readable, devoid of exaggeration, full of detail and full of fun.

From *costumbrismo* it is only a step to the *novela de costumbres* of Fernán Caballero, of which the first example, and one of the best, is *La Gaviota* (1849). The author's dictum, " La novela no se inventa, se observa," [1] signifies the transference of *costumbrismo* into the field of fiction, which turned a large public from fantastically extravagant novels, often historical only in name, and from the translations and adaptations from the French which flooded the market simply because no Spanish author combined a modern way of writing with deep human sympathies. Estébanez Calderón, in his tales and his historical novel, *Cristianos y Moriscos* (1838), had essayed a similar combination, but tended to overweight his stories with *costumbres* till the plot was lost. Fernán Caballero far outclassed him.

Optimistic and idealistic in character, however, she was less of a realist in fact than in theory. She never escaped from herself, whether in characterization, description or moral reflection, and therein she is a true Romantic. But she dropped the characteristic rhetoric and the petty devices of Romantic fiction, and her characters, even at their worst, are not completely un-lifelike. She had a vigorous style, modest and simple like herself, but clear and correct, and an enquiring mind which delved in search of strange regional traditions. The importance of *La Gaviota*, when it first appeared, was compared with that of *Waverley*. In view of the vast superiority of its author over all contemporary Spanish novelists, the comparison, though unjustified by events, was quite understandable.

---

[1] Cit. Mérimée-Morley : *A History of Spanish Literature*, New York, 1930, p. 542.

Chapter VI

THE CONTINUANCE OF ROMANTICISM, 1837-1860[1]

I. Drama[2]

(i) *The Decline in Romantic Drama*

Soon after 1837, romanticism began to show an almost spectacular decline, particularly in the field of drama, where it had won its chief victories. " El público se ha cansado ya de puñales, venenos y ataúdes," wrote a critic in 1839.[3] And not only were there few new original Romantic plays, not only did Hugo, Dumas and the lesser French Romantics become less popular, but there is a falling-off in Golden Age drama too.

The poverty of the stage in original drama is reflected in the depression of critics and commentators. " El teatro va decayendo . . . " begins a characteristic article.[4]

> El rayo fulgente que iluminara aun día a Esquilo y a Eurípides, a Shakspeare y Calderón, Schiler (*sic*) y Corneille despide hoy sus últimos reflejos, y acaso en breve se apague y extinga para siempre. Hace diez años pareció lucir para la literatura dramática un nuevo día, un nuevo y brillante porvenir ; pero ese día ha pasado ya y la esperanza en el porvenir está desvanecida.[5]

This was in 1840. In 1841, Salvador Bermúdez de Castro hopes matters are mending. The Spanish stage needs original genius to purge it of foreign influences, to utilize the best work of the Golden Age and at the same time to make contemporary drama mirror contemporary customs. And,

---

[1] *H.R.M.S.*, II, 160-258.

[2] *H.R.M.S.*, II, 160-191.

[3] *Guardia nacional*, October 1, 1839. The article appears to have been reprinted from a Madrid newspaper.

[4] *Semanario pintoresco español*, 1840, 2ª Serie, II, 198-200.   [5] *Ibid.*

> Por fortuna la extravagante moda se acabó . . . . la manía
> de las imitaciones va pasando lentamente y al volver los
> ojos a nuestro teatro antiguo descubrimos con asombro
> tesoros ocultos, minas abundantísimas que el talento puede
> explotar.[1]

In 1843, however, the level-headed Hartzenbusch is distinctly gloomy.

> Hay . . . . hoy día un género de composiciones algo más
> favorecido de los espectadores que las otras ; y son las
> extranjeras, la mayor parte de las cuales tiene poquísimo
> mérito literario. ¿ Por qué son preferidas a las originales ?[2]

Fortunately, Bermúdez de Castro's confidence was justified. The rise to greatness of Zorrilla in this decade coincided with the appearance of lesser but not insignificant men, such as Rodríguez Rubí, Florentino Sanz and López de Ayala. On the heels of these came a more considerable genius, Manuel Tamayo y Baus, who helped to fill the gap between the early and the late Romantics—between Rivas, let us say, and Echegaray—a gap into which enter also the later plays of García Gutiérrez and his contemporaries. Thus the drama of the forties and fifties reaches, if not a lofty standard, at least a creditable one, while the failure of both romanticism and classicism to dominate the stage gives it a notable variety.

Since it is the history of the Romantic movement, and not of drama in general, that is here being traced, our survey of drama between 1837 and 1860 must be limited to that aspect of it which preserves the Romantic tradition. We shall first look at the chief new Romantic plays staged during 1838-40, and afterwards, in a more general fashion, consider the production of the two following decades.

(ii) *Some Romantic Plays of* 1838-1840

Only two plays of 1838 merit detailed consideration. In his historical verse drama, *Don Jaime el Conquistador*, Escosura

---

[1] " Movimiento dramático." In *El Iris*, 1841, I, 113-14.

[2] *Ensayos poéticos y artículos en prosa, etc.*, Madrid, 1843, p. 235.

tried to avoid both the " transpyrenean " extravagances of his first play and the conventional " languidness " of his second [1]—in other words, he attempted a piece of the Eclectic type which ousted Romantic drama from the stage until the advent of Echegaray. Hartzenbusch, in *Doña Mencía*, endeavoured, with some success, to rekindle the dying interest in Romantic drama with the fuel of anti-clericalism. Character-types, versification and respect for the Unities recall neo-classicism, but the vivid contrasts, the improbabilities, the violence of language and the bursts of melodrama are typical of the Romantics' worst exaggerations.

In 1839, Hartzenbusch's *comedia de magia* in prose and verse, *La Redoma encantada*, makes a Romantic appeal of another kind and José García de Villalta's *El Astrólogo de Valladolid* represents a mild, idealistic romanticism, with a characterization relieved from the most portentous dullness only by the figure of the heroine. It was in this year that Bretón staged the last of his Romantic plays, *Vellido Dolfos*, which was given only four performances.

(iii)   *Zorrilla*

Romantic drama in the years immediately following 1837 amounts to little more than Zorrilla, who produced three of his lesser plays (*Cada cual con su razón, Ganar perdiendo* and —with García Gutiérrez—*Juan Dandolo*) in 1839 and continued writing for the stage for nearly half a century. Though paying homage, as we have seen, to the prevailing Eclectic mode, Zorrilla, in his original works, is an incurable Romantic : he swelled the current of the Romantic revival, prolonged the vogue of the Romantic revolt and became responsible for a vast increase in works bearing the Romantic label.

For the plots of his dramas he turned continually to the Middle Ages. They embrace as much as a thousand years of Peninsular history, extending from the last of the Goths to the last of the Spanish Hapsburgs. He seldom imitates or

[1] Cf. pp. 84, 86, above.

draws material from a Golden Age playwright, preferring to work upon some historical source with his own imagination, but so faithfully does he reproduce the spirit of the Golden Age that the greatest Spanish authority on his work confesses to an occasional feeling, when reading him, that he is reading Lope or Calderón.[1] Zorrilla has much of Lope's fertility and claims Lope's own freedom, He will carry on a plot from one play to another, spurning the Unities and other inconvenient rules whenever it suits him. He is " in the direct line of descent from Lope de Vega, Tirso and Calderón," says Blanco García, and quite rightly.[2]

When, still a boy, Zorrilla stepped on to a stage which had been freed of convention, he found it almost empty of Romantic rivals. Hartzenbusch was still toying with romanticism, while García Gutiérrez, a competitor with whom Zorrilla promptly entered into collaboration, was producing at high pressure with one eye on changing public opinion. There was no one else comparable with these, and it would not have been surprising if Zorrilla had sought notoriety by turning revolt into revolution. But actually, *Cada cual con su razón* (1839) is temperate in tone, and until it becomes Romantic near the end of the second act, it is only a dull and wordy comedy of intrigue. In a preface to it the author expounds the far from Romantic principles on which it is built :

Por si . . . . se les antojara a sus amigos o a sus detractores señalarle (*sc.* al autor) como partidario de escuela alguna, les aconseja que no se cansen en volver a sacar a plaza la ya mohosa cuestión de *clasicismo* y *romanticismo*.
Los clásicos verán si en esta comedia están tenidas en cuenta las clásicas exigencias. La acción dura veinte y cuatro horas ; cada personaje no tiene más que un objeto, al que camina sin episodios ni detenciones, y la escena pasa en la casa del Marqués de Vélez.
Los señores románticos perdonarán que no haya en ella verdugos, esqueletos, anatemas ni asesinatos . . . . [3]

---

[1] N. Alonso Cortés : *Zorrilla, su vida y sus obras*, Valladolid, 1916-20, I, 275.

[2] *La Literatura española en el siglo XIX*, 3rd ed., Madrid, 1909-12, I, 207.

[3] The preface is dated August 27, 1839, and will be found in Vol. VII of Zorrilla's *Poesías*, Madrid, 1837-40.

After producing two more plays of but slight merit, Zorrilla brought out the first part of *El Zapatero y el Rey* (1840), characterized by the diffuseness which is one of his worst faults, as well as by inverisimilitude in characterization and failure to maintain interest of plot. Emotional suggestions, however, are well conveyed and Romantic devices reinforce the author's natural vivacity. The second part (1842) is more properly a second play, with a more closely knit plot and a surprise conclusion. In the same year Zorrilla produced three other plays, the best of which is the one-act Roderick-drama, *El Puñal del Godo*, full of exaggerated language, thunder and lightning, phantoms, stars and the *fuerza del sino*, but noteworthy for its patriotic tone, its picturesque background, its lively action and the melody of its easy verse.

Of the three plays dated 1843 only one need be mentioned —*El Caballo del Rey Don Sancho*, a lively Romantic treatment of Mariana, replete with incident, atmosphere and the interest of the unknown. In 1844 came the frigid Classic-Eclectic "tragic spectacle", *La Copa de marfil* and the play which marks for Zorrilla the limit of ultra-Romantic drama, *Don Juan Tenorio*. The immediate success of this masterpiece, achieved when the Romantic movement was all but dead, confirms the conviction that it need never have declined as it did had it had leaders of force and ability. Don Juan is the Romantic hero carried to the highest degree of dramatic effectiveness, completely dominating the play. The contrast between his audacity, verve, abandon and exaggerated cynicism and his tardy remorse and repentance may not be great art, but is certainly attractive drama. All the other traits of the play illumine this central figure : the highly dramatic use of the religious motif ; the bold introduction of the supernatural ; the masterly technique and the irresistible melody of the verse. Truly Romantic liberties are taken with construction : the two " parts " are not two plays, but one enormous play, with a gap of five years in the middle. And somehow, though the critics frown on this, it seems perfectly in keeping with the drama's other characteristics.

Don Juan Tenorio was followed by a group of mediocre plays, interspersed with much narrative poetry. In the last of his principal dramas, *Traidor, inconfeso y mártir* (1849), he retreats some way from the extreme position for which he had become famous, and gives us a play almost describable as Eclectic. Against the carefulness of its construction, however, and the orderly progress of its action, must be set the essentially Romantic nature of the plot and of the characterization. Don Gabriel, for example, is the Romantic hero pure and simple.[1]

(iv) *Other Dramatists of the period*

For nearly forty years more Zorrilla continued to write dramas, mainly in the Romantic tradition, but none of them can compare with these. Rivas' *El Desengaño en un sueño* (1844), which he terms a " fantastic drama," is fantastically Romantic, packed with Shakespearean reminiscences and not written for the stage. Hartzenbusch made a substantial contribution to the Revival by his twelve-volume edition of Tirso de Molina (1839-42), his Golden Age *refundiciones* and his continuation of the work of Sánchez and Durán in the Biblioteca de Autores Españoles. Most of his late original plays are built on old Spanish themes and combine a superficial romanticism with an intense dullness. García Gutiérrez's historical plays extended into the middle sixties : two of them, *Venganza Catalana* (1864) and *Juan Lorenzo* (1865), are among his best. He cared less for the Revival, however, than the archaically minded Hartzenbusch.

What is true of these two dramatists may be said of Gil y Zárate, Escosura, García de Villalta and nearly all the rest. They derive much of their plot-material from Spanish history, or, if they get it elsewhere, adapt it in accordance with national tradition : in other respects, they merely follow their inclinations, which are by no means exclusively Romantic.

II. PROSE FICTION[2]

The period 1837-1860 falls naturally into two periods. Down to about 1844, production was poor, both in quality

---

[1] Cf., in particular, II, vi : Nací donde quiso Dios, etc.

[2] *H.R.M.S.*, II, 191-202.

and in quantity ; after that date, quantity increased, but quality declined still further.

(i) 1837—1844

Concerning romanticism there is little to say. It would seem as if, in the earliest times, the best story-tellers turned to the medium of verse. The Revival-novel fell upon evil days : " en España," wrote a critic in 1838, " no existe un solo autor que haya aspirado al título de novelista."[1] One of the few exceptions was Estébanez Calderón, whose *Cristianos y Moriscos*[2] partly redeems a weak plot and a violent catastrophe by the charm of its idealism, its local colour and its lyrics. The author attempts to unite romanticism in the outlines of his narrative with realism of detail. Had he had more of the novelist's technical skill, he might have won celebrity.

For six years after this, no fiction of any significance appeared : the least bad of the novels (Rubió y Ors' *Mano-Roja* (1838), Pusalgas' *Nigromántico mejicano* (1838) and Cortada's *El Templario y la villana* (1840) come from Barcelona. In 1844 appeared Enrique Gil's chief contribution to the Romantic movement, perhaps the best novel of the half-century, *El Señor de Bembibre*. This was a genuinely Romantic work : its author, like Zorrilla, had grown up with the Movement and attained manhood during its brief ascendancy. Its special distinction is that of having led the way in the great revival of regionalism for which the later nineteenth century is famous. Gil is the first writer of merit to set a historical romance in his native region. His somewhat languid story is enriched by Nature-scenes of great beauty, conveying a sense of reality which contrasts strongly with the historical background and the characterization. His landscapes are instinct with a truly Romantic subjectivity, sentimentality and melancholy, all of which reappear, though less markedly, in his verse.

[1] A. Fernández de los Ríos, preface to *La Casa de Pero Hernández*, Madrid, 1848, p. viii.

[2] Cf. p. 161, above.

(ii) 1845—1860

After *El Señor de Bembibre*, the historical novel entered a period of frank decline, which ended only with the great revival of some thirty years later. The most frequently recurring names are those of Fernández y González, Ayguals de Izco, Navarro Villoslada and Escosura. All these wrote steadily—the first, voluminously ; his books run into hundreds. He was, however, imbued with the spirit of the Romantic revival, and had a certain distinction of expression and great technical skill. Ayguals de Izco, though hardly less prolific, ranks lower ; lengthy, uninspired and fantastic in theme and treatment, and declamatory in style, he represents not so much the decline of romanticism as its degradation. Navarro Villoslada, the editor of several periodicals in which he serialized his novels, is at his best with an extensive canvas, and writes in a lively style, with more dialogue than description. Much of his technique he learned from the novels of Scott and his own work is continually reminiscent of their plots, characters and methods. Escosura, in his irrelevances and constructional defects, illustrates the worst side of romanticism, though he has pretensions to excellence as a photographer and affects some realism of detail.

The note of Romantic melancholy which continued to be heard in lyric poetry was not entirely absent from the novel. *Cristianos y moriscos* bore the appropriate sub-title " Novela lastimosa." Avecilla, in the theme of his *Conquista del Perú* (1853), found more of melancholy than of jubilation or pride and the disillusion of Nicomedes Pastor Díaz found expression in his markedly Romantic and almost lyrical psychological novel, *De Villahermosa a la China* (1858).

III. LYRIC AND NARRATIVE POETRY [1]

(i) *The trend of poetry after 1837*

The tardy development of the Romantic lyric in Spain, contrasted with the early blossoming of narrative poetry, compels us to deal with each type of verse, so far as is possible,

[1] *H.R.M.S.*, II, 202-58.

separately. We shall first consider the history of the two types jointly from 1837 to their *annus mirabilis*, 1840, and then survey the history of each during the two following decades.

Apart from the early poems of Rivas, Espronceda and Zorrilla, no Romantic verse of any consequence was produced before 1840 and the preceding three years were dominated by Zorrilla. As a lyric poet alone, Zorrilla could never have gone far : even in his shortest lyrics he is always on the verge of narrative, in which he feels metrically freest. In narrative, too, his imagery is richest, and he is more at home in the treatment of native themes : it was as if he could never move at ease save when telling a story.

Yet it was with a lyric that he first sprang into notice,[1] and his lyrics contain all the germs of his complete and mature art. They were in the Romantic mode of the day ; they embodied the double inspiration—patriotism and religion—which in great part accounted for his popularity. They play on ideas and sentiments adopted by the Romantics, such as melancholy, mystery and destiny. They affect a somewhat conventional Romantic symbolism, an incorrigible picturesqueness, a facility in the use of the telling epithet, a power of pictorial appeal. Zorrilla's lyrics, then, can by no means be disregarded even by comparison with the far larger and richer total of his work as a whole.

(ii)   *The Annus mirabilis :* 1840

It was in 1840, when the invasion of the Eclectic ideal had perceptibly weakened the drama, that the full force of the Romantic movement in poetry began to be felt. " A new path is opening before us," wrote a critic in 1839, " and a taste for poetry is becoming general in Spain."[2] The most cursory glance at the collections of verse published in 1840 will bear out this statement.

Campoamor's *Ternezas y flores*, published for their author by the Madrid Liceo, read like the juvenilia of a second

---

[1] Cf. p. 90, above.
[2] Cf. *La Esperanza*, 1839, pp. 197-8.

Zorrilla : nothing in them suggests the *volte-face* of the *Doloras*. Apart from youthful defects, their chief traits are metrical freedom, subjectivity and a kind of Lamartinian melancholy. Nicomedes Pastor Díaz was one of the few writers of the day to absorb, and express with real effect, the spirit of melancholy : he describes his *Poesías* as " plegarias, suspiros, desahogos, gemidos solitarios de un corazón que . . . gime y llora solamente por haber nacido." [1] Arolas' first collection, *Poesías caballerescas y orientales*, published in Valencia, impresses by its brilliance—frequent and sudden changes of metre, an unfailing flow of language, a rich and sometimes ill-controlled imagination. Though he seldom penetrates below any surface, he seemed, in that wonderful year, to show promise of a great future. So did Salvador Bermúdez de Castro, comparable, in the lyric field, with Espronceda, and, for the sincerity of his inspiration and the high level of his thought, superior to all other Romantics earlier than Bécquer. First and foremost, his lyrics are subjective and emotional. " Si algo contienen," he wrote,

es la revelación de las sensaciones internas de mi alma, los pensamientos que me han inspirado el aspecto de la naturaleza, la contemplación de la humanidad.[2]

These sensations and thoughts are closely allied to an Esproncedan *desengaño* and the poet contrives to convey an acute impression of spiritual desolation which at times recalls the French Romantic, Alfred de Vigny. It should be added that, for all his depth of feeling, Bermúdez de Castro was quite capable of pressing his sentiments into the service of Romantic superficiality. In " Sepulcros y misterios," [3] and in " La Duda," [4] the " negras sombras de horrible tristeza " lurk in the " luz sepulcral " of a Gothic church, whose pillars, tombs and " lúgubre altar " provide the conventional background of the day.

Besides these collections, the year 1840 saw the publication of Espronceda's *Poesías líricas*, discussed above ;[5] of García Gutiérrez's *Poesías ;* of some selections from

---

[1] *Poesías*, Madrid, 1840, p. 5.
[2] *Ensayos poéticos*, Madrid, 1840, p. 5.
[3] *Op. cit.*, pp. 271-9.
[4] *Op. cit.*, pp. 239-42.
[5] Cf. pp. 94, 96, above.

Lamartine translated by Juan Manuel de Berriozabal ; of the largely pseudo-Classical *Poesías* of Manuel Rementería y Fica ; and of a number of narrative poems, partly lyrical in tone, to be referred to hereafter.

(iii) *Lyric poetry*, 1841-1860

In 1841 there is again a great output of verse, though narrative predominates. There were Espronceda's *Diablo Mundo*, Zorrilla's *Cantos del Trovador*, Rivas' *Romances históricos*, Rodríguez Rubí's *Poesías andaluzas* and collections by La Avellaneda, Ochoa and Romero Larrañaga.

La Avellaneda, in 1841, had not learned the accents of deeply individual melancholy which were later to characterize her poetry, but, though retaining certain neo-Classical habits, she displayed most of the remaining traits of Romantic art. She shared the Romantics' conception of the poet and interpreted Nature according to her moods. At this stage in her evolution, she must certainly be classed with the Romantics.

Gregorio Romero Larrañaga brought out two collections in 1841, both of markedly Romantic flavour. His *Poesías*, published by the eclectically-minded Madrid Liceo, contains a preface by the Marqués de Molíns, claiming that that body has rescued the young author from classicism and romanticism and " helped to make him a Poet "[1] The claim is hardly supported by the evidence of the volume itself. The poems are inspired principally by the emotions, draw upon mediaeval legend, and are full of colour and sensibility. Their faults of diction are those of Romantic extravagance. The second volume, *Cuentos históricos, leyendas antiguas y tradiciones populares de España*, contains purely Romantic narrative poems in *romances*, achieving a somewhat higher degree of picturesqueness than others of the same period. Historically, their chief interest lies in the verse introduction in which the author, disguised as a troubadour, describes what he finds in the Middle Ages to attract the nineteenth century.[2]

In 1842 appeared García Gutiérrez's *Luz y tinieblas*,

---

[1] *Poesías*, Madrid, 1841, p. xi.   [2] *H.R.M.S.*, II, 220.

enshrouded in an unmistakable atmosphere of romanticism. The light which he invokes is the soft refulgence of slowly fading illusion ; the darkness is that of doubt, despair and the torture of excessive sensibility. With considerable imaginative force he describes the terrified soul fighting its doubts while the hours bear it on towards eternity. A *cuento* of some length, " Elvira," puts the poetry of disillusion into a superficially narrative form and a number of sacred lyrics play upon an essentially Romantic conception of religion.

From now onward, narrative poetry begins to predominate over lyric, which need detain us little further. Francisco González Elipe's *Poesías* (1842) includes both *genres*, together with some verse satires. Campoamor's *Ayes del alma* (1842) foreshadows the development of his simple style into the epigrammatic brevity of the *Doloras* and the metamorphosis of the sentimentality of the early poems into the sententiousness of the later. Carolina Coronado (*Poesías*, 1843) takes themes connected mainly with Nature and veils them in a Lamartinian melancholy. In the same year, Hartzenbusch published some *Ensayos poéticos*, which he prefaced with the confession that he had no poetic vocation.

In the late forties the lyric collections become rarer and of less merit : the most noteworthy, Campoamor's *Doloras* (1846), belongs to the Eclectic movement, with a strong bias in the direction of realism. In the fifties, the nature of the *genre* began to change ; and, before 1860, the properly Romantic lyric had sunk into a decline from which it was redeemed, in a further ten years, by the exquisite poetry of Gustavo Adolfo Bécquer. True, the bulk of verse production remained large and an occasional critic would still become lyrical over the merits and the prospects of the *genre*. But a survey of the field shows that most of the Romantic versifiers either betook themselves to narrative or petered out in vague emotion or melancholy.

From the host of collections published at this time by minor poets, one stands out—the *Composiciones poéticas* (Barcelona, 1851) of three Catalonians, all of whom, like Cabanyes, died young. The most talented of the three is Pablo Piferrer, who justly occupies more space than the two others—Juan

Francisco Carbó and José Semís—combined. His great affection was for the ballad ; his models in subject, and to some extent in form, were Schiller and Scott ; and besides an ample endowment of Romantic sensibility, he had a good ear for melody. Carbó's poems are also of the lyrico-narrative ballad type, and not far below Piferrer's in merit. Semís, at his best, is sentimental but picturesque and melodious, but he stands on a lower level.

The conclusion to be drawn from this survey of the lyric poetry of two decades is only too plain. Striking as was the outburst of activity which reached its climax in 1840, its success lasted no longer than the brief *llamarada*, some five years earlier in date, of Romantic drama. " Este era el momento de la regeneración literaria," wrote Zorrilla, reminiscently, about 1849 :

> Este era el crepúsculo que debía haber sido precursor de un día sereno, esplendente y fecundador para la literatura nacional. Pero . . . . la revolución literaria . . . . se fatigó por mucho tiempo en inútiles y mal dirigidos esfuerzos . . . . Paró al fin en una vergonzosa bacanal, en la que el *demonio de la poesía* embriagó a la juventud, descarriando o embotando su talento, y un enjambre de melenudos poetas nos desparramamos por la Península . . . . Ni un solo genio poderoso, ni una voz pujante y avasalladora se levantó en aquel Pandemonium, capaz de acaudillar aquella juventud, falta solamente de una bandera, privada sólo de un capitán prudente y audaz que utilizase las fuerzas que realmente poseía.[1]

He wrote truly. The glorious company of lyric poets dispersed with surprising rapidity. Zorrilla himself was inclining more and more to narrative ; Campoamor had gone over to his prosaic eclecticism ; Cabanyes, Espronceda, Arolas, Piferrer, Carbó—to name only a few—were dead before 1850. García Gutiérrez, Ochoa, N. P. Díaz and Salvador Bermúdez de Castro practically ceased writing lyric poetry altogether. Some of the remainder degenerated into pseudo-classicism ; others indulged in pseudo-realism, jocularity or satire. As a result, from about 1845 to 1860, few signs were left of romanticism in lyric poetry.

[1] From the preface to *María. Corona poética de la Virgen*, Madrid, 1849, p. 11.

(iv) *Narrative poetry*, 1841-1860

In the field of narrative poetry the case is somewhat different. Through the period 1837-60 there was a steady flow of verse narrative, a little of which was good, a little bad, and the vast bulk simply indifferent. Its quantity will appear even greater if we include the narrative poems which Arolas, Campoamor, García Gutiérrez, Hartzenbusch and others interspersed among their lyrics. And even without these it is quite considerable.

The *Moro expósito*, something of a *tour de force* in its *genre*, had been successful in drawing attention to the possibilities of narrative verse, and also in inaugurating a long series of poems which were essentially narrative. Once revived, the historical verse narrative naturally had a long period of popularity : it was deeply rooted in Spanish history; it had always been independent of Classical precept ; and it was therefore peculiarly suited to the Romantic Spanish genius. But the stanza in which the *Moro expósito* was written did nothing to encourage either a general flexibility in versification or the revival of the mediaeval *romance*. This latter aim Rivas advocated in his *Romances históricos*, five of which he published with it and the remainder in the collection bearing that title (1841). At the time he published this, it seemed to him that the *romance* had made little progress in popularity.[1] But, looking back to-day, we can see that it was steadily re-establishing itself. Numerous versifiers, Romantic and anti-Romantic, good and bad, began to include *romances* among their published works, and reviews of all shades of literary opinion printed them. The best-known stories from Spanish history were retold in this form and a few writers even brought out Romanceros dealing with contemporary happenings.

Before 1840, the output of narrative verse was somewhat disappointing, though it showed signs of the far-reaching character of the Revival. Three notable contributions to it, of quite different types, were the Duque de Frías' "leyenda dramática," " Don Juan de Lanuza, Justicia de Aragón "

---

[1] Rivas : *Obras completas*, Madrid, 1894-1904, IV, xiii, xiv.

(1837), Ochoa's *Tesoro de los romanceros y cancioneros españoles* (1838) and Espronceda's *El Estudiante de Salamanca* (1839). Of the last and most important of these something should be said.

In the *Estudiante* Espronceda impresses the stamp of his personality upon the Don Juan legend. Drawing upon various sources, he treats them in a most individual and effective way : of all the works of the period it is perhaps this which strikes the present-day reader as being the most " modern."

Briefly, Espronceda's method consists in presenting his characters and scenes with the utmost vividness against a background vaguely suggestive and sinister. There is less art in the foreground figures than in the shadows, but the main effect depends upon contrast and variety, found again in the alternation of lyric passages with narrative. Here and there, again, are passages set in dramatic form—a procedure indulged in also by Zorrilla, though a little unconventional for the older and more sedate Rivas. Without going so far as to intercalate snatches of dialogue in his narrative, as Zorrilla did, and content to dramatize one section of his poem, he achieves the same result—the lightening of the weight of narrative—with the greatest facility.

In form, as in content, Espronceda attains the maximum of variety, by means of those experiments in metre which he had been pursuing for some years. In his seventeen hundred lines he uses no fewer than twenty-four measures, nine of which conform to no familiar type. Nor are these measures scattered at haphazard through the poem. Nearly three hundred lines are arranged so as to rise gradually, from a quiet two-and-three-syllable metre, to a majestic climax, conveyed in slow dodecasyllabic quatrains, and corresponding to a climax in the narrative, descending thence, equally gradually and no less effectively, through a series of six groups of *octavillas*, until, at what is virtually the conclusion of the poem, they die away in the familiar

> leve
> breve
> son.

So carefully planned and precisely arranged a metrical scheme might almost be thought of as Classical and superficially it contains no suggestion of revolt. But, historically considered, Espronceda's metrical experiments were of a Romantic type. For generations all but a few verse-combinations had been taboo : of the rest he rescued and rehabilitated a large number, inventing others to set beside them and breaking with the past by arranging his innovations and restorations in a complicated pattern—but in one of his invention and free choice.

In narrative as in lyric poetry, the year 1840 was marked by a great outburst of production. There were Maury's lengthy *Esvero y Almedora*, only a few stanzas of which, on literary theory, have escaped oblivion ; Navarro Villoslada's *Luchana*, a brief " ensayo épico " on the Carlist War ; Mora's *Leyendas españolas*, which, despite its Eclectic preface, at first glance looks wholly Romantic, but which is marred by florid, prosaic language and by a lack of imagination and of a sense of the picturesque ; and the *María* of Miguel de los Santos Álvarez, in which we can detect the influence of the personality of the author's intimate friend Espronceda, with whom, temperamentally, he had a good deal in common.

Espronceda, in his *Diablo Mundo* (1841), still unfinished when he died in the year following, gives the rein both to his intellect and to his emotions, allows himself to be swayed by the influence of Byron, and launches out into a style which, in its total extent, is entirely new. But the poem is in hardly any respect the equal of the *Estudiante de Salamanca*. It repeats some of its devices but lacks its vividness of presentation and its power of pictorial appeal. True, the author introduces himself now, not as an artist, but as a thinker ; but here, too, he fails, for he has no coherent philosophy and few original ideas. The poem has bold and successful tone-contrasts, grandiose tableaux, fine lyric interludes and purple patches of all kinds—lyric, descriptive and narrative. But its defects are even more obvious than its merits : the submersion of argument by pure verbiage ; the dullness of its digressions ; the carelessness of its phraseology ; and the crudenesses, buffooneries and cynicisms from which it is never for long free.

A better book than this was Rivas' *Romances históricos* (1841), an important preface to which eulogizes mediaeval verse narrative and the octosyllabic measure associated with it. Chronologically, if not geographically, the field from which Rivas drew his subjects was a wide one. Mediaeval kings, such as Peter the Cruel and John II, are presented side by side with the Catholic Monarchs, Charles V and Philip II ; yet incidents are described, such as the battle of Bailén, which belong almost to contemporary history. All the narratives have that double inspiration, so typically Rivas', of patriotism and religious idealism. Their attractiveness is enhanced by their artistic qualities : a skilful use of colour, of light-images, of Spanish (especially of Andalusian) landscapes, to say nothing of bold "Romantic" flights into the horrible and the grotesque.

In most of these achievements Rivas was surpassed by Zorrilla, famous for his verse " legends " and his popularization of the Middle Ages. His massive output includes the three-volume *Cantos del Trovador* (1840-1), the three long poems comprising *Vigilias del estío* (1842), the lyrico-narrative *Recuerdos y fantasías* (1844), a number of *leyendas*, such as *La Azucena silvestre* (1845), and the unfinished poem *Granada* (1852). The incoherent form of the *leyenda* suited his temperament well. Of undefined length, it allows unlimited digressions and may be rhymed or assonanced at will. It can use widely divergent metres, and thus, besides avoiding monotony, can register frequent changes of emotional tone. Other of its common devices are the repetition of words and phrases, the use of colloquial asides to the reader, and the alternation of reflective passages with narrative. More typical still is Zorrilla's favourite device of calling in Nature as a background for his narrative, which sometimes, though by no means always, he does well.

If we accept the superficiality of his narrative poems, we shall give them little but praise. Their worst fault is diffuseness—the defect of one of Zorrilla's great qualities : the consummate ease with which he wrote and can be read.

Every reader will admire their magnificently loaded descriptions, their soaring images, their striking scenes and figures. They fall relatively seldom into Romantic exaggerations : their language, for example, compares favourably with that of the drama of the same period. Their twofold inspiration—religion and patriotism—gives them at once unity and power.

The long but unfinished *Granada* (1852) has all the qualities of Zorrilla's other poetry—the religious and patriotic *motifs*, the wealth of imagery, the great metrical variety, the passion for the picturesque—together with a definite object : the same desire to extol Moorish civilization in Spain which so much influenced Rivas' *Moro expósito*. For once Zorrilla took some care with his sources, drawing on mediaeval and modern historians as well as on his imagination. At the same time he contrived to avoid giving any impression of erudition and the poem contains some of his best lyric passages.

The remaining narrative poems of the period may, with one exception, be passed over briefly. Hartzenbusch's *Romancero pintoresco, o Colección de nuestros mejores romances antiguos* (1848) is undistinguished. Romero Larrañaga, in his verse *Historias caballerescas españolas* (1843), traversed Spanish history from the eleventh century to the sixteenth : at its best, his style is indistinguishable from Rivas' ; at its worst, it is surprisingly prosaic. Bofarull's *Hazañas y recuerdos de los Catalanes* (1846) reveals a poetic mind, a dramatic sense, a talent for selection and a quick perception of the picturesque. Ribot y Fontseré's *Solimán y Zaida* (1849) is a "leyenda árabe" comparable in length with the *Moro expósito*.

Rivas' three *Leyendas* (1854)[1], easily the best work in this group, have a historical background, though it is the imaginative element in them that chiefly attracts the attention. "La Azucena milagrosa" is psychologically as impossible as a fairy tale, and its charms are those of colour, grace and wealth of fancy. "Maldonado" has a descriptive power which Rivas had rarely attained in his younger days

---

[1] The first two of the poems in this collection had appeared in 1847 and 1852 respectively. All three were published in book form in 1854.

and which he never again equalled. " El Aniversario "—
the weakest of the three—is in parts somewhat grotesque but
its occasional touches of eloquence give it a certain distinction. These poems, though both in their merits and their
defects highly Romantic, not only belong to the Romantic
revival of the past, but in some respects foreshadow the new
romanticism of the future.

Before leaving this period we must refer briefly to the
growth, during its course, of Romantic freedom in versification. Little progress, if any, was made beyond the point
reached by Espronceda in *El Estudiante de Salamanca*. But, on
the other hand, there was little retrogression. The metrical
freedom claimed by the Romantics persisted long after the
failure of the self-conscious Romantic movement : only a
few typical works need be cited in illustration.

While the extremer manifestations of the revolt in poetic
form found little favour anywhere, the younger generation
fully approved its main trend. Rivas' preface to his *Romances
históricos*, which a few years earlier would have been attacked
for its audacity, appears to have been considered quite
orthodox. The *romance*, "el metro castizo de nuestra lengua," [1]
says Rivas, is the natural metre for Spaniards to use in verse
narrative. But it may be varied with " rhythmical com-
binations and metres taken from other languages," some of
which—the *octava*, the tercet, the sonnet, etc.—are discussed
in detail. [2]   Rivas' *Leyendas* show a still greater metrical
variety.   " La Azucena milagrosa " was suggested by
Zorrilla's *leyenda religiosa*, " La Azucena silvestre," part of
which is modelled on the " escala métrica " (the name is
Zorrilla's) which we find in the *Estudiante de Salamanca*. [3]
Rivas' poem also recalls, though it hardly rivals, Espronceda's.
Its " introduction " is composed wholly of *octavas reales*. The
first part of the poem proper mingles *romances* with a number
of other measures ;   the second, after beginning with
hendecasyllables recalling those of the *Moro expósito*, goes

---

[1] Rivas : *Obras completas*, Madrid, 1894-1904, IV, xxviii.

[2] *Op. cit.*, IV, xviii-xix.   [3] Cf. p. 176, above.

into *octavillas*. By this time such variations of metre were common enough to excite no comment.

Zorrilla's metrical habits differ little from those of Rivas and Espronceda. His very earliest poems—" El Reloj," " A una mujer," " Elvira," " La noche inquieta," etc.— exemplify the freedom which, when he began to write, had no longer to be fought for. The " escala métrica " occurs in several places. In " Un Testigo de bronce " it descends from fourteen syllables to one, and, after a brief narrative interlude, rises again from one syllable to fourteen. In a somewhat longer passage of " La Azucena silvestre," a slow descent, contained within exactly the same limits, is followed by a shorter and steeper rise. In the " Leyenda de Al-Hamar," which forms part of *Granada*, the *diminuendo* and *crescendo* passages each occupy a similarly named " chapter " of a separate " book."

Arolas, Bermúdez de Castro and a number of minor poets will yield further examples of metrical variety, but not until the end of the century was any important advance made on the position represented by Espronceda, Rivas and Zorrilla, and for the full-scale revolution in versification of which even Rubén Darío was only the precursor, we must look to the century following, very far beyond the limits of this History.

CHAPTER VII

THE NATURE OF SPANISH ROMANTICISM[1]

I. RETROSPECT[2]

We have now traced the course of the Romantic movement in Spain from the point, far back in the eighteenth century, where it can first be recognized. We have surveyed the history of each of the two tendencies which grew into the Romantic movement. We have seen how political and social causes delayed the fruition of this movement, and how, when this fruition came, it was short in time, limited in extent and accompanied by sharp opposition. Next, we have traced the early and gradual rise of nineteenth-century eclecticism, described its rather sudden accession to favour about 1836-7 and followed its successful career as far as the year 1860, at which time romanticism, though continuing in some of its aspects to influence literature, was, considered as a movement, quite dead. Since romanticism has never been succeeded by any antithetically reactionary movement, but has remained as a clearly marked tendency in Spanish literature down to this day, we shall glance, in a final chapter, at the influence of this apparently ineffective movement on the later course of Spanish literature, and show that, while it failed to dominate Spain, it successfully permeated every literary *genre* to varying degrees of completeness.

But before this final survey is attempted one further examination of the first half of the nineteenth century has to be made. Many of the numerous definitions of romanticism current at that time have been reviewed—some emanating from its defenders, some from its opponents and some from neutral critics—and in judging the nature of romanticism in Spain more emphasis has been laid on the theories of these

---

[1] *H.R.M.S.*, II, 259-328. [2] *H.R.M.S.*, II, 259-60.

groups of writers than on the practice of those who were primarily creators. We shall now turn to the creators and attempt to describe the nature of the contribution which they made to Spanish literature, and thus to define Spanish romanticism as seen in their original work.

II. Primary Characteristics of Spanish Romanticism[1]

(i) Freedom

Before anything else, the writings of the Spanish Romantics stand for freedom. This is as true of the Revival as of the Revolt. The revivalists claimed the right to return to the Middle Ages and the Golden Age and to make what use they pleased of anything they found there. The revolutionaries claimed the right to go anywhere in search of inspiration and method, or alternatively to invent their own methods and occupy themselves with their own emotions. The ideal of freedom is the only single ideal which can be found beneath all the varied conceptions of romanticism held by the groups and individuals already detailed.

A particular manifestation of the ideal is the domination of Romantic literature by the theme of passion. This was one of the earliest elements of romanticism to appear in the eighteenth century, though at first it was almost imperceptible. There are suggestions of it in Cadalso, Cienfuegos and Meléndez Valdés, and very much more markedly in the plays translated into Spanish from Alfieri. By the time we come to Larra and Espronceda, it is everywhere. For a short period, not only the literary *genres*, but even newspaper articles, threw off restraint and revealed the secrets of the author's heart. Never previously had the Spanish press published anything like the last articles of Fígaro : it has published little approaching them since. The Romantics' feeble attempts at historical prose fiction contain such barely disguised life-stories as those of Larra's *Doncel de Don Enrique el Doliente* and Vayo's *Voyleano, o La Exaltación de las pasiones.*

---

[1] *H.R.M.S.*, II, 261-281.

As to drama, passion strides through *Don Álvaro* and *Don Juan Tenorio*, rants and raves in *Macías* and *El Paje*, sobs its protestations in *Los Amantes de Teruel*, declaims against the existing order in *El Trovador*, revolts the spectator in *Carlos II el Hechizado*, and, despite the excellence of the author's intentions, amuses him in *Fray Luis de León*.

But the supreme expression of this manifestation of freedom in Spanish Romantic literature is Espronceda's " Canto a Teresa," that " desahogo de mi corazón " which—" sin ton ni son "—he interpolates in *El Diablo Mundo* as its second canto. For all its power, it does violence alike to the canons of art and of decency—especially of decency. For, whatever we may think of the insertion into a narrative poem of a completely irrelevant and subjective digression, there can only be one opinion on the propriety of exposing the details of a broken liaison with a woman no longer able to defend herself and in the lifetime of her children.

Yet that is what Espronceda, abandoned to his passions, can bring himself to do. Each act of the drama is staged in turn : the idyllic love-scenes, the bitterness of growing discontent, the fall, the desertion and the final disillusion. Without reticence or shame, the poet not only unlocks his heart, but flings the fragments of it before us :

> Yo escondo con vergüenza mi quebranto,
> mi propia pena con mi risa insulto,
> y me divierto en arrancar del pecho
> mi mismo corazón pedazos hecho.[1]

Here, surely, is the very height—or depth—of romanticism.

(ii) *Patriotism, Christianity, Mediaevalism*

Next to this basic idea of freedom come three qualities which stand out in the Spanish movement from among all others : patriotism, Christianity and mediaevalism. The first, though highly characteristic of romanticism in Spain, is not necessarily a Romantic quality. The second, outside Spain, is generally associated with romanticism, but in Spain

---

[1] *Diablo Mundo*, Canto II.

it is typical of every literary period, though particularly so of the early nineteenth century. The third is a concomitant of romanticism all over Western Europe. These three qualities, then, are of somewhat unequal significance.

At first sight, it seems curious that an outstanding feature of romanticism in Spain should be one in no sense exclusively Romantic. Indeed, romanticism is less often patriotic and national than multi-national and cosmopolitan. Feeling the need for self-expansion, it sets about broadening its own experience. Feeling the need for enlarging the domain of poetic content, it seeks new subjects in the history, literatures and cultures of all parts of the world.

Such needs, felt by Romantic authors in Spain, as elsewhere, were satisfied to some extent by the use which they made of Byron, Scott and Ossian, and also by the importation of an orientalism which they felt to be both highly poetic in itself and closely in tune with the spirit of the Romantic revival.[1] But it must be remembered that orientalism was less of an exotic concept for Spain than for England, France or Germany, and that many of the Spanish Romantics preferred to seek it by invoking the years of Moorish rule in Spain. There was little cosmopolitanism, then, in Spanish romanticism because Spain was so rich in Romantic themes as to make journeys abroad in search of them unnecessary. Zorrilla called it a " petty and ridiculous " practice for a Spaniard to " seek for heroes in distant lands to the detriment of those of his own country."[2] Most of his countrymen, it would seem, agreed with him.

There were, of course, special reasons why the whole of nineteenth-century literature in Spain should be nationalistic. The anti-Gallic reaction which would in any case have followed the dominance of France over Spain under the early Bourbons was intensified by the Napoleonic invasion, so that patriotism in Spanish literature since 1700 is by no means confined to the Romantics. After the War of Independence, the die-hard Classicists opposed Romantic innovations on

---

[1] Cf. Ribot y Fontseré's introduction to Arolas' *Poesías*, Barcelona, 1842, p. ix, and to Ribot's own *Solimán y Zaida*, Madrid, 1849, pp. x-xii.

[2] The whole passage is quoted in *H.R.M.S.*, II, 204-5.

the score of patriotism, using the influence of French
Romantic drama as a stick for the chastisement of their
opponents, though omitting to apply it to those responsible
during the eighteenth century for the grosser subjection of
Spanish drama to French. The Eclectics took much the
same line—there was no greater gallophobe in this period
than Mesonero Romanos—and the *costumbrista* movement,
which they sponsored, was as much inspired by patriotism
as the Romantic revival.

Yet, viewed as a whole, the Romantic movement is more
closely associated with patriotism than is either neo-classicism
or eclecticism. Research has now fully established the
essentially native character of both the Revival and the
Revolt. The *llamarada* of 1835-7 may have owed much of its
luminosity to Hugo and Dumas, but the Spanish Romantics
never drew on the French with anything approaching the
servility of the Spanish neo-Classicists. And if Byron and
Scott influenced Spanish literature more than did any
Spanish writer it was the spirit of Byron's work that conveyed
this influence rather than any one or more of his poems, while
nothing is more notable in the history of the vogue of Scott
than the attempts made by his admirers to transfer him to a
Spanish *milieu*.

Deeply as foreign influence may have entered the Spanish
Romantic movement, patriotism entered it more deeply still.
It was no chance that the three most typical Spanish Romantics should have been intense patriots. Espronceda began his
poetical career with an " ensayo épico " eulogizing the
Reconquest ; from London he bewailed his country's fall
from greatness ;[1] and the deaths of Torrijos and De Pablo
drew from him patriotic poems of considerable power.[2]
Rivas, mourned after his death as the " truest incarnation of
our national spirit,"[3] infuses love for his country into all
his writings. His early poems reflect his patriotic sentiments
during the War of Independence, and in his early play,

[1] " A la patria," a poem dated " London, 1829."

[2] " A la muerte de Torrijos y sus compañeros " ; " A la muerte de Don
Joaquín De Pablo."

[3] *Museo universal*, 1865, IX, 210.

Lanuza, longings for his country's emancipation from tyranny are but thinly veiled. In the *Romances históricos* he gives Spain a portrait-gallery of Spanish history and a text-book of patriotism. Zorrilla is more distinguished even than Rivas as a re-creator of Spanish legend and tradition and a patriotic dramatist. Almost all his narrative poems and dramas have Spanish settings : even in *Sofronia,*[1] where he went for his theme to Rome, he adapted his material in deference to the prejudices of modern Spain. And, not content with indirect eulogy of his country in narrative poems and plays, he continually panegyrizes it in lyric and in prose, declaring his unchangeable devotion to Altar and Throne.

> He tenido presentes dos cosas : la patria en que nací y la religión en que vivo. Español, he buscado en nuestro suelo mis inspiraciones. Cristiano, he creído que mi religión encierra más poesía que el paganismo . . . . [2]

Outside Spain, nineteenth-century romanticism has generally been associated, to a greater or a lesser degree, with the " rehabilitation," or re-introduction into literature, of Christianity. This implies that classicism expelled Christianity from literature, as, for example, it did in France while that country was under the sway of Boileau. There is this amount of truth in the implication : that, since the Classicists' love of perfect form has led neo-Classicists to literatures where perfection of form has been greatest, and since preeminent among these have been the pagan literatures of Greece and Rome, classicism and paganism have become closely connected.

Spain, however, had never withdrawn any of its allegiance from Christianity. Even Luzán refuted Boileau's objections to the Christian epic, and very few Spanish poets, even in the eighteenth century, left religion out of their works entirely. Both the Salamancan and the Sevilian schools were quite orthodox and would have scouted any suggestion that they were pagan. Lista, to take but one example, described Boileau's prohibition of Christian themes in literature as

---

[1] See the " Notas del autor " to this play.
[2] Quoted more fully in *H.R.M.S.,* II, 204-5.

inspired by a " malign genius " and eulogized the "sublime" Milton and the " admirable" Chateaubriand for the use which they made of such themes.[1]

Once Spanish literature felt the stirrings of freedom, it cast off altogether what it considered the incubus of pagan mythology and returned exclusively to Catholic Christianity. Some of the Romantics thought this attitude would be permanent. "El romanticismo había echado de nuestra poesía popular a las divinidades mitológicas," wrote Zorrilla in 1882, " y . . . no volverán a tener altares ni templos en la tierra católica."[2]

Christianity, in the writings of the Spanish Romantics, bears little relation to picturesque religiosity of the kind popularized by Chateaubriand : it is found in a few of Chateaubriand's admirers—e.g., López Soler, Arolas and Boix—but soon passes away. Still less had Spanish romanticism to do with religion of the mystical type. Santa Teresa and San Juan de la Cruz were not rehabilitated, like Lope, Tirso and Calderón.   When Ochoa assigned one of his " Thesauri " to " Spanish mystical writers,"[3] he paid ascetic writers and the ascetic output of the mystical writers disproportionate attention.   The form taken by religion in Romantic Spain is rather a convinced, and at times somewhat florid, institutionalism, of which not the least important characteristics were pomp, picturesqueness and human appeal.   This was quite natural, for nowhere in Europe was institutionalism more dominant than in Spain during those two epochs to which it was the Romantics' delight to return.   So, in a special sense, the Romantics led Spanish literature back to its *madrina*, the Catholic Church, and, besides standing foursquare by the Faith, they made full use of ceremonial, imagery, history and legend to enhance the Church's glories.

Mediaevalism, though not necessarily a concomitant of romanticism, characterized the Romantic movement

[1] *Ensayos literarios y críticos*, Seville, 1844, I, 23-6, 28, 169.
[2] *Recuerdos del tiempo viejo*, Barcelona-Madrid, 1880-2, II, 33.
[3] *Tesoro de escritores místicos españoles*, Paris, 1847, 3 vols.

throughout Western Europe. It could not be said of Spain, as Heine said of Germany, that her Romantic movement " was nothing else than a revival of the poetry of the Middle Ages."[1] But to many early observers something like that seemed to be true, and, as we have seen, many early definitions of romanticism were definitions of mediaevalism, and nothing more. It may be added that the mediaevalism of the Romantic movement in Spain is closely connected with its patriotism and its Christianity. It was in the Middle Ages,

> aquellos tiempos
> en que los hombres de bien
> sólo pensaban en Dios,
> en su dama y en su rey,[2]

that Throne and Altar were most generally and deeply reverenced, and a modern writer, taking a bird's-eye view of the past, would naturally consider the three ideas as inseparable.

III. Secondary Characteristics of Spanish Romanticism[3]

(i) *Subjectivity*

Subjectivity, generally speaking, is less characteristic of Romantic literature in Spain than in other countries. Apart from one or two pronounced individualists, the greatest of whom was Espronceda, the major Spanish Romantics got on quite well with the world and took much less interest in the " satánico yo " than might have been expected. The chief reason for this may have been the predominance in Spain of the Revival, which on the whole was an objective movement, over the Revolt, which tended to subjectivity. Such interests as Scott's novels, the old Spanish ballads, mediaeval history

---

[1] Heine : *Die romantische Schule*, Paris, 1835 (*Sämmtliche Werke*, Hamburg, 1874, VI, 18).

[2] M. A. Príncipe : *Poesías*, Madrid, 1840, II, 161-7. " La Edad media."

[3] *H.R.M.S.*, II, 281-328.

and Golden Age drama all led the Romantics away from any temptation to introspection. Political and social happenings were no less unstable and depressing in Spain than in France or Italy, where the large part played by subjectivity in the literature of the same epoch is commonly attributed to the effect of contemporary events on literature. But in Spain the force of the Romantic revival provided a powerful constructive counter-influence, in which writers who might otherwise have become completely self-centred and correspondingly disillusioned found new inspiration. This is particularly true of Catalonia, where the revived interest in the Middle Ages was accompanied by what, as far as literature is concerned, may be described as the re-discovery of a forgotten native language : the double constructive ideal is stronger than the depressing influence of political disintegration and the age becomes one of highly positive and largely objective literary achievement.

It has been remarked that the abundance of memoirs in this period is suggestive of an age of subjectivity ; but in fact hardly any of the authors of these memoirs were Romantics at all. Alcalá Galiano was a lukewarm and temporary half-convert to romanticism ; Mesonero Romanos, Bretón de los Herreros and Fernán Caballero were Eclectics ; Valera, Chaves and Campillo were later in date than these, and, though not unsympathetic with the Romantic movement, were little more than spectators of its decadence. Further, the memoirs even of the earlier authors appeared long after the movement was over. Alcalá Galiano's *Recuerdos de un anciano* came out in 1878 ; Mesonero Romanos' *Memorias de un setentón* in 1880 ; and Zorrilla's *Recuerdos del tiempo viejo* in 1880-2. But in any case, abundance of memoirs in an age is no proof of the individualism of that age, for memoirs can on occasion be as objective as dramas. Far more of the author's personality may be found in Larra's drama *Macías*, or in Espronceda's narrative poem *El Diablo Mundo*, than in even such substantial memoirs as those of Mesonero Romanos.

There are, nevertheless, some interesting elements in Spanish romanticism indirectly connected with its subjective

aspect. These are the affectations and individual idio-
syncrasies some of which—those of dress, manner, speech
and literary terminology—have already been referred to.[1]
The principal affectation to be found in the Romantics'
thought—if such a word can be used of them—was the idea
that the poet is charged with some kind of " mission," which
makes him a lonely soul and sets on him a seal of apostleship
visible to the whole world. Such sentiments had been
expressed by a French poet, Alfred de Vigny, in lines of such
dignity and beauty as could come only from a writer to
whom they were real : with the Spanish Romantics, on the
other hand, they were at the best only the result of an
ephemeral mood, and at the worst a mere conventional pose.
Their best remembered expression is probably the poem
recited by the youthful Zorrilla at Larra's grave. Its under-
lying theme is that the unfortunate suicide had " ended his
mission upon earth," withering thereupon in the heat of
summer like a plant scorched by the sun :

> Que el poeta en su misión
> sobre la tierra que habita
> es una planta maldita
> con frutos de bendición.[2]

There was much more of this in the poem and it was echoed
by many others—Ribot y Fontseré, Enrique Gil and Miguel
Agustín Príncipe, for example[3]—though the Eclectics, and
even the saner of the Romantics—Lista, Vega, Vera e Isla
and many more—attacked, and sometimes ridiculed, the
affectation.[4] Among the latter was the sophisticated and
unsentimental Duque de Rivas. " I made no attempt," he
declared, " to fulfil any *lofty poetical mission*, by giving lessons
to the world and improving society.[5] On the whole, he was
followed by more Romantics than was the young Zorrilla.

---

[1] Cf. p. 104, above.
[2] Zorrilla : *Obras dramáticas y líricas*, Madrid, 1895, I, 15.
[3] Cf. *H.R.M.S.*, II, 283-5.
[4] Cf. *H.R.M.S.*, II, 285-7.
[5] From the preface to *Solaces de un prisionero* (*Obras completas*, Madrid, 1894-
1904, VII, 8). The italics are in the original.

(ii) *Sentimentality and lachrymosity*

Sentimentality played a large part, both in this conception of the poet's " mission " and in a number of other
characteristics of Spanish romanticism which we shall now
survey—various forms of lachrymosity, sensibility, humanitarianism, vague idealization, all of which were scoffed at by
the anti-Romantics as affectations.

The lachrymose elements in the Romantic *ensemble* have
been traced back to Jovellanos, but no major writer in the
early nineteenth century can compete with him in this form
of sentimentality.   The wanderings of the *emigrados* are
recorded by them in tones of stoical resignation.   Nor was
sentimental literature from abroad popular in Spain during
the Romantic movement.   Kotzebue's vogue was brief and
belongs entirely to the pre-Romantic period.   Richardson
had only the smallest following.   Chateaubriand appears to
have owed his popularity to qualities quite other than the
emotionalism of his novels.   The *comédie larmoyante* had little
vogue in Spain, and the sentimental French melodramas
that were translated there hardly belong to literature.
Further, such sentimentality as can be found in this
period diminishes rapidly as it proceeds.

No doubt the humanitarianism which spread all over
Europe in the eighteenth and nineteenth centuries served as
an occasional outlet for the sentimentality of Romantics—
and of others.   It can be found in Quintana and Blanco
White, and later in Cabanyes ;   and it was upheld as a
justification of Romantic art by some who disliked that art
in other of its manifestations.

But the most characteristic form taken by sentimentality
in the Romantic, and even in the post-Romantic, period is
the idealization of various types of character not in themselves attractive.   Apart from the " Romantic hero " type, of
which we have already studied some examples, these figures
are divisible into two main classes.   The first class includes
the rebel, the criminal, the pirate, the bandit, the adventurer,
the outlaw ;   the second comprises the beggar, the foundling,

the suppliant, the pilgrim, the hermit, the captive, the orphan, the oppressed, the suicide. The figures in the first class attracted the Romantics by their boldness—by the striking way in which they stood out against a drab background. Those in the second class had the appeal of pathos, harmonizing with the sentimentality and melancholy which we find in all nineteenth-century romanticism, of whatever nation.

Both these classes, familiar to readers of Goethe, Schiller, Byron, Hugo and Manzoni—to name only a few representative authors—occur most frequently in that most typical of Romantics, Espronceda. To the one class belong the fearless pirate captain, " King of the ocean " ; the Cossack warrior of the desert shouting those lusty hurras that were echoed by the youth of Spain ; the typically Esproncedan beggar, who must go into the earlier class rather than into the later by virtue of his ownership of the wide world. In the other class are the captive girl—an orphan to boot and awaiting death —the criminal in the condemned cell and the miserable executioner, an outcast from society, a criminal who has committed no crime. And to these well defined types may be added several others only lightly sketched or merely suggested.

The first of the groups is rather the less populated of the two and the less highly idealized. Arolas has a pirate not unlike Espronceda's, but lays his main emphasis on the exotic aspect of his activities—on the booty brought from Tyre and Sidon, Cyprus, Damascus and Brazil and six beauties who had been destined for an Egyptian harem. Arolas also has a Cossack, who proves to be a lyrical transposition of the Romantic hero.[1]

The adventurer, whether or no disguised as a Romantic hero, is less commonly found in lyric poetry than in drama. The best known figure in this group is perhaps the Robin Hood type of noble bandit (often also an outlaw) as we see him in Schiller's *Räuber* and Byron's *Corsair*, who made his re-entry into Spain (for he was familiar to the Golden Age)

---

[1] " El Pirata " and " El Cosaco," in *Poesías caballerescas y orientales*, Valencia, 1843, pp. 233-8, 266-70.

by way of the novels of Scott and frequently occurs in the Romantic novel. Representative examples are : in the novel, the hero of López Soler's *Jaime el Barbudo* ; in drama, Rejón, the great-hearted bandit chief in Bretón's *Elena* ; and in narrative verse, the wealthy, daring, liberal, magnanimous Don César in Zorrilla's " El Desafío del diablo."

The idealized criminal, especially the criminal condemned to death, best known as a type through Espronceda's poem mentioned above, a translation by García de Villalta from Victor Hugo[1] and Larra's realistic article " Un reo de muerte," forms a *liaison* between the first group and the second. Occasionally emphasis is laid upon the criminal's courage, and the daring of his past life, which latter is contrasted, in true Romantic style, with the condition in which he now finds himself. But more commonly the pathetic aspect of the criminal's situation is invoked, in order to excite our sympathy.

> Triste canta el prisionero
> encerrado en su prisión,
> y a sus lamentos responde
> su cadena en triste son.[2]

Boix, who tended to become a literary hypochondriac, drew a criminal of this type in " El Prisionero."[3] Bonilla, his friend and colleague, begins with a model murderer :

> Un arco gótico parte
> la bóveda corva en dos,
> y junto al altar, contrito,
> hay un reo en oración.[4]

but soon passes from the picturesque to the horrible, alternating these notes until the very moment of the criminal's execution.

An interesting variant upon this type is González Elipe's penitent rake, who, like Rivas' Don Álvaro, turns to the religious life.[5] Another is Arolas' parricide, treated somewhat

---

[1] Cf. *H.R.M.S.*, I, 234, 319.
[2] Zorrilla : " Canción " (*Poesías*, Madrid, 1837-40, IV, 220-1).
[3] *Obras poéticas, etc.*, Valencia, 1850, pp. 49-50.
[4] " Un reo en capilla " (*Poesías*, Valencia, 1840, pp. 49-53).
[5] " El monje " : dated 1837 (*Poesías*, Madrid, 1842, pp. 83-8).

floridly in a poem partly dialogue, partly lyric, where all the emphasis is laid upon his remorse.[1]

The Romantics had a strange love of sentimentalizing not only upon the condemned criminal but also upon his executioner. The usual conception of this personage was that of a man whose terrible profession made him a social outcast—a theme on which Espronceda extemporizes with variations typical of his character and genius.[2] But concentration on this trait did not exclude the presentation of gruesome and morbid scenes in which a minority of the Romantics delighted. Morbidity also found ample scope in the presentation of the suicide—sometimes a bold, bad man with sardonic laughter on his lips, sometimes a down-and-out, who begs his Maker to slay him ere he slay himself.[3] Tapia's " El Suicidio " is a conventional piece staged on the banks of the " nebloso (sic) Támesis " and phrased in Romantic language.[4] Agustín de Alfaro contributed to the Semanario pintoresco español one hundred and sixty lines embodying a prospective suicide's ravings on love, Nature and the hereafter ; these duly declaimed, the prospective suicide changes his intention, decides to live on and implores his mother's pardon for causing her pain.[5]

The beggar, a type very attractive to Spaniards, and freely sentimentalized by Hugo, Béranger and other French Romantics, finds an early idealizer in Meléndez Valdés[6] and a distinguished one in Espronceda.[7] The latter's beggar, however, is a sturdy individual, own brother to the Cossack and the Pirate, who excites, not pity, but envy :

> Mío es el mundo : como el aire libre,
> otros trabajan porque coma yo :
> todos se ablandan si doliente pido
> una limosna por amor de Dios.

---

[1] " Los remordimientos de un parricida " (Poesías, Barcelona, 1842, p. 276).

[2] " El Verdugo." [3] Cf. H.R.M.S., II, 296.

[4] Poesías, Madrid, 1832, I, 48-53.

[5] Semanario pintoresco español, 1839, 2ª Serie, I, 392.

[6] Discursos forenses, Madrid, 1821, pp. 273-310.

[7] " El Mendigo," first published in the Revista española, September 6, 1835.

More in keeping with the conception of the beggar then
current in Spain is a somewhat maudlin poem by the
Catalan Juan Antonio Pagés, with a burden characteristic
of its author :

> Yo te lloro porque lloras,
> porque es tan triste el llorar.[1]

and the unhappy child and the starving mother in a poem of
much the same nature, " La niña desgraciada."[2]   It is
perhaps surprising that this type, so common in real life in
Spain, is not found more frequently in the literature of
Spanish romanticism.   But there are numbers of closely
allied types, such as the slave, the captive, the foundling and
the orphan—the last two freely imported, through translations of Bouchardy and Sue, from France.[3]   A foundling is
the hero of the *Moro expósito* ; the type also figures in the
Artista[4] and is the subject of sentimental rhapsodies by Boix[5]
and Arolas.[6]   The orphan—generally female, for greater
pathos—is still commoner.   Francisco Morera y Valls twice
plays upon the theme of orphandom.[7]   García Gutiérrez
broods upon it and treats it in drama.[8]   Salvador Bermúdez
de Castro idealizes the type :

> El huérfano infeliz su suerte llora
> de fe y de amor el pensamiento lleno.[9]

Ros de Olano utilizes the pathos latent in the theme for a
poem in his " Doloridas "[10] Bonilla is mainly lachrymose,

---

[1] " A un mendigo." *Poesías, etc.*, Barcelona, 1852, pp. 377-82.

[2] *Op. cit.*, pp. 349-51.

[3] Cf. *H.R.M.S.*, II, 298, n. 1.

[4] F. Grandallana : " El Expósito." *El Artista*, 1835, II, 269-71.

[5] " El niño dormido en el bosque." *Obras poéticas, etc.*, Valencia, 1851,
pp. 101-3.

[6] " El Expósito." *Poesías caballerescas y orientales*, Valencia, 1840, pp. 285-8.

[7] " El Huérfano." *Cantos poéticos*, Barcelona, 1851, pp. 101-7. " A su
madre." *Op. cit.*, pp. 143-9.

[8] Cf. A. Ferrer del Río : *Galería de la literatura española*, Madrid, 1846,
pp. 258-9.

[9] *Ensayos poéticos*, Madrid, 1840, p. 231.

[10] *Poesías*, Madrid, 1886, pp. 101-3.

though one of his orphans has the additional attraction of mystery :

> Una sombra maldita
> ya persigue mi hermosura.[1]

While Arolas, in the course of a long and sugary apostrophe, actually represents the portrayal of the orphan-girl as part of the poet's " mission."[2] The best picture of the slave is Juan Antonio Sazatornil's " El esclavo griego a sus compañeros," perhaps based on Espronceda's " Despedida del patriota griego."[3] Various Romantic authors portray the captive—notably Espronceda, in his *canción* " La Cautiva," Arolas, in one of his "Oriental" poems[4] and Enrique Gil, who uses the theme in an attractive picture of night.[5]

Perhaps the commonest single type of all is the troubadour, who has a longer life than most, invades every *genre* and displays numerous minor variations, though little variety. In drama, the classical example of the type is the hero of García Gutiérrez's *El Trovador*,[6] while numerous similar characters, such as the pilgrim-troubadour of Pacheco's *Alfredo*,[7] play secondary parts in other plays. In narrative poetry of the *leyenda* type the troubadour is a particular favourite with Zorrilla :

> Yo soy el Trovador que vaga errante ;
> si son de vuestro parque estos linderos
> no me dejéis pasar, mandad que cante ;
> que yo sé de los bravos caballeros
> la dama ingrata, y la cautiva amante,
> la cita oculta y los combates fieros
> con que a cabo llevaron sus empresas
> por hermosas esclavas y princesas . . . .[8]

---

[1] " La Huérfana." *Poesías*, Valencia, 1840, pp. 76-9.

[2] " La Huérfana." *Poesías caballerescas y orientales*, Valencia, 1840, pp. 289-92.

[3] Cf. F. Blanco García : *La Literatura española en el siglo XIX*, 3rd ed., Madrid, 1909-12, I, 177.

[4] " El Cautivo." *Poesías caballerescas y orientales*, Valencia, 1840, pp. 148-54.

[5] " El Cautivo." In *Semanario pintoresco español*, 1839, 2ª serie, I, 39-40.

[6] Cf. pp. 80-1, above.   [7] Cf. pp. 78-9, above.

[8] *Cantos del Trovador*, Madrid, 1840-1, Introducción, I, 5-8.

In the lyric and the short narrative poem there are the troubadours presented by Ochoa and Zorrilla to readers of the *Artista*,[1] Arolas' " El Trovador," in which a lyrical lover assumes the conventional picturesqueness of the troubadour in his approach to his lady ;[2] La Avellaneda's " sleepless troubadour " keeping romantic vigil at his lady's *reja ;*[3] Romero Larrañaga's picturesque singer who enchants a modern audience with the glamour of the Middle Ages ;[4] Salas y Quiroga's variant of the Romantic hero, palpitating with sensibility ;[5] Campillo's " noble troubadour " with his " desmayado acento " and " lira resonante " ;[6] and Barrantes' troubadour, none other than himself—the " troubadour of the soul."[7]

Of religious types, if we except the Templar,[8] the large majority are of the pathetic kind, and this has numerous varieties, of which the commonest is the pilgrim. This type was partly popularized by translations and imitations of Sir Walter Scott and may often be found in novels deriving from him. Examples of it in narrative poetry are the mysterious pilgrim of Zorrilla's " La Pasionaria,"[9] and, in lyric poetry, José Bermúdez de Castro's "El Peregrino," in the *Artista*,[10] the pilgrim of Campoamor's " La Compasión," in *Ayes del alma*,[11] and the " melancholy pilgrim " of Camprodón's *Emociones*.[12] The conventional hermits of Salas y Quiroga[13] and Romero Larrañaga[14] are weak figures by contrast with

---

[1] *El Artista*, 1835, I, 211-12, II, 155-6.

[2] *Poesías*, Valencia, n.d. [1879], II, 45-7.

[3] " La Serenata." *Poesías*, Madrid, 1850, pp. 18-22.

[4] *Cuentos históricos, etc.*, Madrid, 1841, I, 7-8.

[5] " La Hija de Albión." *Poesías*, Madrid, 1834, pp. 23-7.

[6] " El Sueño del Trobador." *Poesías*, Seville, 1858, pp. 50-7.

[7] Preface to *Baladas españolas*, Madrid, 1853.

[8] Cf. *H.R.M.S.*, II, 301, n. 1.

[9] *Cantos del Trovador*, Madrid, 1840-1, III, 5-138.

[10] *El Artista*, 1835, I, 305-6.

[11] *Ayes del alma*, Madrid, 1842, pp. 14-17.

[12] *Emociones*, Barcelona, 1850, p. 27.

[13] " El Ermitaño." *Poesías*, Madrid, 1834, pp. 12-20.

[14] " El Solitario," *Poesías*, Madrid, 1841, pp. 200-4.

the hastily drawn example in Zorrilla's *El Puñal del Godo*. A no less distinctive type, though a slighter one, is the " Cenobita " depicted by Salvador Bermúdez de Castro, who appears to be aiming at picturesqueness rather than at pathos but ends his study somewhat unexpectedly on the note of disillusion[1]. His brother José has an ultra-pathetic pilgrim, turned away by a harsh lord who has refused him shelter, and who shortly afterwards finds him dead from exposure.[2]

As the pilgrims, palmers and hermits were nearly always " ancient," it is convenient to group with them a few representative examples of another of the common pathetic types—that of old age. To this class belong Boix's mournful " viejo solterón " :

> Y es árida mi existencia,
> como el bosque en el invierno ;
> y mi afán siempre es eterno
> sin la magia de ilusión.[3]

Bonilla's " anciano," on the brink of the grave :

> Mis canas escupe el mundo :
> duerme cuando mi alma vela ;
> y ninguno me consuela
> en mi padecer profundo.[4]

and María Josefa Massanés' sentimentalized type of old age, with its idealized portrait, and its moral :

> ¡ Ay del que ultraja en su dolor al viejo
> y sus palabras con desdén recibe ![5]

(iii)   *Melancholy and " pessimism "*

The place occupied by melancholy in the literature of the Romantic movement, though closely connected with the

[1] *Ensayos poéticos*, Madrid, 1840, pp. 191-5.
[2] Cf. *H.R.M.S.*, II, 301, n. 9.
[3] " El Viejo Solterón." *Obras poéticas*, etc., Valencia, 1851, pp. 57-8.
[4] " El Anciano." *Poesías*, Valencia, 1840, pp. 70-4.
[5] *Poesías*, Barcelona, 1841, p. 65.

part played by sentimentality and lachrymosity, is a subject sufficiently distinct to merit separate treatment. Despite the prevalence of sentimentalized types and characters, it will be generally agreed that the literature of the movement, taken as a whole, is neither sentimental nor lachrymose. But it by no means follows from this that a less superficial form of melancholy was not prominent. A strongly individualistic romanticism will always be accompanied by some or other of the manifestations often loosely grouped under the title " pessimism "—*Weltschmerz*, Byronism, *mal du siècle*, *desengaño* and the like—which may differ in a single country as widely as the vague melancholy of *René* and *Obermann* differs from the alternate depression and exaltation of Alfred de Musset and the serene, stoical detachment of Alfred de Vigny. The rarity of exaggerated individualism in the Spanish Romantic movement has its complement in the rarity of melancholy, and this and other causes account jointly for the complete absence of any form of reasoned pessimism. For all Mesonero's irony, far less emotion was generated by ruins and tombs than in either France or England. As we have seen, neither Young, nor Gray, nor Ossian was well known in Spain. Lamartine was thought of less as a poet than as a travel-writer and a historian. Musset, Vigny, Shelley, Leopardi, Hölderlin, Lenau and Schopenhauer had no influence in Spain at all. Heine, until the latter part of the century, had very little. Only the influence of Byron, within this group, is of any importance.

With a few exceptions, such as Cadalso's *Noches lúgubres*, the verse of Meléndez Valdés and Cabanyes, and López Soler's novel, *Los Bandos de Castilla*, there is little of the *mal du siècle* in Spanish literature before 1833. Between about 1833 and 1860 there are some striking manifestations of disillusion, world-weariness and gloom. The authors of some of these, living brief lives of storm and stress, attack the universe with violent passion. Others, with more resignation though not necessarily with less feeling, strike a deeper note of sadness.

Only two men of the highest rank belong to the first of these classes. One is Larra, beneath whose wit, irony and biting sarcasm there lies always an undertone of melancholy. The other, and the more important from this point of view, is Espronceda. Life, to him, is a torment; pleasure illusory; sorrow the sole reality.[1] Man is incarcerated in the prison of this life by an unjust and arbitrary Creator.[2] Or, to vary the figure, he is a traveller at the mercy of every wind, indifferent to a fate which is ruled for him by Destiny.[3] Palliatives may be found in sensual pleasures, but the only remedy is " the peace of the grave."[4]

Between the first class of poet and the second there are many gradations. García Tassara reproduced various moods of disillusion and despair. Ros de Olano, a friend of Espronceda, has been compared, not over-plausibly, with Heine. The *tristeza* of Nicomedes Pastor Díaz has an echo of *saudade* befitting a Galician lyricist. Salvador Bermúdez de Castro feels as deeply as Espronceda, but his plaints are less violent and bitter. La Avellaneda comes into the second class, as the resigned and suffering believer. Romero Larrañaga, going farther, cries : " Yo quiero sufrir."[5] Güell y Renté's collection, *Lágrimas del corazón*,[6] written to " reveal the sadness of his soul," is also untouched by any spirit of rebellion.

Tristeza, then, before 1860, is represented by a few pre-Romantics, two great writers—Larra and Espronceda— and a dozen minor figures. Within each of these groups, they are very much in the minority, and they compare poorly with the corresponding groups in France, Germany and Italy. A study of the unhappy Romantic in the principal countries of Western Europe would show that Spain contributed little to the literature of *tristeza* : her Romantics were more often robust or vivacious than melancholy, pessimistic or sad.

[1] Cf. " A Jarifa, en una orgía."
[2] Cf. introductory stanzas to *El Diablo Mundo*.
[3] Cf. concluding lines of " A una estrella."
[4] " A Jarifa, en una orgía " :
      Sólo en la paz de los sepulcros creo.
[5] *Poesías*, Madrid, 1841, pp. 193-9, 295-301, 309.
[6] Madrid, 1848.

(iv)   *Vagueness, formlessness, love of mystery*

No Romantic movement had more affection than that of Spain for the vague and undefined, the formless and incoherent, the reverie, the meditation and the dream. Of a country always averse from precision this might be expected. Though the Spanish Romantics found in the Middle Ages a close concern for fact and in the Golden Age a certain degree of realism as well as an attentiveness to form, they were never so happy as when tracing the fortunes of some mysterious hero of unknown origin, listening to some " voz admirable, y vaga, y misteriosa "[1] or expressing their love of the nebulous in vague questionings about the ultimate reality.

Sometimes they took refuge in artistry—in elusive images or in word-music pure and simple—and here they often achieved success, for their own sense of beauty was aided by the admirable quality of their medium, a language than which none is more easily attuned to verbal harmony. But too often they sacrificed to their images and their melodies fitness and exactness of expression, verisimilitude and common sense.

With this vagueness appears to be allied the Romantics' love for the fantastic—the principal feature in their presentation of the supernatural. The conjunction of the formless spirits filling the heavens and the " fantastic squadron " of phantasms mounted on goats, serpents and broomsticks which introduces the action of *El Diablo Mundo* is highly characteristic. The vague and the fantastic are frequently allied with the grotesque and the horrible so as to be inseparable from them. Illustrations of this abound in Rivas' *Moro expósito* and Zorrilla's plays and *leyendas*.[2] Precisely what artistic effects are aimed at is often uncertain, but at their best those they achieve are beyond a doubt impressive.

The Romantics in Spain soon acquired a reputation for

---

[1] *Diablo Mundo*, Introduction.

[2] E.g. Rivas : *Obras, ed. cit.*, III, 165, 181, 401, 437 ; also IV, 287-9, V, 297-8, 302-8, 424-6. Zorrilla : *Sancho García*, II, iv ; *La Copa de marfil*, Parte primera ; *El Alcalde Ronquillo*, V, i-ii ; *Don Juan Tenorio*, Segunda parte, III, i ; *El Desafío del diablo ; Las Dos Rosas ; Justos por pecadores*.

" peopling the poetical atmosphere with lugubrious and fantastic visions "[1] and many of them followed Victor Hugo in his quest of deformity and horror, though perhaps fewer than is generally supposed. It so happens that two of the most prolific and famous, Rivas and Zorrilla, were particularly given to portraying horrors ; and it is an interesting fact, which may or may not be significant, that these two authors were by nature particularly expansive and genial and had less in common with the " unhappy Romantic " than any of their Romantic contemporaries. Without pressing this coincidence too far, we may take them as illustrative of this feature of Romantic art : Espronceda, the disillusioned singer, who presents so strong a contrast with these two buoyant painters, generally stops short of the horrible and takes refuge in mistiness and obscurity. He is often grotesque enough, if somewhat conventionally so, but he seldom affects the horrible and is seldom guilty of crudeness.

(v) *Attitude to Nature*

The attitude of the Spanish Romantics to Nature is a much more complicated subject than might be supposed by a superficial observer. Nature is not, like freedom, a primary characteristic of romanticism, nor even a secondary one, like subjectivity, melancholy or passion. A Classical writer can be as deeply moved by the sights and sounds of Nature as can a Romantic writer and can give his sentiments equally eloquent expression. Yet there are essential differences between the attitude of the one and that of the other. With regard to form, the Classic subordinates the intensity of his feelings to the principles of restraint which are part of his creed, while the Romantic flings principles to the winds if thereby he can express all that is in his soul. With regard to content, the Classic maintains an objective conception of Nature, while the Romantic tends to see in her reflections of his own temperament. He looks upon her with more

---

[1] Ramón de Mesonero Romanos : *Memorias de un setentón*, Madrid, 1881, II, 153.

attachment than the Classic : she is, for the time being, his own property ; she can become a part of him.

This distinction is true of Western European literature in general, but it is considerably less noticeable in Spain than elsewhere. Frequent as are the references to Nature in the Spanish Romantics, they are at the worst quite conventional and at the best often completely objective. Rivas, if occasionally moved by some deep personal emotion, is more commonly content to write conventional verses to a stream or a rosebay, and to scatter picturesque figures, derived, at several removes, from Nature, through the *Moro expósito* and the *Leyendas*. Espronceda harangues the sun (" Al Sol ") or hymns a star (" A una estrella "), and often uses Nature decoratively, but the flaming passages in which he is most nearly himself are with few exceptions bare of all imagery. Arolas abounds in Nature-images, some extravagant or artificial, some suggestive of sensibility and taste ; but he is never profound and shows best in comparisons of superficial charm. To Enrique Gil, Nature is bound up with affection for the *patria chica :* he writes with delicate grace of the hedgerow and the country year but seldom penetrates below surface description. Campoamor mingles *ternézas* with his *flores* and moralizes sentimentally on butterfly, streamlet and blossom in the valley.[1] La Avellaneda, still a Romantically inclined young girl, prattles artlessly to her linnet,[2] while Carolina Coronado croons to swallows, nightingales, butterflies and stars, lilies, sunflowers and jasmine.[3] But seldom, when they write of Nature, do these writers reveal any appreciable depth of personal emotion.

It is no exaggeration to say that the Romantics have neither more nor less sensibility to Nature than their predecessors or their followers. Sensibility, as we have seen, runs through Spanish literature in the eighteenth and nineteenth centuries like a thread—not always easily perceptible, but always there. We are perhaps moved by the

[1] *Ternezas y flores*, Madrid, 1840 : " La niña y la mariposa " ; " La flor del valle " ; " El arroyo ".

[2] " A mi jilguero " (1837) : *Poesías*, Madrid, 1850, pp. 9-15.

[3] *Poesías*, Madrid, 1843, pp. 30-1, 66-76, *et passim*.

Romantic Salvador Bermúdez de Castro with his sense of the immanence of God in Nature,[1] but we have an equal appreciation of the " constante amor " and " ternura " for the Guadalquivir of the mainly Classical Jovellanos and we note the close correspondence between his chastened mood and the surroundings of El Paular in which he muses upon it.[2] If we pass on to the Eclectic Ventura de la Vega, we find a melodious and placid little poem on the Pusa endowing that stream with a human personality which seems real to him : at one impressionable moment in his life he can look at it both as a solace and as a symbol.[3] The Eclectic Somoza, again, in at least two of his poems,[4] proved himself a vivid observer of Nature, while in his prose " Recuerdos e impresiones " he recorded long-cherished memories of his native countryside, the sights and sounds of which haunted him like a passion.

But not all the Romantics could share the moods of the Classical Jovellanos or the Eclectics Vega and Somoza. Careful students of the Duque de Rivas, recalling the artificiality of his Nature-references, will not be surprised to hear that natural beauty had hardly any attraction for him. " La admiración de la naturaleza," reports his brother-in-law, Cueto,

> esa conmoción interna que para ciertas almas es a la vez fuerza creadora y deleite purísimo, que hace que el espíritu descubra y sienta la mano divina en el aroma de una flor, en el rumor del mar o en el reflejo de una estrella, tampoco era para el Duque de Rivas manantial de inspiración sincera. ¿ Por qué ocultarlo ? . . . . ¡ Cuántas veces le oí hablar con incredulidad y con mofa de la *felicidad de la vida del campo* ! Él veía exclusivamente tosquedad en la llaneza, afectación vanidosa en el amor a la soledad, y aburrimiento en el sosiego de las selvas y de las praderas.[5]

---

[1] *Ensayos poéticos*, Madrid, 1840, II, 11-31.

[2] " Epístola de Fabio a Anfriso."

[3] " Orillas del Pusa." *Obras poéticas*, Paris, 1866, pp. 562-5.

[4] " A la laguna de Gredos " and " A la cascada de Pesqueruela " : *Obras en prosa y verso*, Madrid, 1904, pp. 208, ff.

[5] *M.A.E.*, 1870, II, 521.

Few of Rivas' fellow-Romantics, perhaps, would go as far as this, but it cannot be denied that many of them look upon Nature with the eyes of the mere spectator and embroider stock themes in conventional language. The Nature poetry of the Spanish Romantics, in short, must be pronounced distinctly disappointing.

(vi) *Romanticism and form*

We turn lastly to questions of form. Here, again, freedom is of the essence of the matter : freedom in language, in style, and in metre. The last of these three " freedoms " has been studied in the chapter on the Romantic revolt. With regard to the first two, more reforms, perhaps, were announced than were actually accomplished, or even attempted : conventional pseudo-Classical language can be found even in Romantic lyric poetry right through the period. Worse still, the Romantics tended to expand into a picturesque grandiloquence and into pseudo-Romantic excesses which were as disagreeable as those of the pseudo-Classics. Even Valera, who regarded the Romantics on the whole benevolently, found them often " hinchados, palabreros y vacíos de sentido." [1] The less benevolent were quick to poke fun at, or heap scorn upon, their dramatic affectations—their " noche tétrica y oscura ", their " siniestros bultos ", their " sonrisa infernal", and, above all, their " ¡ Maldición ! " " Such words and phrases were reinforced by others, of which Zorrilla had perhaps the richest treasury, and by means of which it was vaguely hoped to convey some of the superficial richness of atmosphere popularly associated with the " East". Many authors passed freely from the one type of language to the other. " ¡ Qué versos ! ¡ Qué numen ! ", laughed Abenamar :

> ¡ Qué fantasmas ! ¡ Qué esqueletos !
> ¡ Qué atrocidades ! ¡ Qué horrores !
> ¡ Dominios del infierno !
> ¡ Y qué muchachas tan lindas !

[1] *Obras completas*, XIX, 23.

¡ Y qué amores y qué besos !
¡ Qué jardines ! ¡ Qué palacios !
¡ Y qué zambras y qué juegos !
¡ Qué perfumes del Oriente ! [1]

It was all very magnificent, but it was hardly war—certainly not the war upon pseudo-Classical excesses in which the Romantics had thought they were engaging. In fact, the more closely we scan their record in this field, the more we discover how they eluded or nullified the very reforms to which they had announced their devotion.

[1] " El poeta y el trapero " : cf. *H.R.M.S.*, II, 328, n.1.

Chapter VIII

ROMANTICISM AFTER 1860[1]

I. The Course of Spanish Literature after 1860[2]

To anyone who identified Romanticism with the fallen Romantic movement it would have seemed in 1860 that it was almost dead. But, in reality, the same force which during the eighteenth century had kept the Romantic ideal in a state of smouldering vitality gave it energy to withstand all attempts made to quench it during the nineteenth. The flame had been burning long before additional fuel was heaped upon it by foreign authors, by the returned exiles and by the newly founded literary reviews. When the supply of this fuel decreased, the fire died down visibly, but its flame, though subdued, burned on.

Eclecticism succeeded romanticism as the dominant literary fashion and preserved its dominance until there ceased to be any prevailing fashion at all. The native predilection for the Romantic made impracticable the re-establishment of classicism : a middle course between the two extremes was the most that could be attained. Then came the collapse of such interest as Spain had ever taken in literary theory. It had been one step from romanticism to eclecticism ; it was hardly a longer step from eclecticism to what has frequently been termed chaos.

Out of this chaos came various currents : one was a new type of foreign influence, described by Rubén Darío in 1906 as "la europeización, la universalización del alma española."[3]

---

[1] *H.R.M.S.*, II, 329-376.
[2] *H.R.M.S.*, II, 329-32.
[3] *Opiniones*, Madrid, 1906 (*Obras completas*, X, 201-2).

His summing-up of the state of Spanish literature might suggest that a new romanticism was on the way :

> Se acabaron el estancamiento, la sujeción a la ley de lo antiguo académico, la vitola, el patrón que antaño uniformaba la expresión literaria . . . . El individualismo, la libre manifestación de las ideas, el vuelo poético sin trabas, se impusieron.[1]

This judgment, though true as far as it goes, is misleadingly one-sided. The europeanization of the Spanish mind led not only to a new romanticism but also to a new classicism. Some, though in no mood to follow arbitrary rules, delighted in a subtilized type of restraint and saw the need for curbing the flight of genius lest it should once again lose itself in grandiloquent rhetoric. Some desired to lead Spain back to realities—not to the petty realities of *costumbrismo* but to the stark and serious realities of national decadence and destiny —and to this end they exalted the virtues of sobriety, solidity and precision of expression and style.

What, then, is the affiliation of Spanish literature in this twentieth century ? In practice, it is no doubt Eclectic ; in theory, it has no affiliation at all. It has not merely ceased to attempt a reconciliation of Classical and Romantic ; it has no longer any interest in Classical and Romantic. The average writer adheres to whatever norm he may temporarily set up for himself. Some have embraced the straitest classicism both in form and in content. Some are conscious Eclectics, drawing their inspiration now from this ideal, now from that, and aiming at perfect form and complete harmony. Others are sworn Romantics, with all romanticism's faults and exaggerations. Others, again, try their hand at the imitation or emulation of individual authors, past or contemporary, while still more write with no thought of literary ideals at all. Thus the overwhelming majority of contemporary Spanish writers can subscribe both to the letter and to the spirit of that characteristic declaration of Antonio Machado :

[1] *Ibid.*

¿ Soy clásico o romántico ? No sé. Dejar quisiera
mi verso, como deja el capitán su espada :
famosa por la mano viril que la blandiera,
no por el docto oficio del forjador preciada.[1]

To consider in detail the state of contemporary Spanish
literature would be a task far outside the scope of this History.
It is relevant only for us to trace the persistence of the
Romantic ideal, starting from the year 1860, at about which
time romanticism was at its lowest ebb, and going down to
the present day.

II. Romanticism in Prose Fiction after 1860[2]

During the Romantic and early Eclectic periods, the novel
developed very slowly ; it was not until the eighteen-seventies
that there began that epoch of immense fertility which
continued almost unabated for well over half a century. In
the decade 1861-70, Fernández y González, that Phoenix of
decadent romanticism, dominated the field, producing no
less than twenty-nine novels ; Fernán Caballero and the
superficial *color de rosa* Romantic, Antonio de Trueba, came
a very poor second. In the decade 1871-80, though
Fernández y González showed no slackening of output, the
field belonged to Pérez Galdós, Pereda, Valera, Emilia Pardo
Bazán and Alarcón. The modern period, almost without
warning, had begun.

In this decade, too, romanticism reached its greatest
heights in fiction. Valera dubbed himself a realist and
declared that he " idolized form ", but the idolatry is hard to
discover and the realism was entirely superficial : his novels,
like his early verse and much of his literary criticism, are
idealistic and Romantic. Alarcón, superficially, looks more
like a realist than Valera, but, devastatingly direct though he
can be, he is a Romantic playing at realism. Palacio Valdés,
for over half a century, entertained his large public with a
long series of idealistic novels, diversified by brief interludes

---

[1] " Retrato." *Poesías completas*, Madrid, 1928, p. 103.
[2] *H.R.M.S.*, II, 332-45.

of a benevolently diluted realism. With his inconsequent, rambling plots and his idealized characters, he represents the main current of Romantic art in late-nineteenth-century fiction.

Pereda's novels, too, written in defence of ideals, or in support of theses, are in their essence Romantic, but in choice of words and balance of phrase he is a Classic and his photography of Santander and the Montaña betters the art of the early *costumbristas*. When with his romanticism we compare that of Valle-Inclán, our distance from the Romantics of 1835 becomes evident. Valle-Inclán can be the artist for art's sake, the potent creator of highly original characters, the mediaevalist, the neologist, the devotee of the picturesque. And he can be sheer force, unrestrained and irresistible. Miró has an exuberance of imagination recalling Zorrilla's and his combination of impressionism with symbolism often makes him hard to follow. Romantic in the extreme are his mingling of sense-impressions, his imaginative treatment of inanimate objects, his daring use of epithet and image, his flights of pure fancy, his riotous colour-play, his unconventional plot-construction and his disconnected style.

In these authors Romantic art is to a greater or a lesser extent transmuted. The traditional current is represented by Ricardo León. The atmosphere of his novels, their archaic vocabulary and their lavish use of language recall the Scott-imitations of the eighteen-thirties. His conservative, traditionalist outlook and his turgid, oratorical style are reminiscent of Zorrilla. Of his lesser contemporaries, a few —Concha Espina, Tenreiro, Pérez Lugín—follow this same tradition. Yet, comparing them with the Romantics of the eighteen-thirties, one becomes conscious of the immense growth in complexity of Spanish life and in the europeanization of Spanish literature.

The realists of the post-Romantic epoch are fewer in number than the Romantics ; but, on the other hand, they are less infected with romanticism than are the Romantics with realism. In Pérez Galdós we find sentimentality, sometimes indulged to excess, and a predilection for melodramatic effects and situations which often become stiff, artificial and ridiculous. In other respects his realism is undiluted, though occasionally he varies it by excursions into the realms of the imagination, or even of fantasy. A more thorough-going realist, in her best-known novels, is Emilia Pardo Bazán, who, however, follows the Romantics, though at some distance, in such lesser works as *Morriña*, *El Cisne de Vilamorta* and *Dulce Dueño*. Among her realistic contemporaries not devoid of Romantic affinities are Jacinto Octavio Picón, Felipe Trigo, Leopoldo Alas and Vicente Blasco Ibáñez.

Two very dissimilar writers maintain an effective eclecticism with conspicuous success. Pío Baroja would have been a literary anarchist had he lived in a preceptist epoch. Rebelling alike against academic style and social conventions, he often chooses realistic subjects and treats them in a Romantic way, against the background of a Romantic subjectivity. But there is a detachment about him which objectivizes even the character-types used by the early Romantics, and, though as a stylist he is in the Romantic tradition, he writes with clarity and simplicity, nowhere giving the impression of incapacity for restraint.

Ramón Pérez de Ayala, at first sight, appears to swing towards realism as Baroja does towards romanticism, and intellectually realist in conception of character he certainly is. But occasionally uncontrolled fantasy and a dominant imaginativeness appear in him, and his style, normally of so perfect a balance, sometimes tends to luxuriance. In his masterpiece, *Belarmino y Apolonio*, he gilds his insight into human character with exquisite fancy, working idealistically with real, human types upon an essentially fantastic theme, and thus blending Classical and Romantic into one. He is an author of extraordinary power, deserving of a notable place in each of the two traditions.

III. ROMANTICISM IN DRAMA AFTER 1860[1]

Romanticism in the novel and in drama developed very differently. First, although eclecticism was ruling the stage

[1] *H.R.M.S.*, II, 345-54.

from the mid-century, two of the chief Romantics, García Gutiérrez and Zorrilla, continued to produce plays of merit down to the sixties and the seventies respectively. Then, in 1874, appeared a neo-Romantic of tremendous force, José Echegaray, who, for over twenty years, reigned supreme. Finally, drama was once again transformed by the greatest europeanizing force in Spanish letters, Jacinto Benavente.

The last period of García Gutiérrez and of Zorrilla was marked by the growing success in Eclectic drama of Manuel Tamayo y Baus. His first plays combined a Classical simplicity, severity and unity with the variety, rapidity of action and technical effectiveness of Romantic drama at its best. Then came *La Locura de amor*, Romantic from the sentimental *dedicatoria* to the final melodramatic curtain. But after this, with the exception of the semi-Romantic, historical *Un Drama nuevo*, Tamayo wrote plays of a neo-Classical type, but modern in outlook and concerned with moral or social problems. Contemporary with him were two other Eclectics: Adelardo López de Ayala, a realist who in the main adhered to Classical forms, but used Romantic methods when it so suited him and dealt almost exclusively with problems of morals and society, and Luis de Eguílaz y Eguílaz, some of whose plays are of a lyrical, neo-historical type, while others are bourgeois comedies, excessively realistic and didactic. Another contemporary, Narciso Serra, was prolific in devices, exaggerations and surprises, and wrote fewer studies of real life than imaginative dramas influenced by the Golden Age or the romanticism of 1835.

Echegaray, an impenitent and thorough-going Romantic, was the chief perpetuator of the tradition of the Romantic revolt :

> En el teatro, es la revolución hecha hombre . . . . Abrasó en llamas la escena española. El incendio persiste.[1]

He loved the clap-trap of the past, its sensations and horrors, its melodramatic moments, its grandiose language and sweeping rhetoric, its picturesqueness and colour, its play with coincidence and its grotesque improbabilities. Even

---

[1] Luis Alonso, in *Autores dramáticos contemporáneos*, Madrid, 1881, II, 535.

themes which lend themselves to realism he treats romantic-ally. The contemporary social problems which he discusses are real enough, but as he presents them they seem intolerably artificial.

With Eugenio Sellés, Leopoldo Cano and Joaquín Dicenta the Romantic treatment of social themes continues. Even in the social plays of Pérez Galdós, realism is streaked with sentimentality, melodrama and other Romantic colourings. A strong anti-Romantic reaction, however, provoked by Echegaray, was at hand. By 1880 his plays were being described as the dross which romanticism had left. The so-called Generation of 1898 disowned him. " He is a stranger to us," wrote Manuel Bueno in 1909 ; " he has nothing in common with us ; we do not admire him. We do not owe to him a single emotion ; he has not revealed to us a single interesting aspect of the life of the spirit."[1]

With the beginnings of the reaction came Benavente, a splendid though solitary figure, bringing back to the stage more of the excellences of classicism than it had seen in any dramatist for generations. The sobriety, unity and simplicity of his plays, their intellectualism and their restraint were, to his generation, new and welcome qualities. None the less, he owes to romanticism his subtle use of irony, suggestion and symbolism, and the complexity of his characters, his lyricism, his use of fancy and imagination and his treatment of the marvellous all point in the same direction. Gregorio Martínez Sierra, a sensitive twentieth-century Romantic, the antithesis of Echegaray, also contrasts markedly with Benavente. The brothers Serafín and Joaquín Álvarez Quintero etch themes in the main Romantic with Classical precision. The poetic and symbolic drama of the twentieth century perpetuates the spirit of the *leyendas*, with the almost pure Romantic, Francisco Villaespesa, standing at the one extreme among its exponents and the semi-Classical traditionalist, Eduardo Marquina, at the other. The Romantic tradition also persists in the Maeterlinckian symbolist, Ramón Goy de Silva, in the Valle-Inclán of the *Farsas* and *Esperpentos*, and in certain aspects of the *género chico*.

[1] Cf. *H.R.M.S.*, II, 351, nn. 1, 2.

IV. ROMANTICISM IN LYRIC AND NARRATIVE POETRY AFTER 1860

Lyric and narrative poetry, the last *genre* to be converted to romanticism, remained under its influence longer than any other. If we except Campoamor's short poems, Núñez de Arce and Gabriel y Galán, we may describe romanticism as holding the field until the very end of the century. Zorrilla continued to write verse into the early nineties ; Campoamor paid tribute to the discredited movement with the long, inchoate *Drama universal* ; and a number of the original Romantics—García Gutiérrez, Hartzenbusch, García Tassara, the brothers Bermúdez de Castro and N. P. Díaz—wrote occasional poems not inconsistent with the creed which they had so long before professed.

Younger writers, too, brought up in a post-Romantic world, embraced the tradition. The Galician, Rosalía Castro de Murguía, has all the subjectivity, the doubts, struggles and indefinable aspirations of the true Romantic. The Andalusian, Gustavo Adolfo Bécquer, sounds the truest lyric note of the century, and, almost alone of the Romantics, is completely free from conventionality and bombast. He is a Romantic in his love of distance, of vagueness and imprecision, of aspiration to the unattainable ; in his doubts, questionings and disillusions and in his sensitiveness to every impression, especially to impressions of Nature.

Of lesser poets, Gaspar Núñez de Arce is an Eclectic with many Romantic affinities; Ventura Ruiz Aguilera, Federico Balart and Joaquín María Bartrina are almost pure " unhappy Romantics " ; Manuel Reina and Leopoldo Cano rank doubt and disillusion among their chief inspirations ; Teodoro Llorente and Vicente Wenceslao Querol are two Valencians who preserve the spirit of the romanticism of their native city.

There were many poets, then, in this period, but there was little inspiration. Bécquer, on whom had descended Espronceda's mantle, had died in 1870 ; and it was to a Spain all but destitute of the vital spark that renovation came with Rubén Darío.

15

Like many other great poets, Rubén combined a Romantic audacity with a Classical interest in form. As a metrist, he was a successor to Espronceda—far more fertile in invention, far nimbler in construction, far more sensitive to rhythm, but inspired by the same spirit of freedom. In content, he is even more of a Romantic than in form :

¡ Románticos somos ! ¿ Quién que es no es romántico ?[1]

Daringly subjective, he lays bare his heart to every reader : " si hay un alma sincera es la mía ".[2] His " voces vagas " and " tenues suspiros " mingle with what he himself terms the " sollozos de los violoncelos " of Samain and Verlaine. Even such classicism as he professes is a modern classicism, drawn from France, whose Greeks he loved more than those of Greece herself.[3] This classicism has often mellowed life for him and dissolved its bitterness : without it he might have become another " unhappy Romantic". Yet he could not rest in classicism, powerless as it would be to satisfy the " hunger for space and thirst for heaven "[4] which is part of every Romantic's experience.

As Rubén Darío looked to the future, he saw himself the leader of a new Romantic movement, proceeding, in appearance, from Hispano-America, but grounded in Spain. The modernism which he introduced had indeed many similarities with the Romantic movement, besides those of its inspiration and purpose. It was a combination of revival and revolt ; it was brief in duration ; and it was succeeded, not by one violent reaction, but by a number of diverging tendencies. Such traits of modernistic art as its metrical innovations, becoming progressively more daring, as its subjectivity, scepticism and melancholy, and above all as its vagueness and obscurity, relate it closely to the romanticism of the early nineteenth century in Spain and to the later neo-romanticism of France.

The most fertile descendant of Rubén Darío, and, in his turn, the spiritual father of most of the younger contem-

---

[1] " Canción de los pinos."
[2] " Yo soy aquel . . . ."
[3] " Divagación."
[4] " Yo soy aquel . . . ."

porary poets, is Juan Ramón Jiménez, more truly and completely a Romantic than the majority of his followers. Juan
Ramón showed an early maturity of form which was probably innate, and a variety of mannerisms, in the main
Romantic, and at times somewhat obtrusive. His chief
theme is his own inner life, with its melancholy, aspiration
and unresolved emotion :

> un suspirar por algo encantado y distante,
> por algo más que no se encuentra y que se ignora.[1]

In his later years, he has come nearer and nearer to
poesía pura, in which Spanish poets have seen their almost
mystical goal. The concentration and discipline which that
quest demands belong, not to Romantic expansiveness, but
to Classical restraint, yet in his refusal to be enslaved by form
Juan Ramón is an out-and-out Romantic.

In a general way, the customary assignment of Manuel
and Antonio Machado to Parnassianism and neo-Romanticism respectively seems to be justified. Manuel, however,
can be Romantic enough—self-conscious, self-revealing, sym-
bolistic, emotional—when he chooses, while Antonio has
sufficient sobriety and sufficient sense of form to reject
exaggerated rhetoric. Enrique de Mesa, Enrique Díez-
Canedo and Miguel de Unamuno combine the Classical and
the Romantic. Emilio Carrère, the translator of Poe,
Verlaine and Baudelaire, re-creates some of the first
Romantics' sentimental types.

The latest developments of Spanish poetry, whatever the
names by which they are called, show the same independence of schools of thought as we find in the poets of the
early twentieth century. The " Generation of 1920 " has
been called one of " order and diaphaneity ", but some
would find it hard to see the diaphaneity for the mist and
would judge that the " order " rooted in disorder stood—at
least, if the foremost of these poets are to be taken as typical.
In nothing is contemporary poetry more Romantic than
this : that there is no one criterion or direction generally
favoured by either poets or critics. The wind of poetry blows

---

[1] *Elegías lamentables.*

where it lists and it is impossible to tell whence it comes or whither it goes. But some of it, at least, comes from the early and the late Romantics.

V. ROMANTICISM IN THE ESSAY AFTER 1860 [1]

One of the outstanding phenomena in literature of the twentieth century in Spain has been the vogue of the essay. This has done much to broaden the Spaniard's interests, to stimulate his curiosity and to awaken in him a divine discontent. The achievements of the essay, in a country where personality counts for so much, are largely due to its being so intensely personal. Only in Spain could the vogue of the essay be considered as an extension of the vogue of the lyric. Only of Spain could a native critic write : " The essay is another form of lyricism." [2]

It might be expected, then, that the essay would be entirely Romantic. The *genre* certainly lends itself to romanticism. It leaves the writer completely free as regards length, form and style ; he can be lyrical, dramatic, reflective or critical ; he can tell stories, write letters or air his grievances ; he can string his essays together and call them a philosophical treatise or a *discurso de entrada* for the Academy. But in fact the contemporary essay has been by no means wholly Romantic, and this has been due chiefly to the so-called Generation of 1898. The literary reaction of that group was directed against the " don verbal espléndido," and, in style as in ideas, it began to preach the need for a revision of values, for careful analysis, for economy and restraint. In one sense, then, the Generation aimed at fashioning a new classicism.

But the literature of the Generation of 1898 also evolved a programme which in transmuted form curiously reproduced the main traits of the Romantic revolt and the Romantic revival. It shed new light on mediaeval writers ;

---

[1] *H.R.M.S.*, II, 369-373.

[2] F. de Onís : *Antología de la poesía española e hispanoamericana*, Madrid, 1934, p. xvii.

rehabilitated El Greco, Lope de Vega and Góngora ; and took up traditional themes of Spanish literature, to give them a new meaning, indeed, but also a new life. If the spirit of the age has led some to analysis and restraint, it has inspired others to rebellion. " La generación de 1898," writes Azorín, " no ha hecho sino continuar el movimiento ideológico de la generación anterior : ha tenido el grito pasional de Echegaray, el espíritu corrosivo de Campoamor y el amor a la realidad de Galdós." [1] In other words, it reveals, in fact if not always in appearance, the union of two currents, Classical and Romantic. In some writers one or the other of these ideals predominates ; in others the two unite to form a new eclecticism.

VI. Conclusion

Looking back over the two centuries we have traversed, we may well ask ourselves what the Romantic movement accomplished. To-day it seems so incredibly archaic ; its most vaunted productions are so insufferably crude and childish ; since it passed away, literature appears to have grown up with unparalleled rapidity. Many contemporary critics refuse to take it seriously : "Cosa de broma. Figurones. Oratoria. Escenografía barata." [2] If, as some think, Spain needs a new romanticism, its adherents must at all costs avoid the faults of the old.

But, considered in relation to its own time, the Romantic movement responded to an urgent need : the need for breaking away from rules and conventions which had become arbitrary and meaningless and for substituting for the debased idealism of the eighteenth century a nobler conception of art and beauty. And, from one point of view, the contributions to literature made by its individual representatives matter little. What matters is that it succeeded in inaugurating a new epoch. We visualize the Romantic era to-day as a short period which produced little that is likely

[1] *Clásicos y modernos*, Madrid, 1919, p. 255.
[2] Antonio Espina, in *Revista de Occidente*, 1924, II, 406.

to be immortal, but also as a period which prepared the ground for the far more fruitful one beginning about 1870. It may be that centuries to come will see it as nothing more outstanding than a steepening section in the road leading upwards from the low-lying eighteenth century and connecting the Golden Age of the sixteenth and seventeenth with another such Age of the twentieth or twenty-first, the degree of brilliance of which is as yet undeterminable. Some such transition-value it must surely have : that literature could have jumped from Meléndez Valdés to Bécquer or from Isla to Valera is unthinkable.

At the same time, while the great gift of the Romantic movement to posterity was of a historical and a dynamic character in that it reacted against the past and pointed the way, however uncertainly, to a more brilliant future, it cannot be disregarded as having contributed intrinsically to the content of Spanish literature or as having moulded the writers of to-day. Its failure as a self-conscious movement is of small importance by comparison with its success as a permeating influence. And we can safely prophesy that similar contributions to literature will be made by any Romantic movement in Spain in the future. For we can never lose sight of the fact that the Spanish temperament is " Romantic through and through ". That is a fact which stands out in the treatment of any epoch in Spanish letters and which gives any era, however unproductive, in which romanticism is allowed free play, some abiding value.

INDEX

INDEX

The alphabetical order followed is English, not Spanish, no account being taken of *de* and *y* in the arrangement of names. The name of no individual work is indexed unless its author is unknown. The only periodicals indexed are the *Artista* and the *Europeo*.